Taunton's

BUILD LIKE A PRO®

BUILDING a DECK

Taunton's

BUILD LIKE A PRO®

Expert Advice from Start to Finish

BUILDING a DECK

SCOTT SCHUTTNER

The Taunton Press

Introduction

I've been a carpenter for years, but still enjoy building decks more than any other type of construction project. I like working outside in the sunshine, as well as the fact that no one is inconvenienced by dirt, dust, or disconnected plumbing (unlike in remodeling). There's a low stress level, because I get the chance to do some nice finish carpentry without the exacting demands of interior trimwork. And even though there are some strenuous parts—digging holes and hoisting beams, for instance—they just make me stronger and healthier if I do them safely.

Compared with whole house projects, decks provide instant gratification. Over the course of just a few days, things change radically, as we move from doing the dirt work to laying the decking (my favorite part). A few days more, and we get to create a beautiful railing. And not long after that, the entire deck comes alive with a newly applied finish.

But as with all construction, there is a practical side. Almost inevitably I'm asked, "How can we lower the cost of this project?" My first suggestions are to make the deck smaller, use less-costly materials, or eliminate fancy options, but these are not always the right solutions. Another suggestion is that the homeowners help out, providing some of their own labor, or "sweat equity." This will help lower the project cost, but as I remind the owners, they save dollars only in direct proportion to the amount and type of labor they are replacing. There's no magic.

Of course, if the homeowners are willing to help with some of the project, perhaps they should do the entire project themselves. Now they have eliminated all of my hefty overhead (and my smaller-than-you-would-guess profit), most labor costs, and administrative and design fees. Granted, it is now necessary for them to provide all of these services, and of course, there's also a lot more responsibility, but the potential rewards are greater too.

That brings me to you. Do I think you can do it yourself? Without a doubt! If you have the time and inclination, deck building is a great project for people with all different levels of construction skills and experience. The biggest requirement is desire. And the rewards aren't just financial. Like me, you may find you enjoy building a deck for one (or all) of the various aspects of the job, from the mental challenge of the design work to the physical challenge of pounding nails in by hand. Plus, now you get the sunshine and exercise.

Any new adventure begins with a little trepidation, but that can be overcome with a bit of guidance. That's what this book is all about. What I want to give you is the benefit of my experience as a builder. When I'm building, I use certain methods that have worked for

me in the past, and I'll be sure to point these out to you as tried and true. But as I've learned over my years as a builder, there are lots of different ways to achieve success, so I'll suggest plenty of alternative methods as well. I'll also give you the inside scoop on things that don't work so well. I won't gloss over the difficult details; my goal is for this advice to be clear, definite, and thorough.

I'm guessing that you've done enough carpentry to give this a try. I'm not going to kid you and suggest that the process won't take time and effort, but if you work slowly, safely, and carefully, you can achieve the same results as a professional builder. The process may take a little longer, but I think you'll enjoy it each step of the way. And long after the project's completed, you'll enjoy the fruits of your labor. To me, that's what carpentry's all about.

How to Use This Book

If you're reading this, you're a doer, not afraid to take on a challenging project. We designed this book and this series to help you get that project done smoothly and cost-effectively.

Many doers jump in and do, reading the directions only if something goes wrong. It's much smarter (and cheaper) to start with knowing what to do and planning the process, step-by-step. This book is here to help you. Read it. Familiarize yourself with the process you're about to undertake. You'll be glad that you did.

Planning is the Key to Success

This book contains information on designing your project, choosing the best options for the result you want to achieve, and planning the timing and execution. We know you're anxious to get started on your project. Take the time now to read and think about what you're about to do. You'll refine your ideas and choose the best materials.

There's advice here on where to look for inspiration and how to make plans. Don't be afraid to make an attempt at drawing your own plans. There's no better way to get exactly what you want than by designing it yourself. If you need the assistance of an architect or engineer, this book will explain why and how to work with these professionals.

After you've decided what you're going to undertake, make lists of materials and a budget for yourself, both of money and time. There's nothing more annoying than a project that goes on forever.

Finding the Information You Need

We've designed this book to make it easy to find what you need to know. The main part of the book details the essential parts of each process. If it's fairly straightforward, it's simply described. If there are key steps, these are addressed one by one, usually accompanied by drawings or photos to help you see what you will be doing. We've also added some other elements to help you understand the process better, find quicker or smarter ways to accomplish the task, or do it differently to suit your project.

Alternatives and a closer look

The sidebars and features that we've included with the main text are there to explain aspects in more depth and to clarify why you're doing a step a certain way. In some cases, these features are used to describe a completely different approach to handle the same situation. We explain when you might want to use this method or choose this option as well as its advantages. Sidebars are usually accompanied by photos or drawings to help you see what the author is describing. These sidebars are meant to help, but they're not essential to understanding or doing the process.

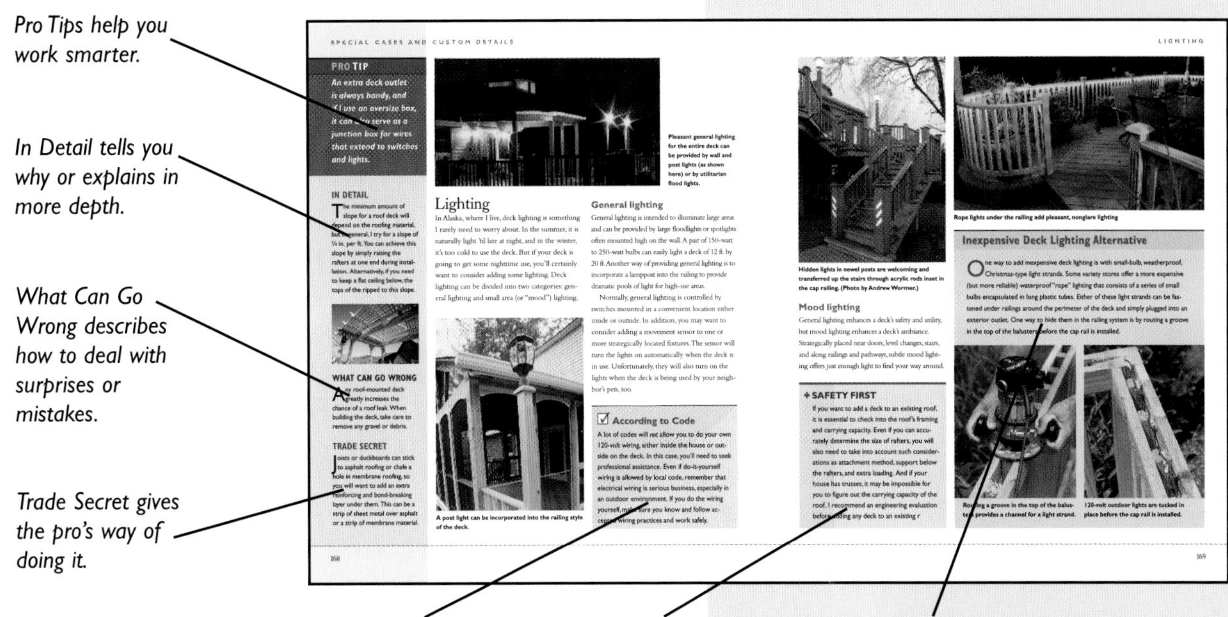

Heads up!

We urge you to read the "Safety First" and "According to Code" sidebars we've included. "Safety First" gives you a warning about hazards that can harm or even kill you. Always work safely. Use appropriate safety aids, and know what you're doing before you start work. Don't take unnecessary chances, and if a procedure makes you uncomfortable, try to find another way to do it. "According to Code" can save you from getting into hot water with your building inspector, building an unsafe structure, or having to rip your project apart and build it again to suit the local codes.

There's a pro at your elbow

The author of this book, like every author in this series, has had years of experience doing this kind of project. We've put the benefits of their knowledge in quick bits that always appear in the left margin. "Pro Tips" are ideas or insights that will save you time or money. "In Detail" is a short explanation of an aspect that may be of interest to you. While not essential to getting the job done, these are meant to explain the "why" of various steps.

Every project has its surprises. Since the author has encountered many of them already, he can give you a little preview of what these unforeseen developments might be and how to address them. And experience has also taught the author some tricks that you can only learn from being a pro. Some of these are tips, some are tools or accessories you can make yourself, some are materials or tools you may not have thought to use.

Building Like a Pro

To make a living, a pro needs to work smart, fast, and economically. That's the strategy presented in this book. We've provided options to help you make the best choices in design, materials, and methods. That way you can adjust your project to suit your skill level and budget. Good choices and good planning are the keys to success. And remember that all the knowledge and every skill you acquire on this project will make it easier the next time.

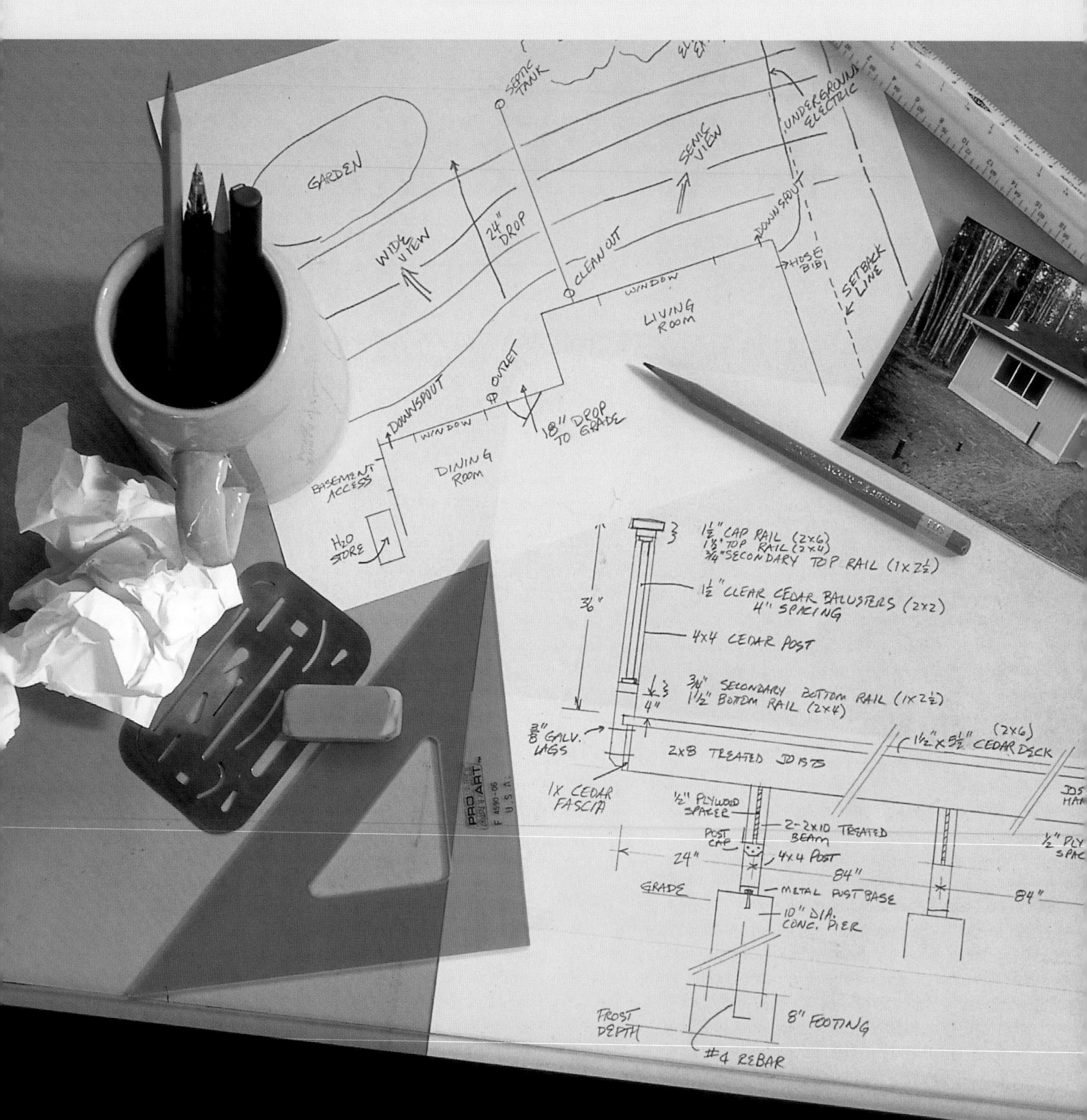

SEPTIC TANK
GARDEN
UNDERGROUND ELECTRIC
SCENIC VIEW
WIDE VIEW
24" DROP
CLEAN OUT
DOWNSPOUT
HOSE BIB
SETBACK LINE
WINDOW
LIVING ROOM
DOWNSPOUT
OUTLET
18" DROP TO GRADE
WINDOW
BASEMENT ACCESS
DINING ROOM
H2O STORE
1½" CAP RAIL (2x6)
1½" TOP RAIL (2x4)
3/4" SECONDARY TOP RAIL (1x2½)
1½" CLEAR CEDAR BALUSTERS (2x2)
4" SPACING
3'6"
4x4 CEDAR POST
3/4" SECONDARY BOTTOM RAIL (1x2½)
1½" BOTTOM RAIL (2x4)
4"
3/8" GALV. LAGS
(2x6)
1½" x 5½" CEDAR DECK
2x8 TREATED JOISTS
1x CEDAR FASCIA
½" PLYWOOD SPACER
2-2x10 TREATED BEAM
POST CAP
4x4 POST
24"
84"
84"
GRADE
METAL POST BASE
10" DIA. CONC. PIER
FROST DEPTH
8" FOOTING
#4 REBAR
PRO ART
U.S.A.

CHAPTER ONE

Decks

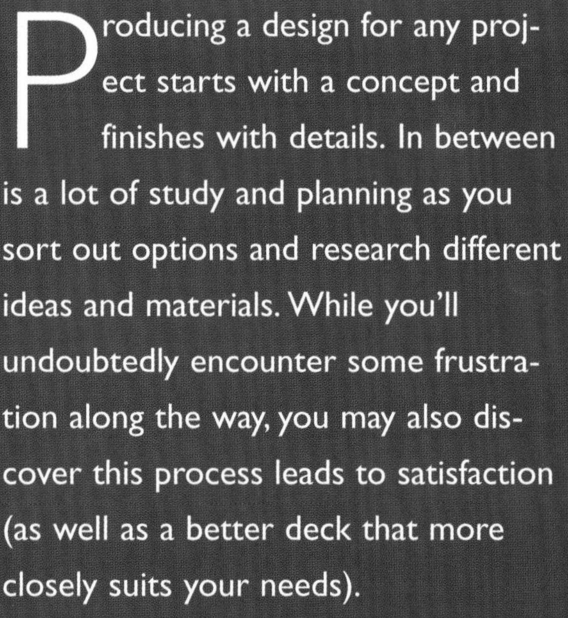

Producing a design for any project starts with a concept and finishes with details. In between is a lot of study and planning as you sort out options and research different ideas and materials. While you'll undoubtedly encounter some frustration along the way, you may also discover this process leads to satisfaction (as well as a better deck that more closely suits your needs).

This chapter focuses on the relationships between setting, aesthetics, and function in the design of a deck. I'll discuss how to turn these considerations into the working drawings that are a necessary communication tool for everyone involved. I'll also introduce some construction terms you'll need for later chapters, and give you some guidelines for estimating the cost of your project.

PRO TIP

Before you start to draw, it's a good idea to prepare a written list of all the general and specific requirements—some obvious, some not—for your deck.

IN DETAIL

Home centers and larger lumberyards sometimes offer deck design services. In some cases, they can produce a computer-generated design and materials list that may be perfectly adequate for a simple deck. But don't expect anything elaborate, and keep in mind that this design will probably suggest using in-stock materials or ones that are easily ordered.

WHAT CAN GO WRONG

While most basic decks aren't complicated, inexperienced deck designers can quickly find themselves in over their heads when conditions get tricky. You should seek an engineer's advice for any of the following problems:

- Highly elevated decks.
- Special seismic requirements.
- Steep or unstable hillsides.
- Ground with poor bearing capacity.
- Large cantilevers.
- Roof decks.
- Foundations with concentrated loading (hot tubs).

Take a photo of the site for reference to assist you in doing design work. A photo provides an easy way to refresh your memory about details.

The completed deck matches the final conceptual drawing fairly closely. The deck's usefulness over the years has proven the value of investing time in the design phase.

Producing Plans

A **set of plans**—or *prints*—is the map that everyone involved in a building project uses to arrive at a common destination. Putting all the dimensions and details down on paper removes most of the guesswork and minimizes—(notice I didn't say "eliminates")—the chances for misinterpretation. I find that getting my ideas down on paper helps me to clarify my thoughts about the design; sometimes problems become obvious only when they are taken from the concept stage and translated into actual lines on paper. And of course, scaled plans will also be required by most local building departments before you can obtain a permit for construction.

So who should produce these plans and do the design work on your deck? Here are your alternatives:

- You—No one knows better what you need and besides, designing a deck can be fun.
- An architect—Architectural services can be expensive, but may be necessary for difficult or complex situations.
- A designer—Although designers charge less than architects and should be adequate for most decks, they may be harder to find.
- A contractor—Contractors are usually experienced, but may offer only simple designs.

The truth is, if you're reading this book, you should be able to design your own deck. As the homeowner, you're the one who best knows how the deck will ultimately be used. All you need is a little tutoring in the planning process, along with some reassurance that your ideas are viable, practical, and relevant. And a deck is an excellent way to hone your design skills.

Admittedly, not everyone has the facility, experience, or inclination to mentally manipulate three-dimensional ideas. This process comes naturally for some folks, only with practice for others, and not at all for a few. I've often found that when a home is owned by partners, one person usually takes the lead in the design while the other may be better suited to the actual hands-on construction, an arrangement that may work for you and your partner.

Of course, if you still feel the need for professional help with your deck design, you have several options. Architects have the most resources to offer and are an obvious choice, but design fees can eat significantly into the overall project budget. However, if you are planning an extensive or complicated deck that must blend with local architectural styling, then an architect's help may be a necessity. If you do choose to work with an architect, find one with plenty of residential experience and references from clients with projects similar to yours.

Designers who are not licensed architects may be better suited to help you with your deck. Some may work exclusively for a specific contracting company; others may be part of an independent design company. Depending on the locality, designers may be subject to certain legal limitations, such as project size or the issuing of engineering specifications.

Many contractors (like myself) do design work at a nominal cost. Although most contractors will design only for projects they will actually be constructing, some may be willing to provide a design on a fee basis. If you do decide to hire a contractor to design your deck, look for those who specialize in deck design and construction; they should be able to present a portfolio full of past deck projects and plenty of good ideas. Another source may be landscape contractors who get involved in exterior projects such as decks and fences. Although I've only seen simple decks produced by these contractors, the right company may be able to provide more elaborate help.

The design process

For me, designing is a process of evolution as I add and discard ideas until a finished product emerges. Later in this book, I'll get into the nitty-gritty of material choices, detailing options, and structure and engineering. For now, I'd like to talk about how to come up with a deck configuration and style that suits your particular needs.

Before starting to draw, you should prepare a written list of all the general and specific requirements—some obvious, some not—for your deck. Carefully observing your daily habits will help you clarify which of these requirements are essential to you and which are pipe dreams influenced by fashion. For example, many times when I'm working with clients on a design, they'll describe a particular feature that they'd like on their deck, but can't tell me why that feature is important to

What You'll Need on Your Permit Application

Here are some of the details that may be required on the plans that you submit for your building permit.

- Overall size of deck and its relationship to property lines, setbacks, and easements.
- Type of foundation including depth, size of footings, and soil type expected.
- Height of deck above ground.
- Size, lumber species, location, spacing, and spans of all joists, beams, and posts.
- Railing design including material, fastener size and frequency, railing height, and baluster spacing.
- Bracing detail on elevated decks.
- Stairway location, railing location, and rise and run expected.
- All structural metal connectors and hardware to be used between framing members.

Deck Anatomy

Decks come in all shapes and sizes, but most are made from the same basic components. Before you can design a deck, you need to know the way a deck fits together and the names of all deck parts. This knowledge will also help you to communicate more clearly with building supply stores, so that you can order exactly what you need.

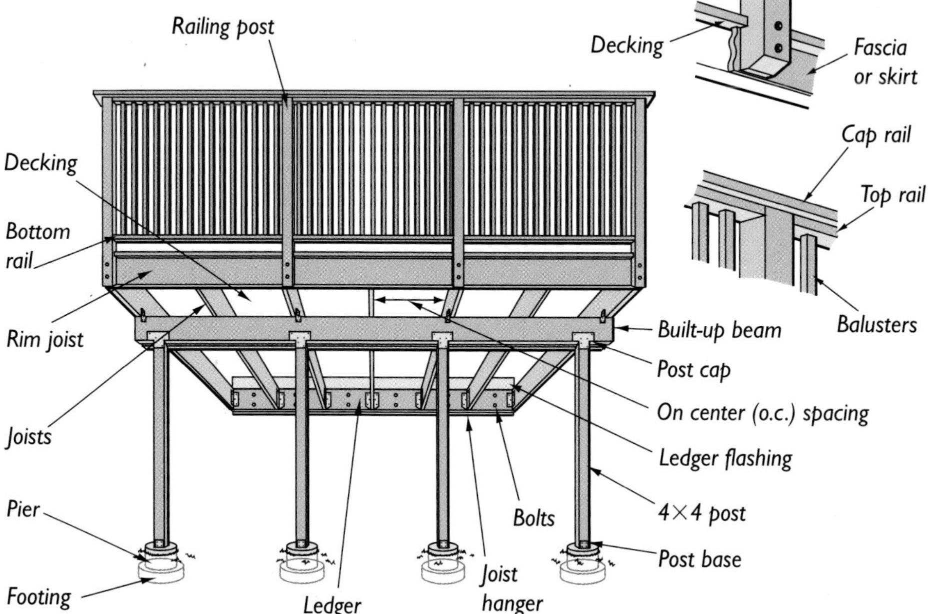

PRO TIP

After doing a site evaluation, draw a scaled map containing all the existing conditions as a reference for rechecking important details.

TRADE SECRET

Putting a few stakes in the ground at your proposed deck site will give you a full-sized outline of the project you're thinking about building. Unless the site is flat, your next step is to refine the site map information and determine more precisely the difference in elevation between the highest and lowest ground points on the staked perimeter to estimate the approximate length of the deck posts.

IN DETAIL

Estimating elevation changes can be difficult, so if you have a sloping site, use a string line level instead of trusting your eye. Another inexpensive tool—called a P-gun or Peep sight—looks like a little spyglass and allows you to make a sighting at the same level as your eye to any distant object.

WHAT CAN GO WRONG

When you're taking site measurements and creating a site map, remember that on sloped sites all measurements should be made horizontally.

them. Often as not, they want that feature because they "saw it in a magazine." While this may be justification enough in some cases, the feature may lose its luster once the extra expense or wasted space has been scrutinized.

The list of what you expect from your deck might begin with simply wanting a comfortable place to relax at the end of the day or a safe and visible play area for growing children. If you like to drink coffee and listen to the birds in the morning, this might call for a smaller, more private deck rather than one suitable for entertaining large groups on the weekends. Do you hope to increase the value of your home for resale, or is this deck fulfilling your immediate personal needs? Is there a crumbling patio or an ugly oil tank that needs to be hidden? If you live in a rainy area, do you intend to be able to use the deck when it rains? Will your deck require lighting for nighttime use?

Site evaluations

In order to answer these questions and build a deck that's well integrated with its surroundings, it's important to do a site evaluation. When I visit the site for a proposed deck, I gather information about topography and drainage, locate utilities, assess easements and covenant zoning restrictions, and then put it all down on one piece of paper. The product of the site evaluation should be a scaled plan detailing all the existing conditions. Having a comprehensive, readily available reference will save you from continually rechecking or even worse, forgetting these important details.

A site plan should show the outline of the house (including dimensions) in bold dark lines, along with the location of existing doors and relevant windows. I also like to note the use of rooms adjacent to the deck. It's a good idea to record the locations of hose bibs and exterior outlets (both of which are expensive to move) and to note all buried and overhead hazards such as utilities (electric, gas, phones, cable TV) and tanks (water, fuel, septic) and represent them with dashed lines. Don't forget to sketch in large natural objects, such as trees and gardens, as well as the locations of neighboring houses and easements. Downspouts that will need extensions to carry water away from new footing should also be located. In addition to these physical considerations, your site plan should include compass directions, prevailing wind conditions, and the location of the sun during the day, noting in particular any shadows cast by the house or nearby trees that will affect shading on the deck.

Topography plays a very important role in determining deck design. A site plan for a sloped site should note the natural elevation changes of the land around the site, drawn as contour lines. Drawing the contour lines absolutely correctly is not as critical as accurately determining the total drop in elevation over a certain horizontal distance. Steep slopes may allow for more level changes and will require more or longer stairs as well as taller support posts that will need closer structural analysis to determine their size and frequency.

Along with your wish list and site evaluation, photos taken of the site can be invaluable. Not only are they useful when you're sitting at your desk and need to check on exterior details, they can also help you see things in a refreshing way.

✓ According to Code

You may live in a neighborhood where there are covenants dictating your deck's architectural style, size, visibility, location, and materials. These covenants can be quite lengthy, and may require that your deck plans be reviewed by a neighborhood board. There may also be easements or other restrictions on the use of your property. Be sure that you know what these are before you begin your project.

A well-designed deck includes consideration of deck furnishings and clearances around them.

Drawing solutions on paper

With my site plan and photographs in hand, I begin putting my ideas down on paper by establishing the areas will best meet the requirements of the wish list. Solutions to simple wants are usually obvious, but often a deck will be serving more than a single need. If I don't have a preconceived idea for the overall project, I like to first design a solution to each individual requirement on my list. After I've produced an array of small designs, I attempt to integrate them into a whole.

For example, I'll sketch an ideal eating area—which may include table, food prep counter, storage, and grill—then separately sketch a perfect hot tub deck with privacy screen, sitting bench, and changing booth. Next I might draw small sketches for a planter garden or a reading/meditation area. I then arrange all of these drawings in a logical pattern and

✓ According to Code

A setback is a locally prescribed buffer zone around a property's perimeter that must be free from all new structures. Even if the deck's foundation is not in the setback area, setback restrictions may apply to deck overhangs, so check with local building department representatives for their exact interpretation.

The Evolution of a Deck Design

A deck design evolves over time out of some core ideas and a lot of sketches.

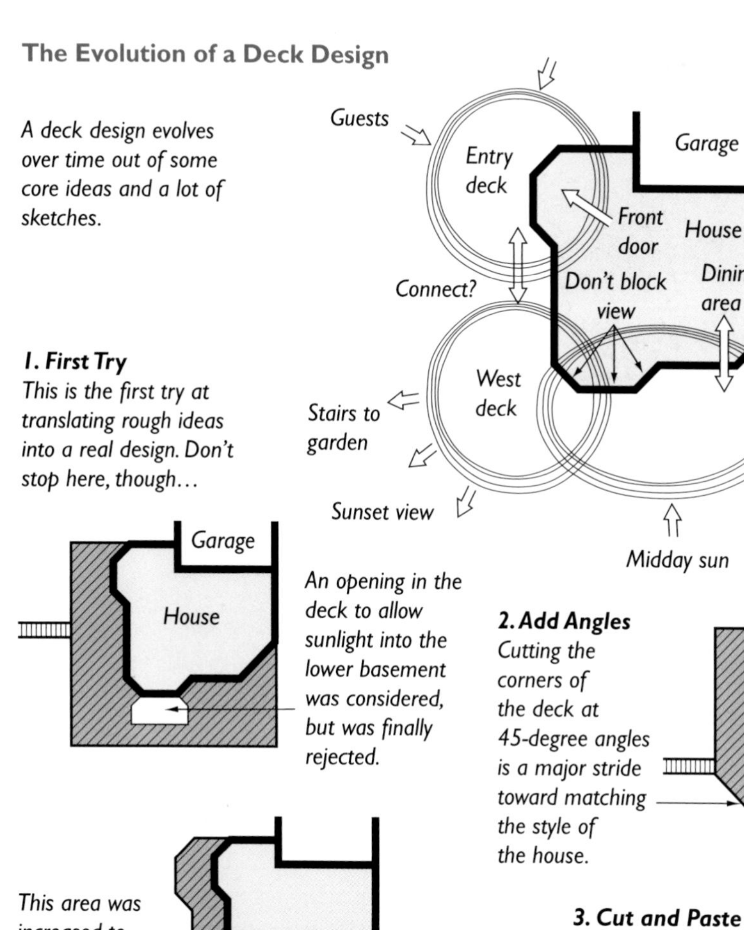

1. First Try
This is the first try at translating rough ideas into a real design. Don't stop here, though…

An opening in the deck to allow sunlight into the lower basement was considered, but was finally rejected.

2. Add Angles
Cutting the corners of the deck at 45-degree angles is a major stride toward matching the style of the house.

This area was increased to provide room for a future hot tub.

Cutting back this section allows a view out of the southeast windows.

3. Cut and Paste
Reducing this area emphasizes the distinction between the main entry and the west deck. It now serves as a walkway rather than as a full section of the deck. But one problem still remains: The main area of the deck interferes with the southerly view from inside the house.

4. Add Levels
The next step separates the deck into three distinct levels—A, B, and C. Level A is even with the entry floor level, Level B is 15 in. below Level A, and Level C is 22½ in. below Level B. This allows a better view of the yard from inside the house, complements the downward slope of the land, and prevents the deck from towering above the ground.

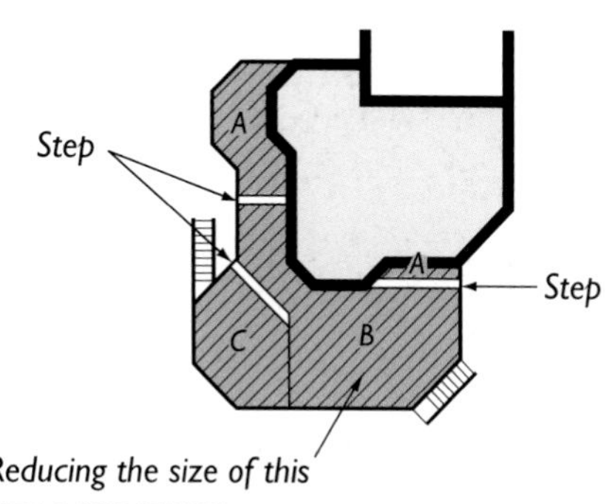

Reducing the size of this area saves money.

5. Final Design
The final step in this design process directs the stairways into the front lawn and garden areas, and a ramp is added near the front door. Rather than use built-in seating, which might block the view, the design relies on broadened level changes that can also be used for seating.

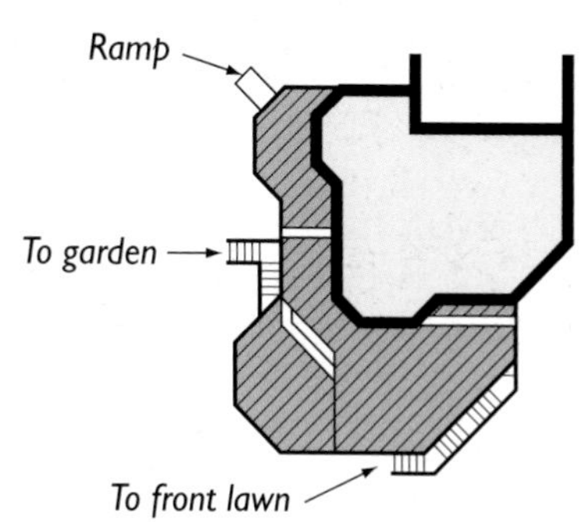

PRO TIP

I find that photos taken of the site are especially useful when you're drafting your plan, so you won't need to go far to check on exterior details.

IN DETAIL

While I do most of my drafting by hand, there are plenty of simple but powerful computer-aided design (CAD) programs for home computers that you can use to help you design your deck. They can create views from different angles or take you on a three-dimensional walking tour using your drawing as the guide.

TRADE SECRET

Some triangular architect's scales have as many as ten different scales (beware of similar-looking engineer's scales that have the markings in tenths of feet instead of inches). While drafting, I usually have to fumble for the correct scale every time I pick it up. Put a sticker or mark a red dot on the scale you're using to cut down on errors.

A Site Plan

A site plan is an attempt to consolidate all the information about the site on one sheet that is readily available to jog the memory during the design process. The site plan should include easements, setbacks, terrain, elevation changes, and house features that will be important to remember.

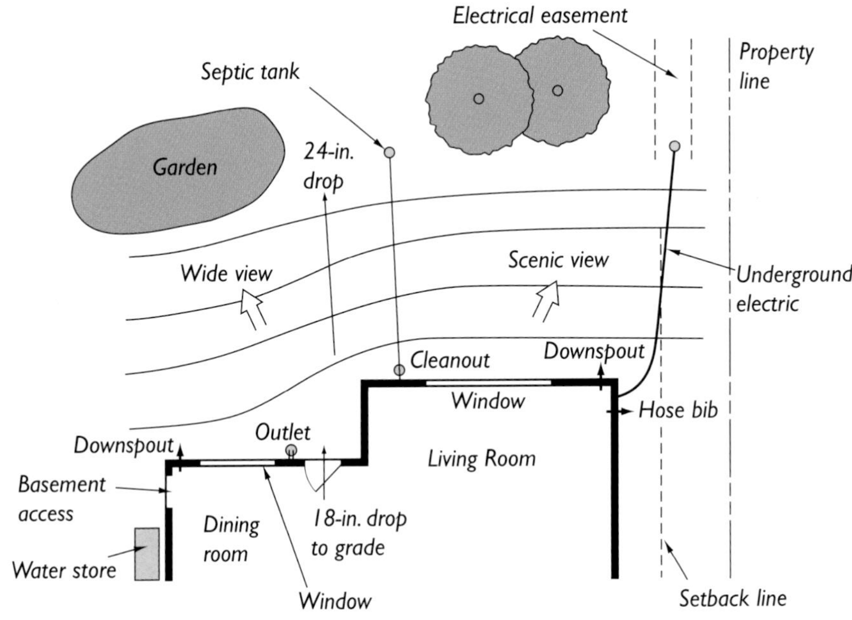

tape them together, trying to problem-solve as I go along. For instance, the eating area might be best located near a door to the kitchen so that food doesn't have to be carried a long way. On the other hand, the hot tub would probably work best in a more obscure corner, especially if privacy is an issue. If you've sketched a play area for kids, you might want to situate it under a kitchen window from which a parent can keep a watchful eye on activities. (See the drawing on p. 11.)

As your deck begins to take shape, you need to find a creative way of linking the separate areas together. Start thinking about level changes, broad stairways, connecting walkways. Give close scrutiny to size requirements. Benches, trellises, railings, and other features combine form and functionality, while specific finishing details—a classic or contemporary balustrade, for example—help ensure the deck's style matches your home.

At this stage of the process, I like to let my wish-list considerations take precedence over cost and structural details. I've yet to see a design that couldn't be built, but in the real world cost is usually a consideration, so now's the time to go back and modify some great—if impractical—ideas to bring them in line with the budget. One problem most novices encounter is that the difficult-to-build design elements, such as curves, are not always readily apparent. If you're doing your own construction work, this can be a mixed blessing, for you may enthusiastically tackle something out of inexperience that a contractor would know will be difficult (and therefore costly) to build.

While compromises can be frustrating, it's important to bring into focus exactly what isn't working about a particular design. Sometimes this means setting the whole process aside for a while until clearer heads and calmer emotions can prevail. Often, it's just a single, knotty problem that makes the entire design seem faulty. If you can recognize this and focus on solving that one problem, it may clear up the misconception that the whole design is defective and help you see that your design is a good one. A good design usually seems obvious, while a bad design keeps nagging at you to fix it. This process should be fun, rather than tedious or stressful, so allow yourself plenty of time. I often spend weeks on a deck design as my clients assimilate the latest alteration and respond with new suggestions.

Plans and views

Formal plans typically give views from several different perspectives. The basic bird's-eye view—called a *plan view*—includes the outline of the deck and maybe that part of the house to which the deck is attached. Usually drawn to a ¼-in.- or ½-in.-equals-1-ft. scale, this view is the most useful because it can be packed with information. A house or other complicated structure might require several plan views to show such information as room layout, foundation outline, and floor framing; your deck plan, however, should be able to show foundation locations, post and beam locations, joist spacing, and railing post locations on a single plan view. Putting all this information on one sheet isn't essential, but it will save you the trouble of organizing multiple sheets and redrawing outlines for additional plans.

Your plan view should include all important dimensions, including overall size and locations of beams, house corners, doorways, and windows. This view will also show locations of stairs, changes in level, deck features, and relevant lot and boundary considerations.

The view from the side is called an *elevation* (drawn 1 in. equals 1 ft.) and shows heights of the various deck components, their vertical arrangement, and other information not easily conveyed on the plan view. The elevation also should indicate the depths of foundations, the deck height off the ground, and the sizes of posts, beams, joists, and cantilevers. It may show the relationship of the railing posts to the joists as well as railing heights above deck level. It isn't essential to draw tall elements to full size, as this may require a scale that renders other elements too small to be useful, but do keep labels on dimensions accurate.

Detail drawings will illustrate those specifics that are too small or intricate to show on the plan view or elevation view. These drawings are often done full size, if possible, in order to include all the

Drawing From Photos

One trick that may help if you're having trouble visualizing a design is to take a photo of your home while you are standing in the yard. Then take this photo to your local copy store, and for just a few dollars, have an enlargement and some color copies made.

Now draw your ideas directly on the copies. It's not important to get the scale exactly right because these are serving as temporary aids, not building plans. Draw railing details, foundation posts, stairways, and anything else that will have an impact on the ultimate look of the deck.

A Plan View

This plan view contains most of the information needed to build a fairly typical, simple deck. More-complex decks may benefit from additional plan views illustrating railings or difficult framing solutions.

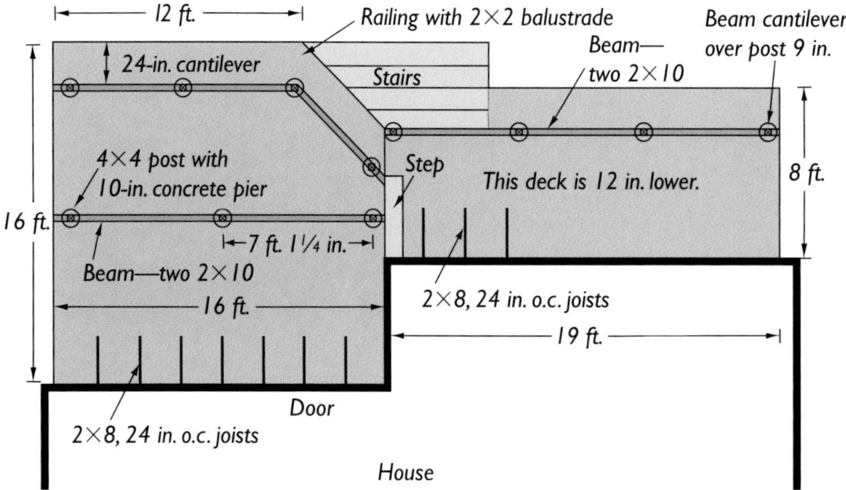

PRO TIP

A rectangular or square design is certainly the easiest to build and is often the best choice for a simple deck of small size.

IN DETAIL

Rather than a deck that feels like a stage, most people want their decks to offer a degree of privacy. One way to make a deck harder to look into from the outside is to add privacy screens to shield the deck's occupants from unwanted stares. It helps to think of these screens simply as sections of railing with different heights.

WHAT CAN GO WRONG

Long, continuous decks that try to provide economical access to public areas of the house as well as bedrooms too often create a privacy problem: Anyone can walk right up to a bedroom door or window and stare in. The obvious solution is to build two separate decks, a remedy that probably requires only a little more foundation and railing work than one deck.

An Elevation

Elevations show the deck plans from the sides and illustrate vertical arrangement and dimensioned heights of components that wouldn't show in the plan view. One side view here shows everything needed for this simple deck, but level changes and stairs may require extra drawings.

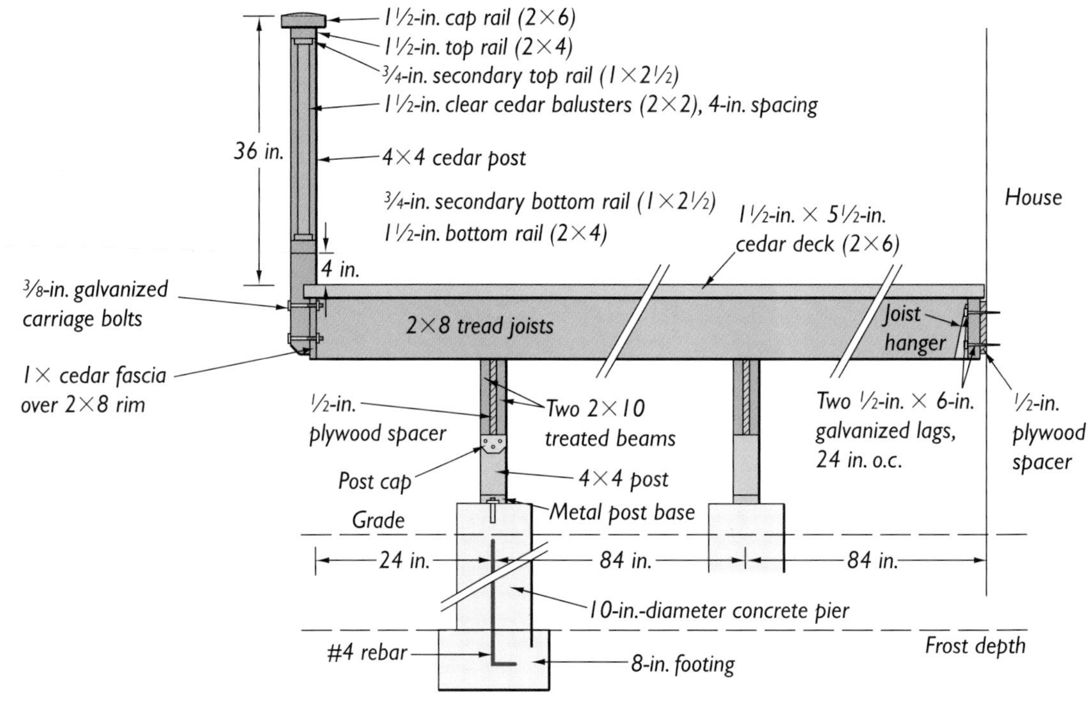

Sample Detail Drawings

Detail drawings are essential when you are trying to work out exactly how everything will fit together. Detail drawings convey specific information about dimensions, fasteners, brackets, and unusual components and their arrangements. These drawings show a side view of a railing (left) and a typical beam–post connection (right).

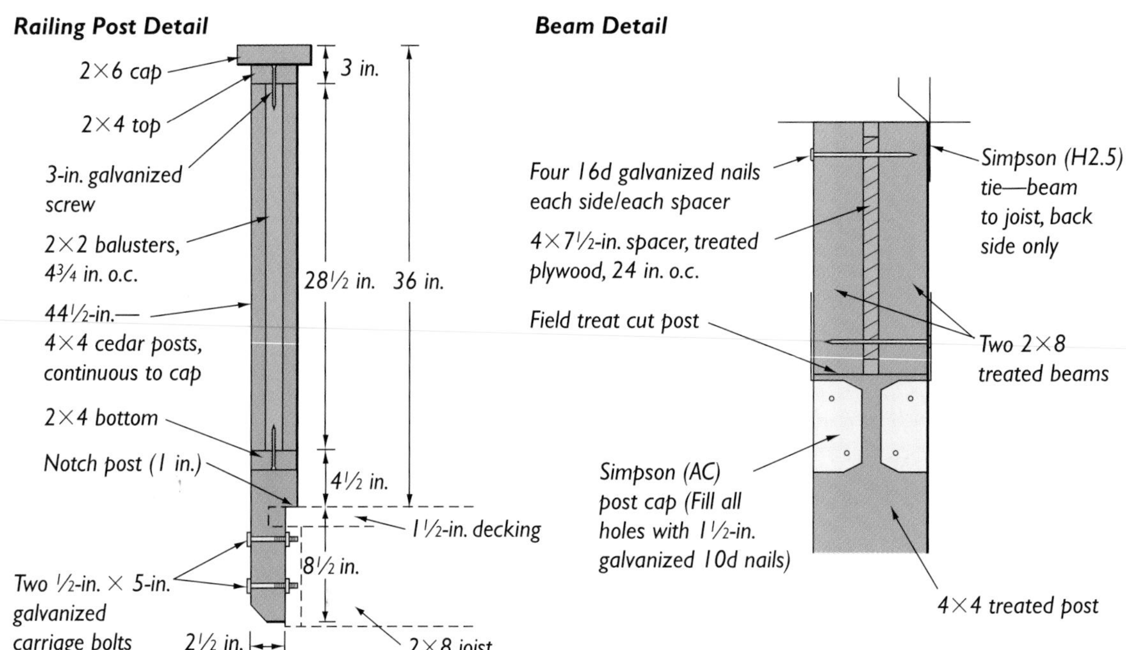

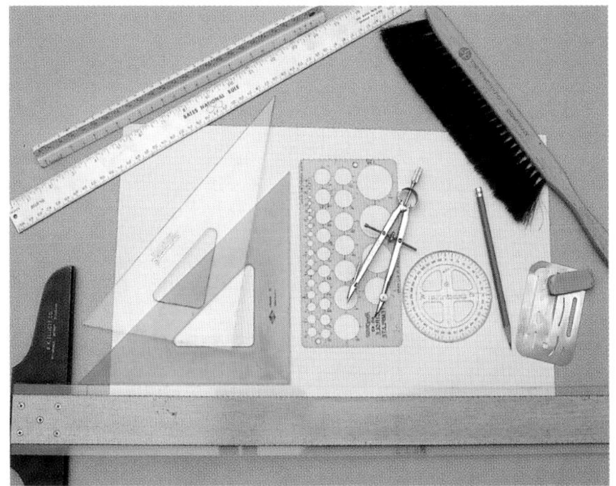

A basic drafting setup consists of a board, T square, rulers or an architect's scale, triangles, and a pencil. A circle template or compass, protractor for angles, an eraser for mistakes, a shield, and a brush to sweep without smudges will make drawing quicker and more accurate but aren't essential.

information needed to properly assemble a particular connection. Sometimes, a builder will work out these details at the job site on a sketchpad or a scrap of lumber in order to figure out how something is supposed to fit. To help avoid mistakes, however, it's best if most details are provided by the designer before construction begins. Detail drawings are important because they specifically spell out how the deck will be assembled.

Drafting your plan

Whether you do your drafting by hand or with the help of a computer, it can be a fun technical exercise as you formalize all of your notes, sketches, and ideas into a real plan. I prefer to use pencil and paper, an approach that may be a bit more time-consuming but doesn't take a lot of equipment.

The basic tool is a T square of wood or plastic that allows you to draw parallel lines. T squares are available in a number of different sizes, but I find the 24-in. length adequate for small projects such as a deck. Also handy to have (but not essential) is a drafting board. My 22-in.-by-26-in. melamine board is easy to keep clean, has a flat and smooth

A Deck With a View

When there is a beautiful view, houses are almost always sited to take full advantage of it. A common problem is that an added deck often interferes with the view from inside the house. Not only does the railing of the deck get in the way visually, but the deck floor often does too. Minimal railing styles or cable rails can go a long way to keeping the view open. Another solution is to lower the deck so that it is several feet below the floor level of the house. A small landing and cascading stairs can make up the difference in heights as well as add interest to the deck.

My particular view on views is that they shouldn't be squandered. Rather than expose an entire deck to a vista, provide for a special area that requires a little effort to take in the scenery. Says Christopher Alexander in *A Pattern Language* (Alexander et al, Oxford University Press, 1977), "one wants to enjoy [the view] and drink it in every day. But the more open it is, the more obvious, the more it shouts, the sooner it will fade. Gradually it will become like the wallpaper; and the intensity of its beauty will no longer be accessible."

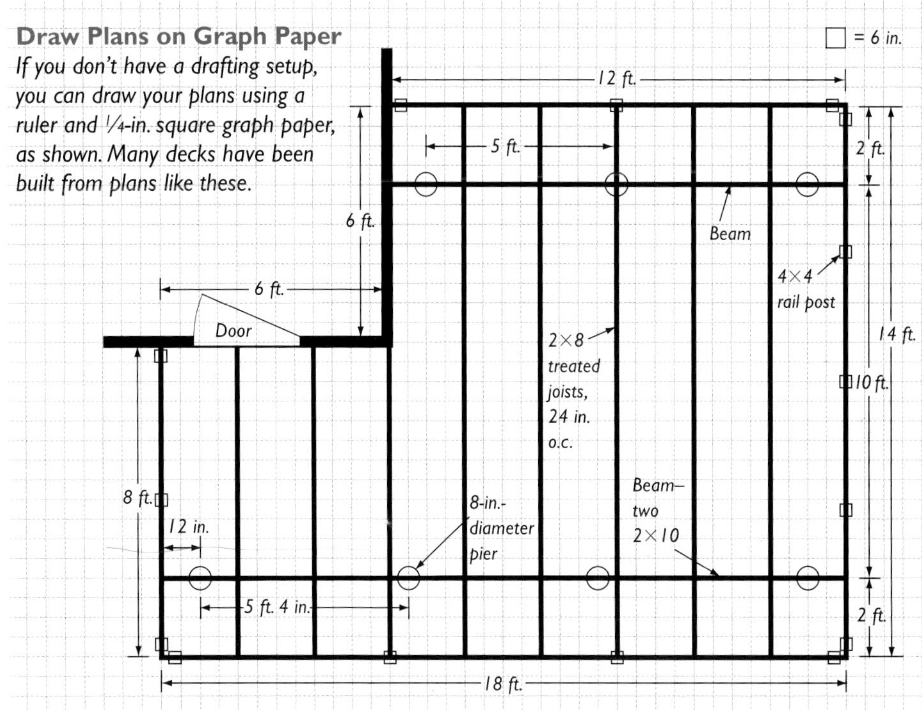

Draw Plans on Graph Paper
If you don't have a drafting setup, you can draw your plans using a ruler and ¼-in. square graph paper, as shown. Many decks have been built from plans like these.

PRO TIP

If your door location is okay but the existing door has no windows, the door blank itself can usually be swapped out for a glazed door without modification.

IN DETAIL

Most interior hallways are between 3 ft. and 4 ft. wide, but deck walkways that are the same dimension tend to look and feel fairly narrow, especially when they're elevated. I like to make connecting walkways and almost all smaller areas of a deck at least 5 ft. to 6 ft. wide. I like exterior stairways to be 4 ft. wide, although a 3-ft. width will work on little-used stairs. Remember that deck railings and handrails tend to be somewhat bulky and intrude quite a bit on narrow spaces—one of the reasons I like to add plenty of width to stairs and walkways.

surface and straight sides for the square to ride on, and holds an 18-in.-by-24-in. sheet of paper perfectly—(you'll want a board that is at least 4 in. wider and 2 in. longer than the paper you're using).

Other tools that are handy to have include a smaller 90-degree square (made of transparent plastic) for drawing lines perpendicular to those drawn with the T square, a good eraser, a pencil sharpener, and an eraser shield. Garden-variety No. 2 pencils are okay, but I suggest using a harder lead that is less likely to smear. You'll also need an architect's scale. In addition to the usual 12 in.-equals-1-ft. marking, an architect's scale includes various other scales, from 3⁄32 in. equals 1 ft. to 3 in. equals 1 ft.

You can also use 8-in.-by-11-in. graph paper (it also comes in other sizes). I favor the kind with four or eight squares to the inch as it easily lends itself to different scales, depending on the size of the project. Over the years, I've probably seen plans produced with graph paper, ruler, and pencil as often as professionally drawn ones, and have found them to be perfectly adequate when accurately drawn.

Design Considerations

Having been involved in the design of my own construction projects for the past 20 years, I have learned that design is a very subjective undertaking. However, there are a host of routine, objective factors that must be considered in every deck design—exposure concerns such as sun, wind, and weather; functional considerations such as traffic patterns and connection to the house; and ultimately, the aesthetics of shape, contrast, and color.

Siting for climate and exposure

The influence of local weather conditions—your microclimate—needs to be considered when you locate and design your deck. Temperature

This sturdy trellis of sculpted timbers provides a large shaded eating area.

and light can be controlled with the flip of a switch inside a house, but not on a deck. A deck serves as a transition area between the environment we maintain inside our homes and the external world, so consider carefully how the external elements will affect your use and enjoyment of it.

The position of a deck in relation to the daily path of the sun is one of the most critical considerations. If a deck is too cold or hot to use comfortably, then it won't be used at all, no matter how great the view. For good reason, every deck that I've built in Alaska has avoided the northern

✓ According to Code

Avoid building on an easement, which grants some other party (besides the owner) access to or use of the property. Typically the other party would be a utility company having the right to use some property for wires or pipes, but an easement also could include a neighbor's right to cross some part of your land for a driveway. Other easements may refer to solar rights, views, or drainage. All easements should have been disclosed to you when you bought the property (and should be detailed on your deed), but sometimes they aren't.

Wind and Privacy Screens

Screens provide protection from wind, sun, and curious neighbors. Because pressure on a screen quadruples when wind speed doubles, all screens need to be firmly anchored. Gaps slightly reduce a screen's effectiveness, but facilitate air circulation on calm days. The height of a screen determines its effectiveness: The sheltered area downwind of a screen is equal to about twice the height of the screen.

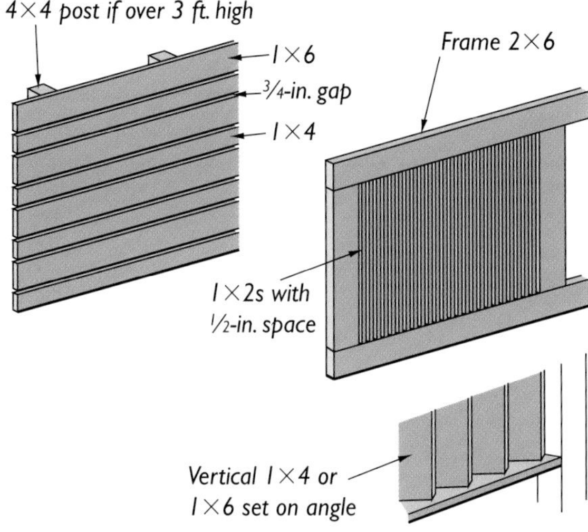

and cooler side of the home. Most decks in far northern climates are situated on the southern and western sides of the house to capture the afternoon and evening sun, the times when decks are at their peak use. In colder climates, even shade from trees is unwelcome.

In warmer climates where decks can be used year-round, the primary goal may be just the opposite—to provide shade by location. This may mean situating the deck on the eastern side of a home to take advantage of shade in the late afternoon or early evening. In very hot climates, the north face of a building would be the coolest side at midday.

Because decks may experience completely different temperatures over the course of the day, you must also carefully consider when and how you will optimize heating and cooling on your deck. For a deck with a southern exposure, trellises or awnings can be used to block the sun when it is high overhead, but are less effective when the sun is lower in the sky during mornings and evenings. While this may not be a problem in the winter months, it can cause significant overheating in the summer.

Sometimes a deck can be designed to make the best of both sun and shade—for example, a deck that wraps around a corner of a house. Moveable screens are useful for shading small areas, while a fixed overhead trellis or awning can provide shade for larger areas. Trellises (see pp. 170-172) can be designed to provide maximum shade at certain times of the day while letting some sun through at other times. And trellis posts can be used to support additional sun-blocking screens to the west, so the deck can be enjoyed in the early evening.

Wind changes direction and strength frequently and can be a particularly difficult element to design for. Wind-shielding options include using well-anchored screens and large plantings, as well as locating the deck on the side of the house opposite the prevailing winds. Two other features that I find helpful in windy areas are changes in level and railings that have few or no openings. By combining these two features, you can create small protected areas on lower deck levels and block the wind with an adjacent high-level deck and railing. Of course, if you need as much breeze as you can get to cool things down, then elevating the deck, moving it away from wind-blocking structures, and making the railing as unobtrusive and open as possible will all help.

If you get lots of rain during the warm months when deck usage is high, you may want to add a partial overhead structure. (A full roof would make the structure a porch; in either case, foundation design must address the extra load.) If you need to clear the deck of snow during the winter (particularly important in areas where a full winter's snow load can exceed the deck's structural capacity), you must consider where the snow will go and provide a railing design that will make snow removal easier. This may mean having a railing section that can be removed to facilitate snow removal.

PRO TIP

Stairways should be located so that frequently used areas off the deck don't require a long walk. A large deck may need more than one stairway.

A spa surrounded by an elegant railing leaves no doubt about the focus of this small deck area.

IN DETAIL

Focal points are single-function objects or areas that can add interest to a simple deck. These might include small bump-outs in the deck for cooking areas, a central outdoor fire pit, hot tubs, gardening workbenches, or fountains and pools.

IN DETAIL

Level changes are a great way to introduce contrast and interest. They can punctuate transitions from one function to another. Varying levels can also help introduce changes in style (as from wood decking to a rock walkway), or provide a great place for accessories. Level changes also allow a deck to follow the contours of the land, preventing a hillside home from having a deck that towers high above ground level.

Getting an Angle on the Sun

Morning Sun
Except in the hottest climates, early morning sun is always welcome, and decks can be open to the east. Overhead trellis boards oriented along the north–south axis will let the sun penetrate back to the deck and house at this time of day but will block midday sun.

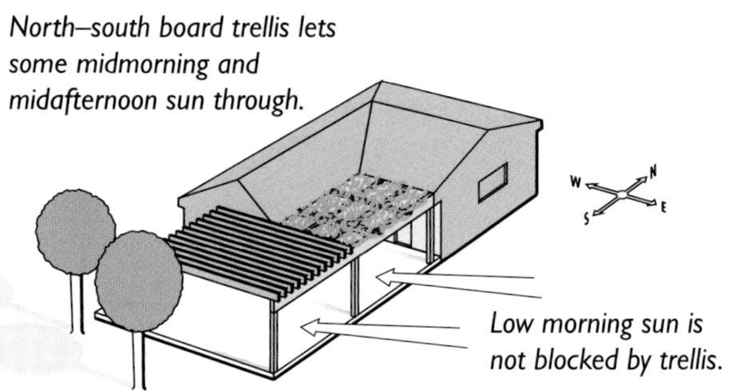

Midday Sun
Midday sun is the hottest everywhere. A trellis can provide shade during the hot summer, but unfortunately it works during the winter, too.

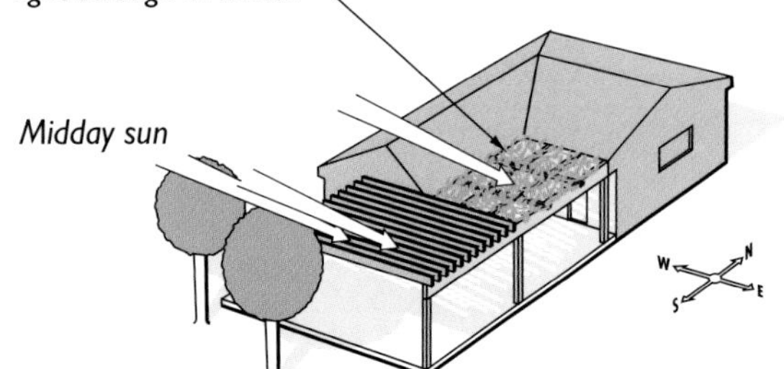

Evening Sun
To block evening sun, add screens to the west or keep the deck exclusively on the east side of the house to provide shade from the lower sun. Locating a deck to utilize trees and natural greenery for shade is a good three-season solution without winter-time complications.

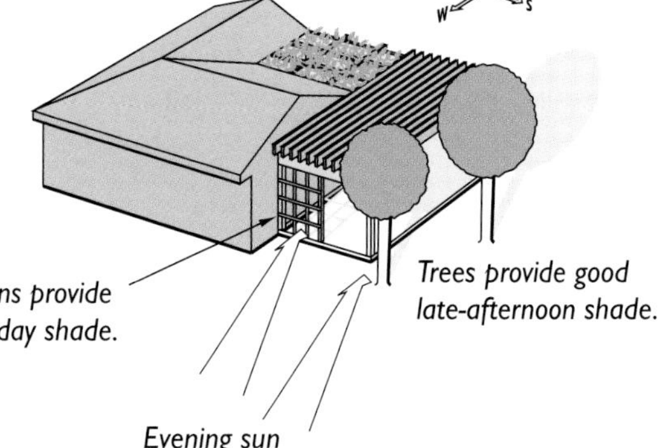

This covered deck extends along the whole side on the house. Although translucent panels were used in the central area to let in light while keeping out rain, any part of the roof system could have been omitted in sunnier climates.

Doors and traffic patterns

While climate and other outside factors certainly influence where you choose to locate your deck, you also need to consider how the deck relates to the *inside* of your house. If eating on the deck requires you to haul food halfway through the house, you can bet there won't be many picnics. If a parent inside can't keep a watchful eye on youngsters playing outside on the deck, the kids will end up staying indoors. A deck is—or should be—an extension of the house, a transition area between a "wilder" natural setting (albeit some lawns are wilder than others) and the more-protected indoors. A deck with easy and obvious access will entice guests to wander out at parties, or simply encourage you to step out and check the weather or admire the view. If a deck isn't to become a seldom-used hideaway, it should be a fully integrated, but outdoor, part of the house.

Obviously, a door (or doors) leading from the house to the deck is a necessity. Some smaller decks serve only bedrooms, but most decks serve many purposes and people, so the door will usually be located in the living, dining, or kitchen areas. When locating a door, think in terms of walkways that route traffic naturally around the perimeter of a room, rather than directly through it.

With luck, you may have an existing door in the right location. If there isn't a suitable door, consider creating an exterior walkway or boardwalk or adding a narrow, connecting deck to an existing door. This can be a good solution on some elevated decks because it may eliminate the extra stairway needed to connect a too-distant door with the new deck. Almost invariably, however, it's worth the trouble to add a new door rather than live with a door that is poorly located.

As for the actual door, the one I prefer for deck access is a full-glass, 5-ft.-to-6-ft.-wide patio unit with one hinged door and one fixed panel. In more moderate climates, a French door (where both halves open) can help make the deck seem more of an extension of the interior space. To avoid air leakage at the door, I always choose a hinged type with compression weather-stripping rather than a sliding door; recently, however, some sliding door manufacturers have alleviated the infiltration problem by using different hardware and weatherstripping.

Just as access from the deck to the house is an important traffic consideration, access to the lawn or yard also needs some thought. Stairways should be located so that frequently used areas off the deck are easy to get to. If the deck is large, this may mean having more than one stairway. Analyze existing traffic routes and important work areas to be sure you will have the necessary access to such areas as driveways, garages, clotheslines, trash collection, gardens, and dog houses.

While stairways and paths are the most common ways to provide access to a deck, a ramp may be useful in some instances. Although not required in most residential construction, a ramp will certainly be appreciated by a friend or relative confined to a wheelchair. And a ramp can also make it easier to wheel heavy garden carts, barbecue grills,

Traffic Patterns

When choosing a location for the deck, consider how access points will affect walkway traffic both from inside the house and outside to other areas such as lawns and storage.

Trash

Deck door conveniently located to busy areas

Deck visually accessible from inside

Barbecue close to kitchen

Out of traffic area for hot tub or benches

Could be gated to restrict access

Table out of traffic flow

Traffic flow is conveniently and centrally located, but maintains large areas for other uses.

The large glass wall and French doors blur the boundaries between inside and out, and the spacious deck extends the living space when the weather cooperates.

PRO TIP

If you need the square footage of a large deck to accommodate several different functions, consider breaking it up into two (or more) smaller decks.

IN DETAIL

Changes in materials are a great way to introduce contrast and interest. You might connect two wooden decks with a small stone walkway, for example, or incorporate copper post caps into your railing. The same materials installed in a different direction or stained a different color will also attract attention and can be a useful technique to signal a level change or a set of stairs. Foundations provide another opportunity for contrast. Instead of standard wooden posts, consider concrete columns or a partial wall system veneered with brick or stone.

This low railing uses stone work that contrasts with the wooden deck but matches the house and ties the two spaces together.

A ramp is easy to build and may be a necessity for handicap use, but it can also help with access for carts, bikes, or wheelbarrows.

or bicycles onto the deck. However, ramps can be slippery in wet or winter climates and should be considered an adjunct to, not a replacement for, a set of stairs.

Architectural considerations

Now that you've determined the functional characteristics of your deck design, you need to consider the "look" of the deck and how it will blend with the existing style of the house. Some of the factors to take into account are contrasts and continuity, as well as shape, elevation, and materials.

Contrasts. How can we best blend the functional and aesthetic to produce a visually successful deck? In *The Good House*, Max Jacobson writes that good design "is the production of harmony through the orchestration of strong contrasts." In my experience, good designs are full of contrasts: short and tall, open and enclosed, dark and light. Colors can be warm or cool. Spaces can be wide open or secluded. Railings can be bulky and solid or unobtrusive to the point of near invisibility. In fact, planned contrasts can actually be wonderful solutions to necessary compromises. Just as the deck is a transitional space between indoors and out, sections of the deck serve as transitions to other deck areas, and these transitions offer opportunities for introducing contrast.

Although the wooden posts and wrought-iron railing contrast in size, texture, and color, they complement each other and match the rustic setting.

Why is contrast desirable? Because differences sharpen our experiences and let us adjust our environment to our momentary needs. We can choose warm and sunny or dark and cool. We may want a maximum of social interaction or seclusion. At the very least, decks should have small areas that are more isolated than others, such as a hidden bench in a strategic location, screened by a level change or greenery.

Continuity. Another important consideration is *continuity*. New elements must make sense in the context of the existing structure. Tongue-piercing and pink hair may not seem out of place on a city street anymore, but in a very formal situation—in another context—these styles still raise eyebrows.

While perhaps not as novel as pink hair, decks are a relatively recent architectural creation. Though a deck on a contemporary home rarely seems out of place, adding a deck to an older house demands special considerations and restrictions. This may mean that the deck be somewhat understated and conservative in design or located in the back of the house to minimize visual discontinuity with other homes in the neighborhood.

Be sure the mass or heaviness of your deck matches the mass of the house. A deck with large, exposed foundation timbers and posts will not be a good complement to a small and refined

A large landing (rather than a set of steps) directly outside of an exterior door creates a contrast in deck levels without adding a lot of extra foundation work.

For some decks, promoting continuity is preferable to creating contrasts; this log railing perfectly complements the log house.

Matching the style of an existing structure is important. This substantial covered deck over a sunroom perfectly complements the heft and vintage of a traditional Victorian home.

cottage. If the deck's foundation is going to be highly visible, then create continuity by matching deck materials to those used in the house. For example, a brick-veneer house might be well served by a deck that incorporates brick in the foundation or railing columns or features a brick walkway. A deck for a Victorian home could include a railing design that mimics an ornate trim detail from the house. If attaching the deck directly to the house creates too much visual and stylistic confusion, then perhaps a freestanding deck connected with a walkway would be a better solution.

If your deck is to seem a natural part of your house, it must reflect the house's "personality." Colors used on the deck should match or complement those used on the house or house trim. Visual elements of the house—for example, horizontal or vertical lines of siding—can be repeated on the deck. A strong feature such as a round window can inspire a visual "echo" in a curved element on the deck. Railings and accessories—benches, screens, trellises, built-in planters—are two easily manipulated features that significantly

The steel-pipe railings match the contemporary styling and trim color on this Seattle home, and don't interfere with the view from inside (although they may not meet code in all areas).

Lighten Up

A deck can have a major impact on the amount of light available to any room under it. This may not matter in an unused basement, but it will have a significant affect on a frequently used living area. Sometimes shade is desirable, but if creating a cool, dark space sounds uninviting, then consider some alternatives. One solution is to build a freestanding deck 10 ft. to 12 ft. away from the house, then connect the deck to the house with a boardwalk or bridge. This type of deck will require more foundation work and probably a lot of extra bracing. Another solution is to simply leave off the decking in some areas and protect the openings with railings. A third solution is to replace some of the wood decking with thick sheets of Lexan™ or other tough plastic. A matte finish will still let light through but won't show as much wear as it ages. The plastic should be installed so that it can expand and contract without cracking. A glass supplier can help with appropriate thickness information and installation details.

PRO TIP

Your deck can enhance the house's exterior by adding visual interest or correcting deficiencies.

IN DETAIL

I use the following minimum dimensions (as measured away from the house) as general rules of thumb when planning decks:

- 8 ft. for special use areas.
- 12 ft. for general and social areas.
- 4 ft. for ground-level connections, paths, and stairs.
- 6 ft. for elevated connections with railings.

Matching the style of the home may require more than a visit to the lumberyard for materials. Although a different railing could do the job, it's hard to imagine one that looks more appropriate than this log design.

affect the final appearance of your deck. However, use discretion in your quest for contrast and continuity; the finished result should look inspired and subtle, not overdone or heavy-handed.

An overhead structure offers another way to create continuity. As I've mentioned, a trellis is a good choice when sun must be blocked; in cloudy regions, a simpler, more skeletal structure can be used to suggest a protective ceiling overhead without actually blocking the sun. A trellis can help create a feeling of enclosure for an intimate deck and also serve to extend the house form outward. The trellis can be simply a few posts and beams forming an outline over part or all of the deck and provides a great place to hang baskets of flowers.

Shape. The *shape* of a deck can help correct deficiencies in the house's appearance. A very vertical house or one with a tall side can be visually lowered by a deck that uses strong horizontal elements in the railing and foundation. A short deck perched high on long foundation posts accents the height of the house. A long ranch house can be shortened visually by a deck placed at the middle of the house, whereas a deck situated at one end would only exaggerate the house's length.

A rectangular or square deck is certainly the easiest to build and is often the best choice for a simple deck of small size. But if I'm building a larger deck that has changes in level or serves multiple functions, I'll often incorporate angles to add interest. This may mean simply cutting the two outside corners at 45 degrees, or it may mean setting one side of a deck at an angle. Keep in mind that chopping off corners should be done with some discretion as the effect can quickly become

Suggested Minimum Sizing Guidelines

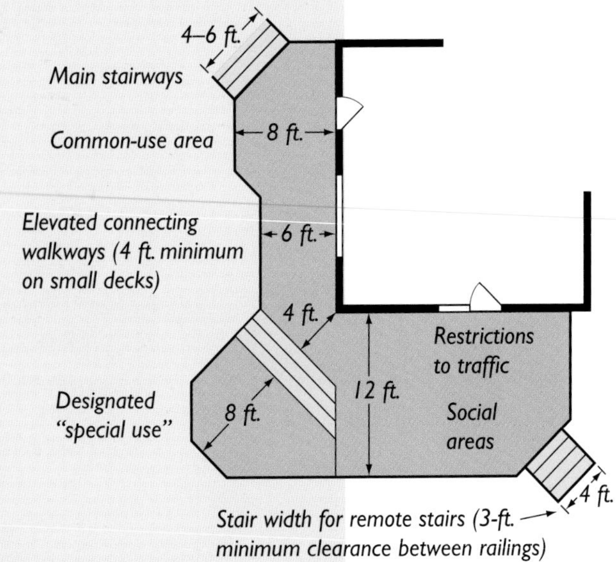

This multilevel deck serves several different functions. The elevated deck serves the second floor while the lower level—which is structurally a good place for the hot tub— finishes the underdeck area and helps make use of a sloping site. The generous stairway connects the two levels into one unit.

chaotic-looking and will not be in keeping stylistically with older, more formal homes. Adding angles also increases foundation and framing complexity and doubles the number of corners in the railing design, both of which may significant affect the amount of labor required (and the cost).

Local building codes

One design consideration that should not be neglected is a practical one. Is the construction strategy sound? In most areas of the country, local building codes establish a uniform set of minimum requirements for safe construction. These requirements are usually based on one of the widely recognized national codes, such as the Uniform Building Code (UBC)®, Building Officials and Code Administrators Building Code® (BOCA®), the Council of American Building Officials Code (CABO), or the new nationwide building code called the International Building Code®. Your local building codes also apply to deck construction, and cover details ranging from railing heights and stair dimensions to handrail locations. If you're installing any plumbing or electrical work for hot tubs or lighting, you'll also need to comply with the mechanical and electrical aspects of these codes. Your local building department will also have its own set of rules for such items as foundation depths and seismic requirements.

Your local building department can help you steer your way through the code requirements by answering your questions and suggesting solutions to problems. I've found my local building department officials to be helpful, friendly, and professional. Throughout upcoming chapters, I'll be discussing elements that need to comply with most building codes; I will call attention to the specific details as they arise.

Most cities and some rural areas require that you obtain a building permit before construction can begin. This permit will be issued only after you have satisfied your local building department that your project *intends* to meet all applicable requirements. This intention is represented by your set of plans. While the plans required for a deck may be relatively simple, building departments vary in how much detail they require before granting approval. During construction and after project completion, building department representatives will make inspections to insure that the project is built according to the plans they approved and that any deviations from the plans meet code requirements.

Estimating Size and Cost

A deck should be sized so that it is both in scale with the house it is attached to and adequate for the functions it needs to perform. As with most building projects, enlarging the deck makes it easier to accommodate all the features you want, but it makes the deck more expensive too. Although deck costs vary with materials chosen, complexity of design, and local labor conditions, there are ways to increase deck size without breaking the bank. Regardless of your budget, shop carefully and keep exotic extras under control, but spend lavishly on creativity.

✓ According to Code

A variance is a waiver of one or more zoning requirements (such as setbacks) that your property is subject to. A variance is awarded or denied on a case-by-case basis and is obtained through a sometimes lengthy process at your local building department. If there is any doubt at all about whether or not your proposed deck project is compliant, don't be surprised if the building department requires a survey of your property.

Adding angles is probably the most common way to change the look of a rectangular deck. Simply styled homes may only need the two outside corners of the deck clipped off, but busy exteriors can support complex shapes with multiple angles.

The basic rectangular deck is easy and the most cost-effective to build. This low-level, attached deck uses a straightforward ledger installation and little extra bracing for stability.

PRO TIP

Some types of decking will require extra joists, special fastening systems, and more labor to install, making a big impact on cost.

TRADE SECRET

Doubling the size of a deck doesn't necessarily mean that it will cost twice as much. When it comes to framing and decking materials, cost is almost directly proportional to size, but it's harder to generalize about labor. It doesn't take much longer to cut, fit, and hang a 12-ft. joist than a 10-ft. joist; on the other hand, a 16-ft. joist is heavy and may require handling by two people (and therefore double the labor). Doubling the deck size may increase the amount of railing needed only by 50%, and there may not be a need to add another stairway, access door, or deck accessories. And increasing the dimension away from the house may require only wider joists but no extra foundation work.

WHAT CAN GO WRONG

If you've designed your dream deck only to find that it will cost way more than you can afford, you have several options. The most obvious is to adjust the size and appearance to fit the budget. But perhaps a better long-term solution is to start with a core deck and add peripherals as time and money allow.

Wrapping a deck around a corner of the building helps provide climate control, adds interest, or may allow the main deck area to be located on a different side of the house than the access door.

Size

In addition to affecting cost, the size of a deck has a lot to do with its overall feel. Besides being more expensive than a smaller deck, a large deck that tries to answer too many needs can feel like a parking lot rather than a cozy and inviting space. Remember too that size is relative. A small house is better served by several small decks, either separated or on different levels, whereas a large house might need to be balanced by a big, unbroken expanse.

If you need the square footage of a large deck to accommodate several different functions, consider opting for two (or more) smaller decks. While level changes can play a part in delineating different decks, decks can just as easily be located on the same level but accessed by separate interior doors. What I like about smaller decks is that they keep things on a human scale.

I use some general sizing guidelines to help me when I design a deck. One rule of thumb suggests about 20 sq. ft. of deck per person for social situations. On top of that, you'll need to add extra square footage for furniture, grills, and planters. I like a minimum dimension of 12 ft. in both directions for all social areas.

Decks that extend more than 14 ft. to 16 ft. from the house will probably require additional foundation and structural work (and more expense), so consult span tables and your pocketbook before deciding to go this route. I think that anything over 16-ft. wide feels too large for a residential deck and should be broken into smaller decks. Smaller doesn't have to mean inadequate. It's quite easy to incorporate a food area, seating, and a hot tub on a 12-ft.-by-12-ft. deck if you don't need large spaces for many people.

Cost

Like cars, decks come in a wide range of prices. Material prices can vary by 10% to 20% or more

This simple ground-level deck doesn't require a railing and offers plenty of extra living space for a relatively low cost per square foot.

Cost Comparison of Common Decking Materials

	Cost per lineal foot
Treated southern yellow pine, 5/4, radius-edged, premium grade	$1.25
Treated hem–fir, 2×6, brown-stained, select	$1.00
Treated hem–fir, 2×6, brown-stained, standard grade	$0.80
Western red cedar, 2×6, select, tight knot	$1.10–$1.40
Western red cedar, 2×6, clear	$2.25
Western red cedar, 5/4×6, radius-edged, select	$1.20
Alaska yellow cedar, 2×6, select, tight knot, usually KD	$1.20–$1.50
Alaska yellow cedar, 2×6, clear	$2.75–$3.00
Redwood, 2×6, decking grade, all heartwood	$2.00
Redwood, 2×6, B grade, all heartwood	$3.00
Redwood, 2×6, clear, all heartwood	$4.00
Ipe, tropical wood, 5/4×6, clear	$2.25
Meranti, tropical wood, 5/4×4 (Add approximately 20% for certified wood)	$1.70
Trex®, recycled, 2×6	$1.60
Trex, 5/4×6	$1.45
Nexwood™, recycled, 2×6	$1.70–$2.00
Brock Deck®, polymer material 2×6	$4.50
Dream® Deck, vinyl	$4.00

Prices will vary depending on shipping distance, discounts, and local availability.

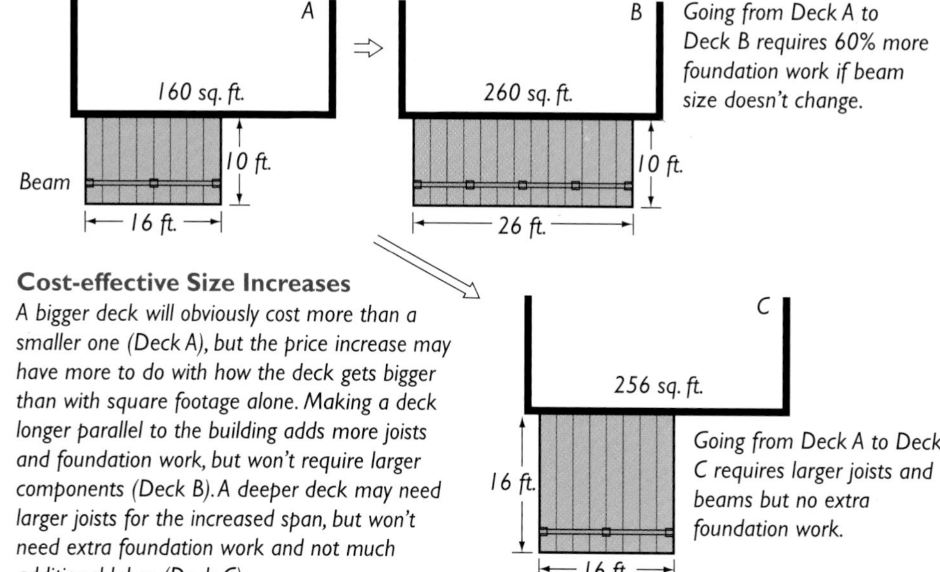

Cost-effective Size Increases

A bigger deck will obviously cost more than a smaller one (Deck A), but the price increase may have more to do with how the deck gets bigger than with square footage alone. Making a deck longer parallel to the building adds more joists and foundation work, but won't require larger components (Deck B). A deeper deck may need larger joists for the increased span, but won't need extra foundation work and not much additional labor (Deck C).

from year to year, and if you need to hire help, the cost of labor can fluctuate as well. Availability can also affect the cost of your deck, as local suppliers tend to stock "best sellers," which aren't necessarily the most appropriate materials for your deck or of the best quality. If good materials aren't available locally, they usually can be found elsewhere, but shipping them across the country may increase their cost significantly.

Built-in seating, elaborate railings, curves, trellises, exotic materials, and multiple coats of finish all add significantly to the price of even the most modestly sized deck. The desire for clear lumber, extensive landscaping, and problems with the site (such as steepness or drainage) are other factors that can drive up the price. And if you require the services of an electrician and a plumber to add lighting or a hot tub, this will also increase your cost.

Even the method you choose to fasten the decking can have a significant impact on your budget. For example, high-quality stainless-steel fasteners cost several times more than standard lumberyard-variety galvanized or coated fasteners, but because the more expensive fasteners won't chip and corrode or stain your decking, I think that this is one area where it doesn't pay to economize. Switching from nails to screws may almost double the amount of labor required to fasten down the decking; using an elaborate hidden fastening system may double the labor again, besides adding to the hardware cost.

Building the

CHAPTER TWO

Foundation

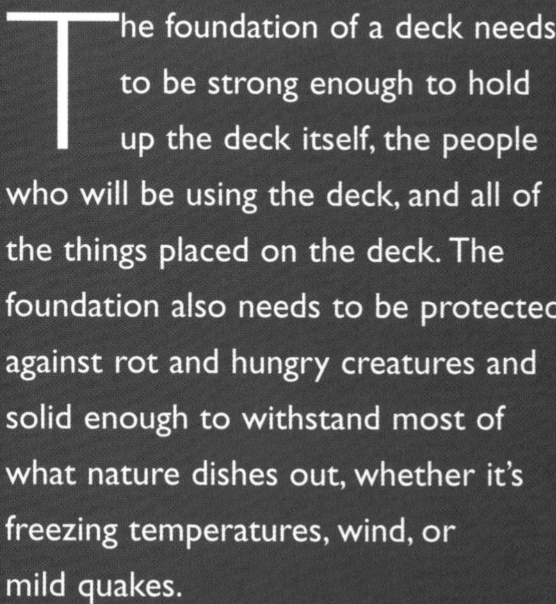

The foundation of a deck needs to be strong enough to hold up the deck itself, the people who will be using the deck, and all of the things placed on the deck. The foundation also needs to be protected against rot and hungry creatures and solid enough to withstand most of what nature dishes out, whether it's freezing temperatures, wind, or mild quakes.

In this chapter, I'll help you choose a foundation that will fulfill these needs without breaking your back or your budget. After a look at some foundation choices, I'll show you how to size your foundation for the weight (or *load*) it will be expected to carry and for different types of soil conditions. Once the foundation is figured out on paper, we'll start the real work of layout—digging holes, making forms, and finally placing some concrete.

PRO TIP

Put a buried concrete footing on solid, undisturbed ground so it less likely to be affected by groundwater and runoff.

IN DETAIL

If you live in an area where seismic activity or frost isn't a problem, precast pier blocks are quite handy. Some have two open, perpendicular grooves cast into the top, sized to allow a 1½-in. wide board to slide in on edge. These grooves don't do much to keep the wood anchored to the block and are used only on ground-level decks, but the blocks are easy to work with in circumstances that don't require a buried footing. I've also seen pier blocks with wood blocks cast into them, but avoid these. The wood blocks (usually untreated) will rot quickly in contact with the concrete. They'll also split when a post is toenailed to them and don't provide a secure connection to the deck.

A typical pier-type deck foundation. Batter boards and stringlines help to precisely locate the position of the pier, which is supported at its base by a footing buried below frost level.

Typical Concrete Footing-and-Pier Foundation

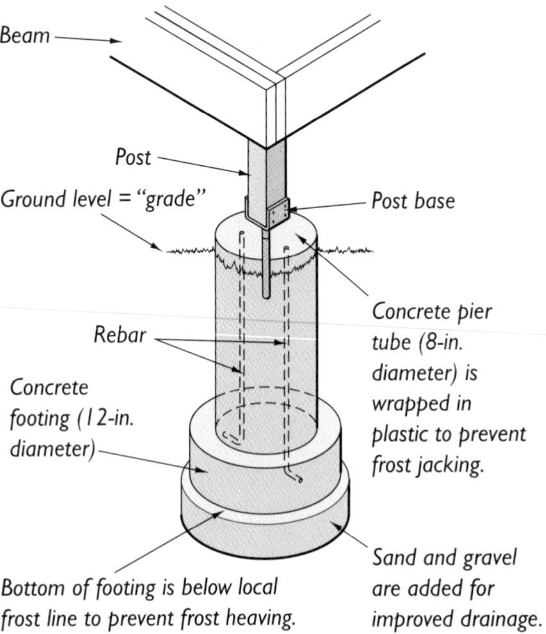

Choosing a Foundation

Deck foundations are different from house foundations because the load is concentrated at specific points on the ground rather than being spread around the whole perimeter. Even though a deck weighs a lot less than a house, this point loading means that you must give some thought to foundation design.

With the exception of solid rock, no soil type can hold a point load for long without some settling. That's why all types of foundations have thickened weight-bearing supports—called footings—at their base to help spread point loads over a larger area. Depending on climate conditions, footings may be very close to the surface or may need to be deeply buried 4 ft. or more to get below frost level. If you live in a mild climate, your footings may be on the surface or only need to be buried a little, and you may be able to start your deck-post framing right from the footing itself by buying (or making) a simple one piece block (called a pier block). But if your footings need to be deeper than about 12 in., you'll need to add a concrete column (called a pier) or a buried post to get to above-ground levels. If you have any doubt about the right foundation for the conditions, consult an engineer.

Combination footing-and-pier foundations

My favorite type of deck foundation is a footing buried below frost level with a concrete pier that brings the foundation up to grade (or finished ground level). In cold climates, the buried footing is required by most building codes because it helps avoid frost heaving. A buried concrete footing is also permanent, and putting it on solid, undisturbed ground makes it less likely to be affected by groundwater and runoff.

For most of my decks, I pour the footing and pier at the same time with an internal piece of rebar. This kind of one-piece foundation that is wider at the bottom helps spread the point load and act as an anchor against frost jacking, another cold climate concern. With large or complicated footings, it is sometimes easier to pour the footing first and the pier separately. Casting an L-shaped piece of rebar in the footing in the first pour and leaving the vertical part sticking up to catch the pier in the second pour will provide the same anchoring effect. (See the drawing on p. 43.)

Continuous-post foundations

Sometimes a single pressure-treated or decay-resistant wood post may be used to get from a buried footing up to grade and then continue on to the deck framing. This system would be a good choice in areas with a lot of seismic activity that need the additional lateral stability gained by eliminating the connection from foundation to post at grade level. The post can simply sit on the footing if the post is buried several feet to resist lifting forces. Sometimes the base of the post, spiked with stainless-steel nails, is cast into a thickened footing to prevent uplift. In both cases, it is essential to backfill with gravel around the post when damp, freezing soils are present to ensure good drainage and help resist frost jacking. Finishing the backfilling with several inches of regular dirt helps seal the hole against water intrusion.

While the continuous-post foundation can be easier to build and may be necessary for lateral stability, it does have one big disadvantage. Below-grade inspection of the wood and any subsequent repairs needed will require removing the entire post down to the footing. Although modern treated lumber is of good quality, I am suspicious of larger timbers that "check" or crack open as they dry and expose poorly treated interior sections to moisture, rot, and bugs. An alternative is to use steel posts, which are stronger, can be made rust-resistant, and are comparably priced. Steel posts will need a bracket at the top to allow attaching wood beams but these are easily added by your steel supplier.

A treated buried post that rests on a concrete footing below frost level and runs up to a beam is easy to install and provides good lateral stability, but is harder to maintain.

Pier-block foundations

In certain situations, a combination footing/small pier—called a precast pier block—offers a simple foundation solution. These pyramidal shaped blocks can be bought at most building supply stores and are usually cast with some type of

✓ According to Code

Building codes vary across the country and may require different types of foundations, depending upon local requirements for frost protection, high winds, earthquakes, and environmental issues. Your local building department will probably request a foundation detail showing foundation type, depth, sizes, and any reinforcements. During the construction process, you should count on at least a couple of visits from the building inspector, who will want to make sure that your deck conforms to code.

Steel beams provide durable support with longer spans than wood beams, but they need holes drilled for attaching wood. Steel posts with a rust-preventive coating can be buried for continuous-post footings that won't rot and can withstand abuse.

PRO TIP

If you're unsure about how strong a foundation you'll need, just err a little on the side of stronger: "When in doubt, build it stout."

IN DETAIL

A *design load* of 50 psf is composed of two elements. The first part is the *live load* of 40 psf, which is the average weight of furnishings and people expected on the deck. The second is the *dead load* of 10 psf, which is the weight of the framing and decking materials themselves. This is a fairly typical minimum specification for most codes. However, if you expect lots of snow to sit on your deck all winter or plan on having large groups of people, you'll want to use a larger design load of 70 psf. Remember that a hot tub will need special considerations since it may produce loads of 100 psf or more.

Determining Loads

Shown here is a sample post-and-beam layout. Each shaded area, or *supported load* area, indicates the amount of deck that bears on each post, and is measured in square feet. The supported load area extends halfway to the next support member in each direction, usually another beam, post, or ledger.

Perpendicular to the beam in one direction, each post will support from the beam halfway back to the ledger, and in the opposite direction will include a small cantilevered area. Parallel to the main beam, each interior post supports the area halfway to its neighboring post. Notice that the end posts, having neighbors only in one direction, support less area than do the center posts.

The end posts have a supported load area of 28.5 sq. ft. (9 ft. × 3 ft. 8 in. minus 4.5 sq. ft. for the missing angled corners); the center posts have a supported load area of 66 sq. ft. (9 ft. × 7 ft. 4 in.).

If these areas are multiplied by the load I anticipate per square foot—called the *design load*—I will get the total load for each supported area. This is the load that is transferred to the footings. The design load on this deck is 50 psf. To get the total load for each end post, multiply this by 28.5 sq. ft., which results in a load of 1,425 lb.

To get the load for the center posts, multiply the deck's design load (50 psf) by 66 sq. ft., which results in a total load of 3,300 lb. For the sake of simplicity, I usually make all the footings the same size as needed for the heaviest load.

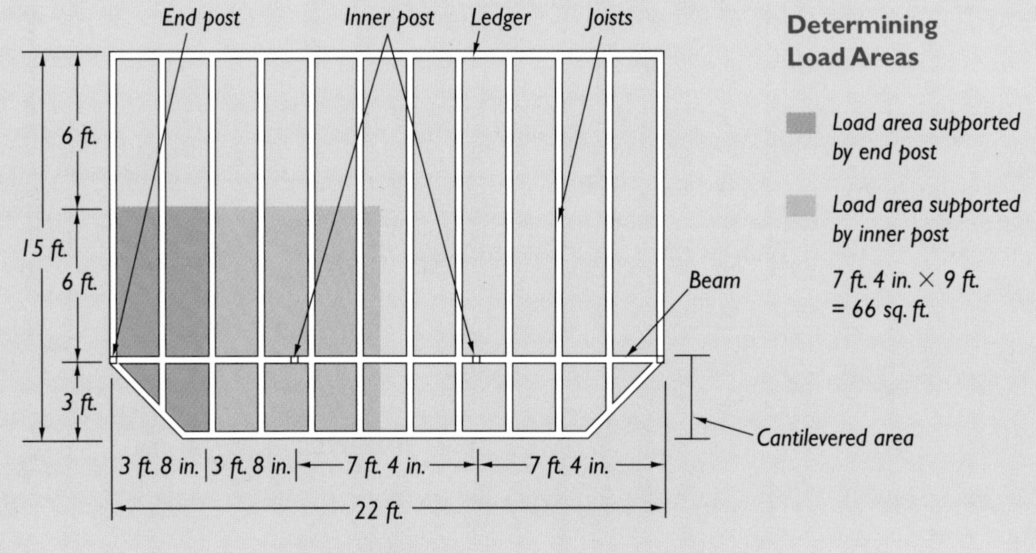

bracket on the top for attaching a wood post. These piers should be used only on stable soil and in warmer climates with a shallow frost line, but there are ways to improve your success in less than perfect conditions. For example, it is always a good idea to dig down about 6 in. to 12 in. deeper than the pier block to get to solid ground. Then refill the hole with compacted gravel to aid drainage, set the pier so a few inches are above grade, continue filling around the pier with gravel, and finish with a layer of dirt. Partially burying the pier will add to its stability and help make it less noticeable.

Keep in mind that the bases of these pier blocks are usually not very big and so might settle unevenly in weak soils. If your calculations call for a larger footprint than the pier block provides, it helps to dig a little deeper, add the layer of gravel, and then pour a larger footing for the pier block to sit on. While pier blocks have their limitations, they can provide a good, easy foundation if frost depth isn't deep and drainage is good. If soils are dry, I often use pier blocks for small details like the bottom of stairs, even in my cold Alaskan climate.

Sizing Footings

In order to determine the size of the footprint (the area at the bottom of the footing in contact with the ground) needed for each footing, we need to consider both the the total supported load on each footing (see the sidebar on the facing page) and the soil conditions (see the chart at right). But to find the load on each footing, we must know the number of posts that will be supporting the deck. So, to begin our footing calculations, we must first decide the basic framing plan for the deck. (See Designing and Sizing Beams and Posts, pp. 62–67.) The framing plan will determine the number, size, and location of posts as well as other structural considerations like beams and joists. Consider your framing plan to be tentative until you are content with the results of your footing calculations.

Soils

Let's say, for example, that each of the footings on a deck must support a load of about 3,300 lb. The size of the footing needed to support that weight will depend on the bearing capacity of the soil. If I divide my supported load (lbs.) by the bearing capacity of the soil (pounds per square foot, or psf), the result is the size of the footing (in sq. ft.). Soil capacities range from 400 psf (not so good) to 8,000 psf (very good). Dry soils that are composed mainly of inorganic clays and silts or those that are sandy or gravelly typically have a bearing capacity of at least 1,500 psf and allow for average-sized footprints. If the soil contains a lot of organic material (as with peat or certain clays), then the bearing ability can be significantly lower, and the footprint will need to be increased to handle the load.

Soil that has a large amount of sand, no organic material, and bedrock that is within a few feet of the surface is typical. It's great for support, but it's hard to dig.

This type of soil has a bearing capacity of at least 3,000 psf, so the footings need only be 1.1 sq. ft. (3,300-lb. load divided by 3,000-psf capacity). Either a 13-in. by 13-in. square footing (169 sq. in.) or a 15-in. diameter round footing (176 sq. in.) would be adequate for this load on this soil.

Bearing Capacity of Different Soil Types

Soils are usually a mix of different types. Water, soil particle size, and layering are all factors in bearing capacity.

Type	Bearing	Frost Action	Drainage
Compact gravel or compact sand, loose gravel-and-sand mix; gravel-and-sand mix	12,000 psf	None	Excellent
Hard-dried clay	6,000 to 8000 psf	Slight	Fair to good
Medium-dry clay, fine loose sand	4,000 psf	High	Fair to poor
Soft clay, silts, broken shale	2,000 psf	High	Poor
Organic soils	Unacceptable		

psf = pounds per square foot 1 sf = 144 sq. 1 in.

Spotting Poor Soil Conditions

Remember that soil can lose some of its bearing capacity when it gets wet. Clay can expand and fine silts become squishy. Check for cracks in your or your neighbor's foundation, notice if nearby sidewalks and driveways are moving and cracking, and look for large cracks in the earth during the dry season. All of these may be symptoms of moisture-retaining soils. If soils are permanently wet or have low bearing capacities, then you should check with an engineer.

PRO TIP

In areas where the ground freezes in winter, avoid frost heave by burying your footings so the bottom rests on soil below the frost line.

IN DETAIL

A good gravel for use under footings (and one that won't settle later) needs to contain a variety of sizes from sand up to marble size. The small sizes can also be provided by *fines*, the small particles left in the mix after larger rocks are mechanically crushed. A 50/50 sand-and-rock mix or crushed gravel and fines will both pack well using a little water. Larger rocks (from about ½-in. to 1-in. diameter) without fines or sand will allow better drainage but are harder to compact. These are a good choice for backfilling posts or piers in damp soils to prevent frost jacking.

Downspouts that dump water next to footings cause settling and frost movement from wet soils. Using a flexible drainpipe to lead the water away is a simple but often neglected fix.

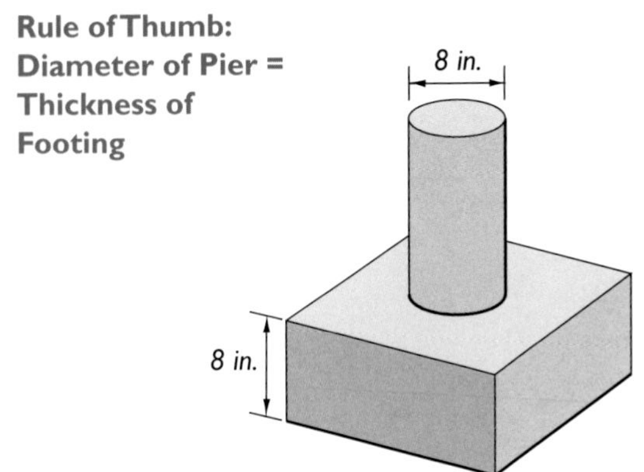

Larger or extra footings?

If you have a lot of weight to support or soils with poor bearing capacity, you will need larger footings, but these are practical only up to a certain point. It may be better to add extra posts, which decrease the load on each and keep the footing size smaller. While the extra holes add expense (and work), using more posts means shorter beam spans, which may allow you to use smaller (and less expensive) beams. Adding a second beam parallel to the first will certainly decrease the load on the footings, but this probably won't be necessary or cost-effective until joist spans are too high. The optimum number of posts will depend on spans, sizes, soils, and loads, all of which are different for each deck. As a general rule, I make the thickness of my footing the same dimension as the width of the pier it supports, but seldom less than 6 in. Extra-heavy loads like hot tubs or roofs will need footings that are 8 in. to 12 in. thick.

Avoiding frozen feet

If you live where the ground freezes in winter, you'll need to bury your footings so their bottoms rest on soil below the frost line to avoid frost heave (this measure will be required by your local building code). Frost heave causes footings to be lifted as water in the soil beneath them freezes and expands. Frost heave can be a seasonal problem that causes the foundation to rise and fall every year, or it can have a cumulative effect that will require major deck repairs after a few years. It takes three things for frost heave to occur: freezing temperatures, moisture, and soil conditions that hold the moisture. Effective foundation design attempts to avoid all of these conditions whenever possible.

Burying the footings helps protect them from the cold. Your local building code will have minimum foundation depth requirements (or recommendations) based on the average depth to which the ground freezes during the winter. The bottom of your footings must be below that depth. In northern climates, the situation is complicated by the fact that deck footings have little snow cover and aren't close to a heat source (such as a basement), so the freezing depth may be even greater than expected. And if you have moist soil conditions, you should bury the footings even deeper to be sure.

Since it can be difficult (or expensive) to avoid freezing temperatures, the most cost-effective solution is to eliminate moisture through drainage control. If you reach rock or well-drained gravel as you approach frost depth, then you need go no deeper. The footing in these cases would be sitting on material that won't hold moisture, so the soil can't heave. If you have well-drained soil with a shallow frost depth, it is acceptable to dig down below frost depth and then refill the hole with compacted gravel, referred to as NFS (non-frost-susceptible) material. Then you can use a simple pier block or other premade footing.

✓ According to Code

Local building departments can have specific and differing foundation requirements. For example, steel reinforcement may not be required in all footings, while some areas with loose soils will not allow earth-formed footings. Be sure to check first.

Even if you don't need to bury your footings deeply, it is still necessary to remove the top layer of soil, which retains moisture and contains organic materials that are not able to support a load. It is quite likely that the dirt surrounding a newer home has been disturbed during its construction and final grading, and it is likely to settle under footing loads. As you're digging footing holes, look for clues of recent soil disturbance—a change in the color of the soil, obvious layering, or a noticeable difference in the amount of effort required to dig. Generally speaking, soil that is easy to dig through won't hold much weight.

Unfortunately, the requirements for a problem-free deck footing are the same as for an expensive home. You might think with a deck you can reasonably cut your margin of safety and use a less elaborate foundation to save expense, but remember that it will cost twice as much to fix a problem as to prevent it in the first place.

Laying Out the Foundation

Use stringlines and batter boards to help locate the position of piers.

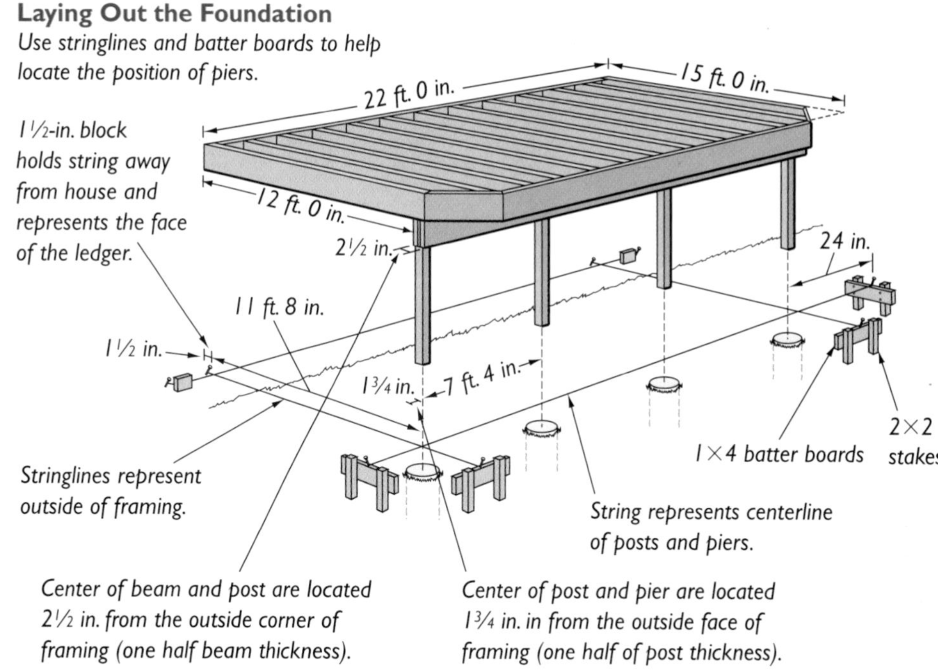

Layout

With the details for the deck's foundation worked out on paper (and drawn on the plans), it's time to transfer this information to the job site. Here we'll use stringlines and simple geometry instead of pencil and paper to lay out the location of the footings. Layout work can sometimes be done by one person if the site is flat, but on a hilly site or a high deck where a plumb bob is needed, a second helper is essential.

Start with the ledger

The first thing you'll need are some fixed reference points—a wall of the house, for example—to represent one side of the deck. Usually this is where the ledger will be located. If the deck is simple and the reference wall is fairly flat, you can simply mark the ledger's position directly on the surface; to get an accurate reference, however, be sure to remove siding or other trim down to the sheathing where the ledger will be attached. On most decks (especially those that aren't simple rectangles), I like to actually install the ledger board before laying out the foundation. (For more on installing ledgers, see Chapter 3.)

Sometimes, if a wall is wavy or has obstructions, it may be necessary to use a string to represent one face of the ledger. If you plan to install a 2× ledger tight against the house's sheathing, use 2× blocks to space your line 1½ in. out from the house to represent the outside face of the ledger (see the drawing above). Alternatively, if you plan

✓ According to Code

If there's any uncertainty about soil conditions, your building department might want to inspect your excavation before you do any concrete work. If inspectors do visit your site, ask plenty of questions because their soil opinion will be relevant and valuable… and free. Local foundation engineers may give out general information but will need to take soil samples if there's any uncertainty, and that can cost hundreds of dollars.

PRO TIP

Generally speaking, soil that is easy to dig through won't hold much weight.

TRADE SECRET

When I'm working with someone and making measurements, I do a lot of talking out loud. I ask my helper to repeat whatever number I might be calling out and to double-check my mental math as I add and subtract while adjusting diagonals for square.

IN DETAIL

Frost jacking is similar to frost heaving and occurs in moisture-bearing soils in cold climates. The frozen ground can freeze to the sides of a post or pier, lifting the entire column as it expands. The best defense is to keep moisture away and backfill around the post with gravel or other well-draining materials. I've also found that it helps to wrap the buried post or pier with several layers of heavy polyethylene before burial so the freezing ground can't get a grip. This solution is only effective for as long as the plastic remains intact (which can be forever if it is treated with care).

Batter boards are usually screwed to pointed 1×2 or 2×2 wooden stakes, which are readily available at most lumberyards.

on putting drainage spacers between the house and the ledger—for example, if the ledger will be installed over the siding—then use blocks that are the thickness of the spacer. The string will then represent the house side of the ledger. Just be sure to remember which side of the ledger is represented by the string for the rest of your layout measurements.

Using strings to lay out the deck

After establishing a reference on the house, the next step is to construct a large rectangle (usually with strings) to represent the other three sides of the deck. On most decks, I will represent the first of these three sides with a string set parallel to my ledger and directly over the centerline of the footings supporting the beam. For the remaining two sides, I set strings that are perpendicular to the ledger and beam string. Usually I install the two side strings at the outside dimensions of the deck framing and measure in to locate the corner footings. (I also use side strings at these locations to help establish angles and other deck features.) But if the deck is simple, you can set up the two side strings directly over the centerlines of the corner footing. In either case, I measure in from these corner footing locations to get my inner footing locations.

I use batter boards to hold the ends of any lines that aren't attached to the house. These are 3-ft. to 4-ft. long pieces of 1×4 attached about a foot off the ground to a pair of 2×2 stakes. The stringline is then tied to a screw driven into the top edge of this batter board. Keep batter boards at least 24 in. back from the digging locations so that they won't be in the way, get bumped out of position, or covered in excavation dirt. You'll use them often to check the locations of forms and for putting in post bases after the concrete is poured.

When setting the outside strings, remember to allow 1½ in. in your dimensions for the missing end joists, which will lap the end of the ledger (see Chapter Three; also, see the drawing on p. 36.) Alternatively, if the strings represent the centerlines of the corner footings, set this string back on the ledger the same distance that the centerline of the corner footings are set back from the edge of the deck. These lines should be parallel to each other and reasonably close to square to the ledger—(we'll soon adjust them to be perfectly square). Each corner footing now has a pair of batter boards perpendicular to each other and a pair of crossing strings.

1. For most deck layouts, run your first string (representing the centerline of the beam) parallel to the ledger and attach it to a batter board at each end. Note that the tape measure is held level and a plumb bob used on this sloping site to accurately locate the string.

2. Because this particular deck will require two beams, we next run a second string parallel to both the first string and the ledger to represent this second beam.

3. To serve as a reference in aligning the joist framing to the walls of the house, attach a separate string to a far house corner and extend it out to a batter board. Keeping the string equidistant at all points to the house wall makes it parallel to the house.

4. Parallel to this reference string, set another string representing the outside of the deck framing, first attaching it at the ledger end and then keeping it equidistant out to the batter board. If the house walls are square to each other, this string should now be at right angles to the ledger; this gets double-checked by comparing diagonals (see below).

Check for square

Now that there is a large rectangle defined by the ledger and three strings (or by four strings if the ledger isn't up yet), it's time to make sure the strings are square to each other and square to the house. On a rectangle with parallel sides, this is easily done by making sure that the two diagonals are equal to each other. If the measurements are not the same, move the ends of the strings repre-

PRO TIP

If a wall is wavy or has obstructions, don't use it as a reference. Instead use a string to represent one face of the ledger.

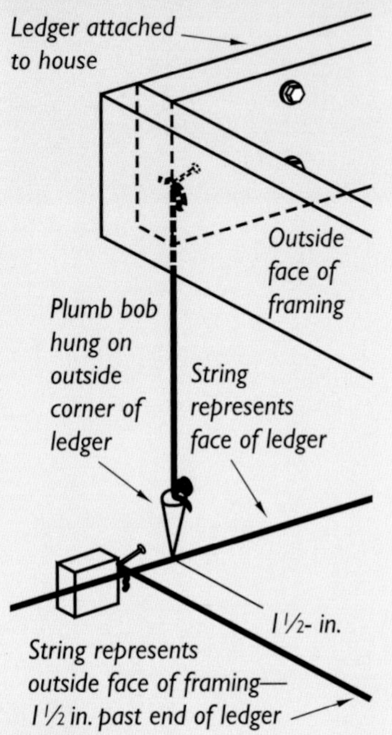

IN DETAIL

For high decks, it is easier to lay out the foundation if you first reference your high ledger closer to the ground. I set up a separate ledger string directly below the actual ledger by dropping a plumb bob as shown.

WHAT CAN GO WRONG

When measuring diagonals, be sure to always measure from the same points at each end. For example, don't hold the tape measure on the back side corner of the ledger on one end and the front side on the other.

Checking for Square by Measuring Diagonals
You can check that a rectangle is square and lines are perpendicular to each other by measuring the diagonals. When $A_1 = A_2$, $B_1 = B_2$, and $C_1 = C_2$, all corners will be 90 degrees.

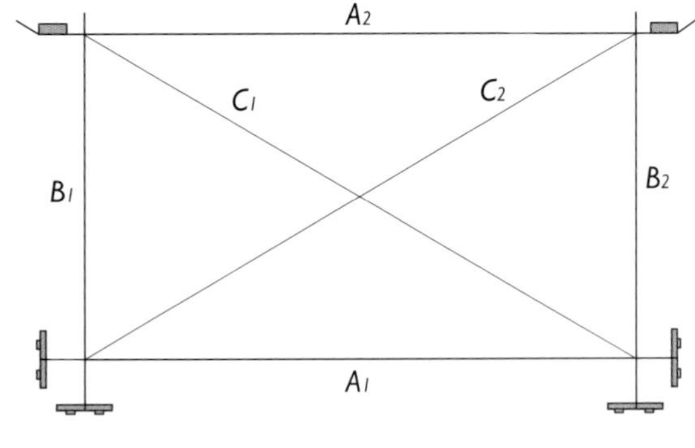

senting the sides by the same amount in the same direction, keeping them parallel. This will shorten one diagonal and lengthen the other; (it may take a couple of tries to get them the same). I've found that this procedure is a lot easier to do with two people.

When everything is square, I normally use a plumb bob to mark the center of the corner footings. If your corner footing strings were set on centerlines in both directions, then drop the plumb bob directly down from their intersection to the ground for the center of the footing. Mark this spot with a 16d nail and a bit of brightly colored surveyor's flagging. However, if your side string represents the outside of the framing, then measure in to the center of the corner post (making sure to account for post width and any beam cantilever over the post) and drop a plumb bob. This is done by holding the zero end of your tape measure at the side string and pinching the plumb bob string at the correct measurement.

Once the corner footings are located, measure in from them along the ground the correct distance to the central footings. Make sure that these also fall directly under the stringline by dropping a plumb bob next to the tape measure. Again, mark these with a nail and flagging. Double-check the location of each inner footing by measuring in from both corner footings to be sure everything adds up correctly.

Once all the footing locations are established, the strings can come down. I leave the batter boards up though, because they'll be needed again shortly to check the locations of the forms.

Use a nail and surveyor's flagging to mark the plumb bob location.

Hold the zero end of the tape measure at the side string and pinch the plumb bob at the measure.

Measure along the ground to find the correct distance to the central footing.

Excavation

If you need just a few holes not much deeper than 2 or 3 ft. or not too big around, then a good sharp shovel and a post-hole digger will be the only tools you'll need. Throw in a pair of boots or shoes with stiff soles to keep your feet from getting sore. And remember that big rocks should be moved by rolling, not lifting, even if it means digging a bigger hole. But if you have quite a few holes or they need to be deep, then consider mechanizing the process. There are a couple of options that can help save your back (and your spirit).

Power augers

The first option is to rent a handheld gasoline-powered auger. The one-person model is fine for small fence post holes, but the two-person model is essential for larger holes. I've found though that even in ground that doesn't have too many rocks, a 12-in. diameter bit is really about the upper limit for two people to handle. I've also found that a power auger is not a user-friendly tool; I almost prefer digging these holes by hand. Be prepared for some abrupt stops as you hit roots and snags, and this tool really gets heavy when you're lifting it out of the hole with an auger full of dirt. It may be quicker than handwork, but not necessarily less painful.

Drill rigs

My favorite option is to hire a local fencing installer to come over with his drill rig. Depending on the contractor I contact, I'll get a small, self-contained unit with plenty of mobility to get around obstructions or a slightly less maneuverable one mounted on the back of a vehicle. Drilling holes on moderate slopes isn't a problem because usually both vehicles have four-wheel drive. These rigs can drill up to about 24-in. diameter holes that are up to 5 ft. deep if there's not too much rock. Prices in my area run about $125.00 per hour, but it only takes an hour or so (plus travel time) to drill the holes for an average-sized deck.

If you have a steep site, lots of rocks, or some other onerous complication, then check in the yellow pages under electrical contractors or drilling companies. They'll have track-mounted machines that can do 30-in diameter holes as deep as you'd ever want them for a deck, though these services cost twice as much as the small rigs. If it's the only way to get the job done, however, the cost differential is well worth it.

No matter how you drill your holes, a few inches of loose dirt will be left in the bottom of the hole. Try to remove as much as you can with

+ SAFETY FIRST

Loose clothing is dangerous around power augers, so keep your sleeves rolled up and shirts and jackets buttoned in front.

PRO TIP

Spray paint sold specifically for putting lines on the ground is handy for marking buried utilities or the dimensions of a large hole.

TRADE SECRET

When I'm putting together batter boards, I find it easiest to pound my stakes in first and then attach the horizontal 1×4 to the stakes with drywall screws instead of nails. Although nails will work too, the pounding often loosens the stakes and also makes adjustments more difficult. You can make stakes or buy pointed 2×2 stakes at the lumberyard (but they may only come in bundles of 25 or so).

Using screws instead of nails to secure strings to batter boards will help you make small changes more easily and avoid knocking the layout out of alignment.

This maneuverable drill rig costs me about $150 per job but will save a day's back breaking labor when I have more than a few holes to drill. It can easily drill 12-in. diameter holes 48 in. deep in most soils.

This larger drill rig on tracks can go up the side of a hill and drill 24-in. diameter holes 8 ft. deep, all day long (or until you run out of money).

In addition to a shovel, a post-hole digger will make hand-digging for deep pier holes easier.

Compacting dirt or gravel in layers during backfill will discourage future settling.

the post-hole digger, and then compact whatever's left. I do this with a 2×4 or a 4×4 that is long enough to reach the bottom of the hole and still allow me to grab it without bending over. I pound the board up and down until the bottom of the hole feels solid. Fine soils will compact better with addition of a little gravel.

This is also the time to add a thicker layer of gravel if needed for drainage, and this gravel can be compacted the same way. A 6-in. to 8-in. layer of gravel will allow for easy compaction and aid drainage. Adding a little water to the gravel until it is moist, but not puddling, is important for solid compaction. But avoid too much water; you'll just make mud, and that won't compact at all.

Forms for Footings and Piers

Once the holes are dug, a form system will need to be constructed to contain the wet concrete for the footings. This can be done with manufactured forms, wooden forms or earthen forms. Pier forms aren't required for many types of deck foundations, including post-type foundations, shallow foundations, and pier-block foundations. But here I'll show you how I build pier forms.

I generally try to pour my footings and piers at the same time. Although this requires a bit of extra work building the forms, it allows me to avoid the significant costs and delays of separate concrete pours.

Footing forms

I generally use earth-formed footings, which are shaped simply by digging the hole to the size of the needed footing. If the footing isn't too much larger than the pier tube diameter, both can be poured at the same time. To do this, the pier tubes can be simply suspended in the hole above the widened footing area, then braced at the top. Since there isn't a lot of room for the tubes to move around down in the hole, there's no lower bracing to add or remove later; a little extra care when pouring will suffice. When footings and pier are poured together, very wet concrete may tend to rise around the outside of the pier form. To inhibit this, I just give the concrete some time to set up a bit in the footing before I continue pouring the pier. If the footing is quite a bit larger than the pier, I pour all of the footings first and allow them all to set up overnight. Then I add the pier tubes on top and pour the piers separately.

It can take a surprising amount of concrete to fill the bottom of a big hole, so in some cases, I build wooden footing forms to contain the concrete. I use 2×8 or 2×10 boards (depending on

Suspended Tube Pier Form on an Earth-Formed Footing

In good soils, you can simply dig a hole to the diameter required by the footing and suspend a pier tube as shown.

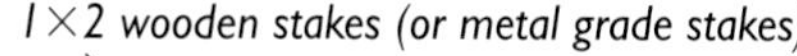

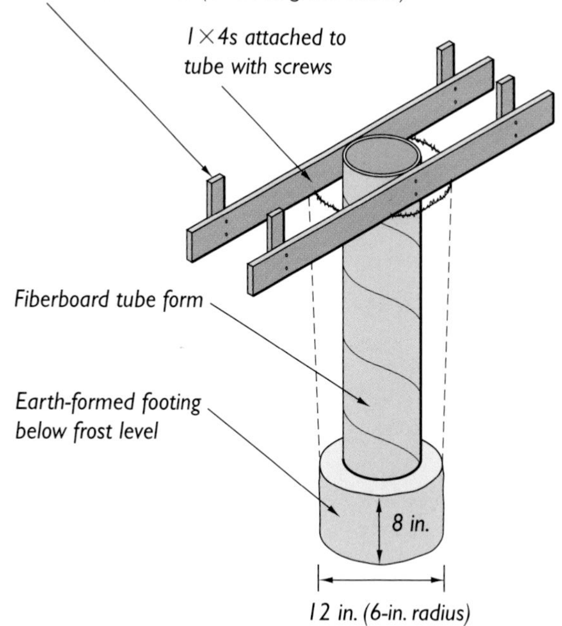

> **+ SAFETY FIRST**
>
> While it is possible to buy precast footing pads, don't be tempted to buy any that are larger than about 14 in. square by 4 in. thick. Precast concrete that is any larger than this is very heavy, and trying to set even small footing pads solidly in a hole while you are bent over can ruin a good back. It's better to cast your footings in place.

PRO TIP

Utility companies are happy to locate buried power and phone lines that might be on your site, usually at minimal cost.

IN DETAIL

I almost always use lightweight fiberboard tubes—known commonly as Sonotubes®, but made by other companies, too—for my pier forms. These tubes come in 12-ft. lengths and in diameters from 4 in. up to 4 ft., and are readily available at lumberyards or concrete suppliers. They will get soft if left in the rain, so be sure to keep them under cover before using them.

TOOLS AND MATERIALS

Rebar size is designated by its diameter in eighths of an inch. That means that ½-in. diameter rebar—the type you'll use for most decking projects—is called #4 and ⅝-in. diameter rebar is called #5.

Manufactured Footing Forms

Bigfoot Systems® footing forms (see *Resources*) is a plastic cone-shaped footing form that comes in sizes ranging from 20 in. to 28 in. in diameter at the base. The forms can be used with 6-in. to 12-in. diameter pier tubes, and while they're not cheap (a midsized form costs about $15), they'll save you plenty of time and energy as you build your deck's foundation. And as an added bonus, you can turn a Bigfoot form over, cut out the bottom, and use it as a funnel for the concrete pour.

This system works best when the bottom of the hole is level so that the pier tube will stand up straight. It also helps to dig the hole larger than the form itself, because both the footing and the attached tube form will have to be moved together as a unit in order to get the pier in the right place. Once in position, the forms should be backfilled before pouring begins; this not only keeps the forms from moving but also helps to reinforce the connection. You can add extra rebar to Bigfoot forms by tying separate lengths to the horizontal leg of the L-shaped piece connecting the footing to the pier.

A handsaw is used to trim the plastic footing form to match the pier tube form size.

The pier tube is attached with screws.

Once a level, compacted base of gravel has been provided at the bottom of the hole, the assembly is dropped in the hole. The top of the form is then secured as usual.

Combination Footing-and-Pier Foundation

Concrete piers and wider footings can be formed in a single pour. The pier tube must be suspended so that it is level with the top of the footing. The footing here is built with wood forms. This method is used when the footing and excavation are significantly bigger than the pier tube.

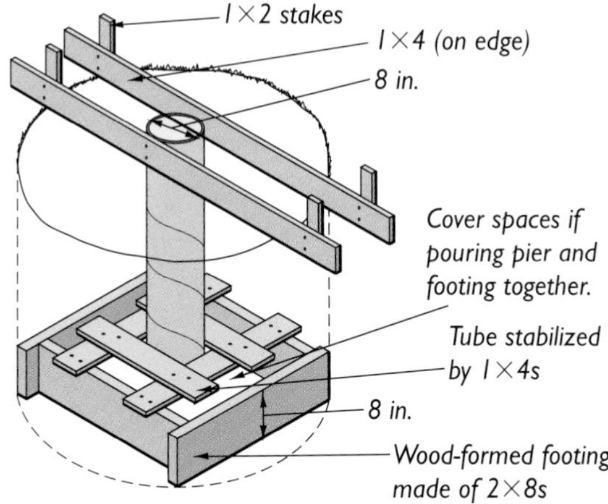

the needed thickness of the footing) and nail them into a square with 16d duplex nails. Then I place the form in the hole, staking it around its perimeter to keep it from shifting laterally. Check the top of the form for level before nailing or screwing it to the stakes.

After the footing form is in place, I place a pier tube form on top of it, holding it in place with 1× material nailed across the top of the footing form and to the outside of the tube. It's a good idea to close off most of the opening to the footing form or some concrete will escape when the pier form is being filled, unless the pier is poured separately. Wider 1× material or a one-piece plywood top with a hole for the tube form are common solutions. The top of the tube form should be braced and locked with screws, boards, and stakes.

Pier forms

In this example, I'll use 8-in. diameter pier tubes to support 4×4 posts; (I would use a larger 10-in. diameter tube to support 6×6 posts). Larger tubes allow more leeway to place the post bases if the piers aren't located exactly right, but they also require considerably more concrete to fill. Larger-diameter tubes can also be used as forms to surround a concrete-encased continuous-post foundation from footing to grade instead of letting the earthen sides of the hole become the form. The smoother forms may help protect against frost action, especially they are wrapped in plastic, but backfill will still be necessary.

I cut sections of tube to length with a handsaw so that the tops will be at least 6 in. above grade when they are installed. It's not important that the tops of all the tubes be at the same level, as it is much easier to adjust the lengths of the wooden posts later on.

If I'm taking the precaution of wrapping the tubes in plastic sheeting, I do this before I place them in the hole. I wind several layers of 6-mil

Cut the tube form with a handsaw.

To help prevent frost jacking, wrap tubes in plastic.

Secure with staples or duct tape.

PRO TIP

A concrete hoe: It has a larger head than an average garden hoe and a hole in the blade to aid mixing and decrease resistance.

IN DETAIL

Concrete forms are easier to take apart if you use a double-headed nail—called a *duplex* nail—to put them together. The nail is driven tight up to the first head, while the second head is left protruding and available for a hammer or crowbar to grab onto later. I use 16d nails for 2× forms and 8d for 1×s.

Immediately after the forms are full and rebar placed, use a trowel to smooth the concrete on top. Gently tapping down the gravel will help the cement rise and give a smoother finish.

1×4 blocks and stakes hold tube forms in place.

Tubes are attached to the 1×4s with screws.

Do a final checking of a row of forms before taking down the strings and filling with concrete.

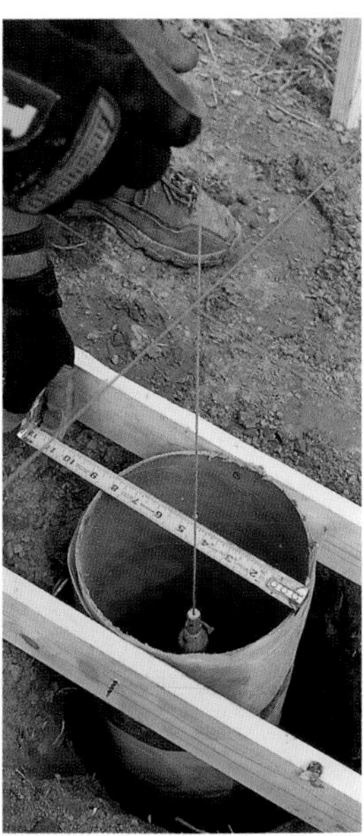

Corner forms are often located by a pair of crossed strings.

polyethylene around the tube and use duct tape and staples to hold the sheeting in place.

After cutting the tubes to length and placing them in the hole, I brace the top of each tube with 1×4s on edge attached to stakes at each end. A couple of drywall screws from the inside of the tube out through the 1×4 will lock the top in place. Before taking down the strings and filling the forms with concrete, I double-check that they are all in alignment, particularly at the corners.

Tube forms are definitely the cheapest and easiest solution, but you can make piers or any other form shape out of ¾-in.-thick exterior plywood. A square column can be built to any size using 1×2s on the outside of vertical corners and stitching the whole assembly together with 8d duplex nails or screws. Columns larger than 12 in. square will need some extra reinforcement, such as horizontal 1×4 bands attached to the corner 1×2s or several tight wraps of wire. Be sure to remove wooden forms after pouring concrete, because the decaying wood can attract insects later on.

Steel reinforcing

If there is a vertical pier/footing combination (as on this deck), I use a #4 L-shaped piece of rebar in the pier to connect it to the footing. The base of the L should be placed approximately in the middle of the footing (not higher) without touching the form; the vertical section of the L should come to within a few inches of the top of the pier. I use two Ls in 12-in. diameter tubes, but this is a detail that should be checked with your building inspector.

During the pour when the pier tube is about half full, I add the rebar, keeping it in the center of the tube and off the bottom and pumping it up and down a little to insure good concrete-to-steel contact. If you're pouring footings and concrete piers at different times, don't forget to add the L bar when pouring the footing.

Small footings that are only a few inches wider than the pier they support will usually not require separate pieces of rebar reinforcement in the footing alone. Deck footings more than a few inches wider than the pier should have rebar in the footing (see the drawing on the facing page). I use 2 pieces of #4 rebar oriented in an X for footings

Adding Rebar to Footings

The need for extra rebar depends on loads carried as well as size. For most typical deck footings, the examples shown here are adequate.

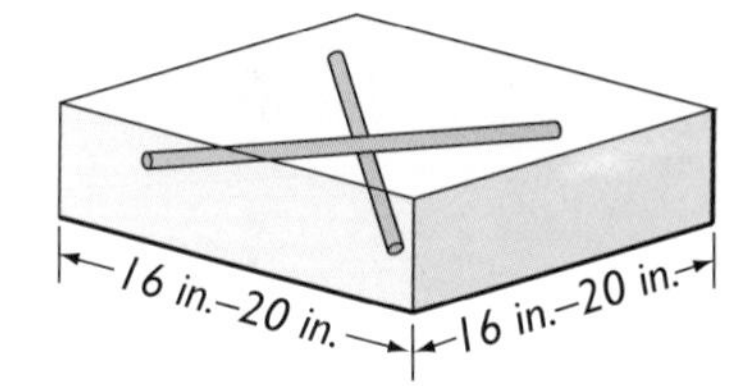

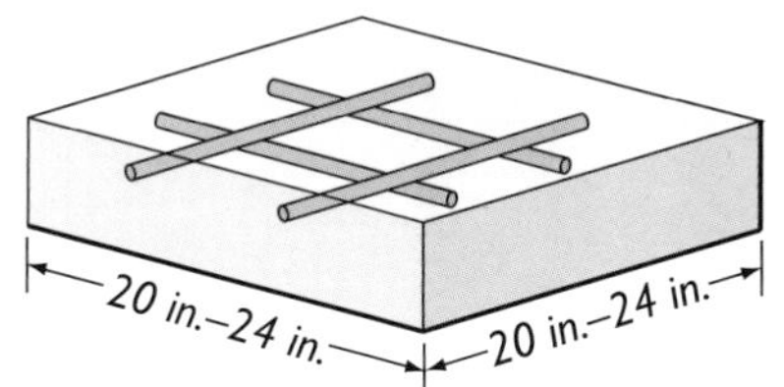

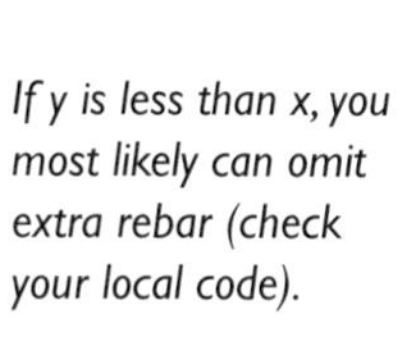

If y is less than x, you most likely can omit extra rebar (check your local code).

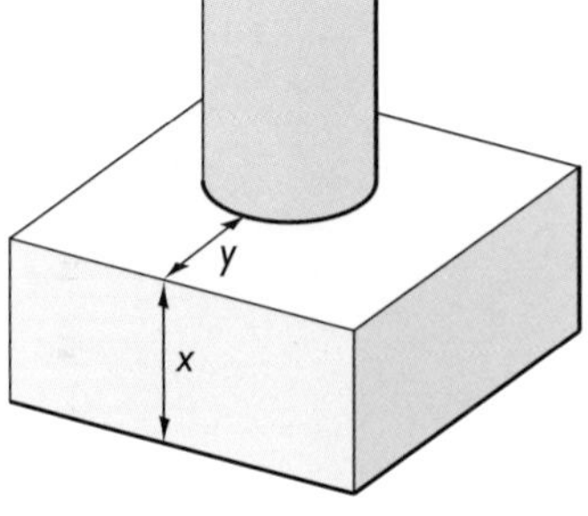

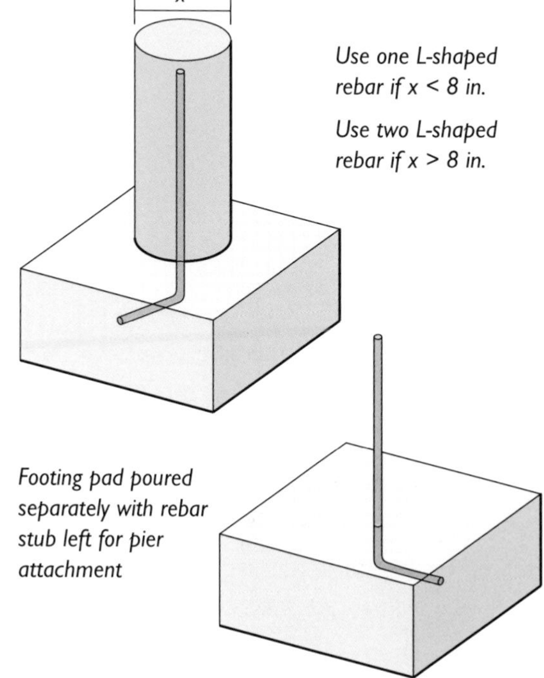

Wooden Pier Forms

Forms can be built on site using ¾-in. plywood and 1×4 stock.

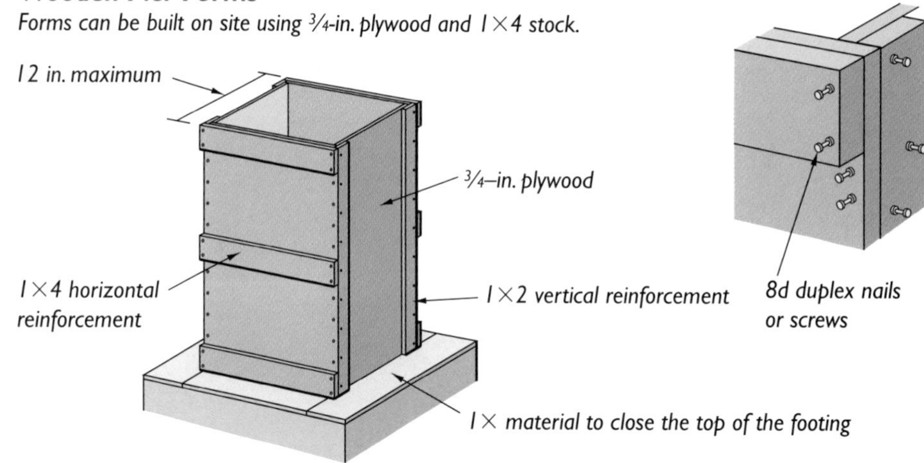

Footings for Hot Tubs

Hot tubs filled with water and people are heavy, and support for them needs to be carefully planned. Depending on the size of the hot tub, support can be provided either by a reinforced section of the deck or by a separate concrete slab. Hot tubs full of water and people can weigh a couple of tons, requiring framing that can support loads in excess of 100 psf. Additionally, hot tubs are considered permanent loads, and are used in wet conditions, both factors that require an increase in the number and size of framing members. (See Framing Deck Openings, p. 91, for more on framing for hot tubs.)

Footing sizes for hot tubs can be calculated normally using larger design load factors, but with the precaution of thickening footings to 8 in. with extra rebar reinforcement. Using a 10-in. diameter or larger pier size is also a good precaution, as is extra care with drainage and gravel. If you choose to put the tub on a slab, the loads will be spread over a much larger area than if separate footings are used. A well-prepared, reinforced 4-in. thick slab should be adequate, but the area under the slab should be excavated down to frost depth and refilled with compacted gravel. The tub supplier should be able to give you the weight of tub and users when full.

Hot Tub on a Concrete Slab

Check with the tub manufacturer for specific plumbing and electrical details, which must also meet local code requirements.

100-plus-psf load is supported by slab, not by the edge of the tub.

4-in. thick reinforced concrete slab

Compacted, well-drained, frost-protected gravel base: Bottom of gravel is 6 in. below frost depth.

PRO TIP

Mixing your own concrete in a wheelbarrow one batch at a time can get you some exercise, but mixing more than a yard will take you the better part of the day.

IN DETAIL

The water content of concrete can determined by a *slump test*, where a sample cylinder of concrete is turned upside down, removed from its container and allowed to settle. If the concrete settles 4 in., it has a 4-in. slump (this is the slump I order from the batch plant). While this test is usually done on critical commercial jobs and isn't a necessary test for your deck, it points out that stiffness—and therefore water content—is important because it's related to strength.

TRADE SECRET

When cutting a round shape such as a pier tube, I wrap a piece of heavy paper (15-lb. asphalt–felt paper works great) around the tube and trace along the edge to get an accurate line to follow. You can also leave the tubes a little long and not fill them all the way to the top with concrete, but this makes it a little harder to finish the concrete.

When forms are almost full, slide in a piece of rebar and give it a good wiggle to settle the concrete around it.

from about 16 in. to 20 in. across; for larger footings, I use 4 pieces in a square pattern. It's easiest to make the pattern before placing the rebar into the footing; you simply fasten the steel together at the intersections with steel tying wire. Unusual situations, such as much larger footings, heavy loads, or poor soils, will require engineering help.

Pouring the Foundation

Once the forms are built and set in place, it's time to pour concrete. Anyone who likes construction usually loves to mess around with concrete. It represents that first immutable step in a project's life, and we like to scratch our initials in fresh concrete because we know it will last a long time. I admit that I even enjoy mixing the stuff by hand…once in a while.

Concrete is a mixture of water, sand, aggregate and portland cement that hardens during a chemical reaction between the cement and water called hydration. If we used just enough water to satisfy the hydration process, the concrete would be too stiff to handle easily. So extra water is needed to make the concrete slide down the chute or pour from a wheelbarrow and conform to the forms. This extra water slightly weakens the concrete, so add only the minimum amount of water needed for easy handling.

Versatile, durable, and inexpensive, concrete can be mixed by hand with a few simple tools. If your

Estimating and Ordering Concrete

Concrete is sold by the cubic yard, which equals 27 cu. ft., but you can often order it in half-yard increments. First you'll need to calculate the volume of your forms, and then add up all the volumes. I like to be safe, and round up figures in all of my measurements, then add 10% to the total or round up to the nearest half-yard.

Here are some formulas that I use for calculating volumes:

- Volume of a box = length × width × height
- Volume of a cylinder = Pi (3.14) × radius (½ the diameter) squared × height of tube
- A 6-in. diameter tube uses 0.20 cu. ft. of concrete per foot of tube length
- An 8-in. diameter tube uses 0.35 cu. ft. of concrete per foot of tube length.

If you do your calculations in inches, divide your answer by 1,728 to get cubic feet. Divide the number of cubic feet by 27 to get cubic yards.

For example, the volume of a round footing that is 6 in. thick and 14 in. in diameter equals:

3.14π × 7 in. squared (radius squared) × 6 in. (height) = 923 cu. in. ÷ 1,728 = 0.53 cu. ft.

The volume of an 8-in. diameter by 42-in. long Sonotube pier equals:

3.14 × 4 squared × 42 = 2,110 cu. inc. ÷ 1,728 = 1.22 cu. ft.

Together, this footing-pier combination has a volume of 1.75 cu ft.

If there are four footings, the total needed concrete is 7 cu. ft. (4 × 1.75 cu. ft.), or .26 cu. yd. (7 cu. ft. ÷ 27 = 0.26 cu. yd.).

deck foundation calls for a large quantity of concrete, however, you'll want to consider either renting a mixer or having your concrete delivered.

Mixing concrete by hand

Mixing your own concrete in a wheelbarrow one batch at a time can be a satisfying way to get some exercise, but mixing more than a yard will take you the better part of the day. I can mix about 1 or 2 cu. ft. of concrete per wheelbarrow load, enough for a small footing. Separate batches of concrete going to the same footing or pier should follow one another quickly to avoid "cold joints" that weaken the pour. You may want to consider renting a small mixer, which will be easier and faster, or plan on getting some help if you need to pour a larger form.

You can buy bags of dry, premixed concrete—one brand name is Sacrete—at your local hardware store or lumberyard. Each 60-lb. bag yields about 0.45 cu. ft. of concrete (or about 60 bags/yd.), so besides being relatively expensive, these bags are only practical for very small jobs. They are a lot cleaner and more convenient to haul around in your car than loose gravel and sand, though.

Another option is to buy the ingredients separately. My concrete supply yard has a big pile of sand, premixed with the gravel in the correct proportions and ready to shovel right into my truck when I go to pick up a few bags of portland cement. You can buy sand and gravel separately, but be sure to get washed material specifically intended for this purpose, as dirt, salt, and organic materials will weaken concrete.

The sand should be a mix of fine particles no larger than ¼ in. (beach sand is not a good alternative), while the aggregate should be washed gravel that varies in size from ¼ in. up to ¾ in. For deck footings and piers, I specify concrete with a maximum gravel size of ¾ in., which makes it easier to fill my forms. Each 94-lb. bag of portland cement will yield about 4.5 cu. ft. of concrete when mixed with 500-600 lb. of sand and gravel.

Get all of the dry mix out of corners by hoeing from different sides. The final consistency should be just wet enough to pour out of the wheelbarrow and fill the forms without a struggle.

The first step in making concrete, whether premixed in bags (as shown here) or made from bulk ingredients in piles, involves mixing the dry ingredients thoroughly with a hoe.

If I'm mixing by hand (and not using premixed concrete), I first add the dry ingredients in the following sequence: three shovelfuls (by volume) of aggregate, two of sand, and one of cement. I try to keep the shovel loads about the same size, but when in doubt I err towards adding more cement. Start with a small batch, but depending on the size of your wheelbarrow or if you are using a mixer, you can probably at least double the recipe. I mix the dry ingredients thoroughly with a hoe before starting to add water a little at a time (a starting ratio is about 1 qt. of water per shovelful of cement), mixing and adding a little water at time until the mixture is just wet enough to spread out and fill the forms. The mix has a tendency to get too soupy all of a sudden, but if that happens, just add more dry ingredients until the mix is right. The mix should briefly hold distinct ridges when you chop it with a hoe.

Add about three-fourths of the estimated water at first and mix again. Then continue adding the rest of the water until the mixture is the right consistency. Just add more dry mix if the batch is too soupy.

PRO TIP

Whenever you use a treated post in or near the ground, always put the uncut factory end toward the footing.

TRADE SECRET

Some builders kerf the horizontal 1×4 of their batter boards with a handsaw rather than drive in a screw for the string. Simply tie a knot in the end of the string and drop it into the kerf. The knot holds the string in place in the kerf, but allows the string to be easily removed and replaced again.

In rocky ground, 1×4 batter boards screwed to rented metal foundation stakes work great.

IN DETAIL

If you have rocky ground, steel grade stakes (sometimes called *form stakes*) are a good alternative to wooden stakes. Available at most tool rental stores, these are 18-in. to 30-in. long steel rods with holes for nails; the stakes are usually used to anchor concrete forms in place and are stronger and easier to drive into hard ground.

Delivered concrete

If you need more than a yard and have limited time, then getting a ready-mix delivery may be the way to go. On my jobs, I never even consider mixing my own concrete (except maybe for a single footing) because the labor for rounding up all the tools and ingredients, to say nothing of the mixing time, would quickly cost more than buying ready-mix concrete.

I don't think that the price per cubic yard of delivered concrete—currently about $90.00 in my area—varies much from place to place, but the extra charges might. For example, I pay a surcharge if I order less than five yards, or if I'm more than ten miles away from the mix plant, or if I take longer than five minutes per yard to unload their truck. When you order concrete from a ready-mix plant, be sure to ask about these extra charges. At the site, be ready with all your forms in place and have helpers standing by when the truck arrives. And because it's unlikely that you'll be able to back a truck up to each individual form, have a wheelbarrow (two for more than a yard of concrete) and shovels at the ready.

Delivered concrete is more expensive but a whole lost easier. Having three or four helpers available can minimize "excess time" charges.

Filling the forms

If you're mixing your concrete by hand, then you'll be hard-pressed to keep up with your curing concrete. But if you're pouring footing/pier combinations with delivered concrete, and if it is convenient, you may want to fill all the footings first, and then go around and fill the tubes.

Forms can be filled one shovelful at a time directly from your wheelbarrow, but to speed the filling I tip the wheelbarrow up on its nose—use a half-filled wheelbarrow; concrete is heavy stuff—and pour the concrete directly into the tube. A makeshift chute can be formed by pairing two shovels together (see the photo at left), but for longer drops, it's not a bad idea to have a small plywood chute with 2×4 sides on hand to help

+ SAFETY FIRST

Never reach into a turning cement mixer with an arm or even a shovel to grab a stick or poke a lump, and watch those loose shirtsleeves. Using a mixer can be pretty dusty, so a dust mask is a good idea. Mixers also tend to splash, so wear safety glasses when you're operating one; concrete is caustic and will burn your eyes if you get splashed. Concrete will also dry and irritate your skin, so don't forget to wear rubber gloves and boots if you're the messy kind. Prelubricating your hands with a heavy cream or lotion will help keep them from cracking.

guide concrete into your forms. If I'm lucky, the concrete truck can deliver the concrete directly to my forms from the truck's chute. If the concrete is a little reluctant to spread out in the form, just pump a long 2×4 around in it and it will start to flow sideways. And don't forget to place or position any required rebar.

After the tubes are poured full, I use a small trowel to smooth the exposed top of the pier. Pushing the rocks down a little first leaves a cement-rich slurry that is easier to smooth. If I'm adding post bases to the top of the pier, this is a good time to do it. Concrete needs to cure slowly, which normally isn't a problem for buried footings and piers. Still, plan on covering any part exposed to the hot noonday sun; periodically giving the concrete a light misting with a garden sprayer will help if it's really dry out. Let the concrete cure at least overnight before you resume work. It will still be "green" the next day but able to take light loads. (It takes about 28 days for concrete to reach its maximum strength.) Be sure to wash all your tools as soon as you're done.

After the concrete piers have been poured, we still have a few more steps before we can start framing the deck. First, we'll attach post bases to the piers. Then, we'll backfill and grade the site.

After concrete is smoothed on top but while it is still wet, reattach your stringlines and mark the exact footing centers for inserting bolts with a plumb bob.

If the concrete has already cured, use a felt tip marker to mark bolt locations.

Post bases

Metal post bases not only anchor the deck framing to the piers, but also hold the bottom of the posts off the concrete. This space helps keep the post out of any standing water, prolonging the life of even pressure-treated posts.

There are a number of different types of post bases. One-piece steel saddles aren't adjustable, which means they are more likely to stay where you put them for a long time, and they must be installed in wet concrete. Other post bases attach to a bolt that is either installed while the concrete is wet (which is easier) or added later. These usu-

One-piece post bases are set in wet concrete and held a little above the pier top to help keep post ends dry.

PRO TIP

Always flash the ledger board when it is recessed into the siding, even if there is a protective overhang.

TOOLS AND MATERIALS

Self-adhering, waterproof bituminous tape combines a sticky layer of waterproof bituminous material—that black stuff used on the outside of basements and as ice dam protection on the lower part of roofs—with a durable polyethylene or aluminum backing. This tape is perfect for providing backup waterproofing under ledger flashings, where it's hard to make complicated bends that won't leak. I use bituminous tape around thresholds and corners, as well as for covering the tops of posts and flashing and any untreated wood not exposed to direct sunlight. I also use it over the tops of built-up beams that have been nailed tightly together without spacers.

WHAT CAN GO WRONG

You can avoid having to put holes in your ledger flashing by installing an extra row of 2×6 blocking parallel to the ledger but spaced away by several inches to allow water to drain through. Fasten the decking to this row of blocking and allow the ends to cantilever the short distance over onto the flashed ledger.

Calculating Joist Spans Supported by Beam

The span of a joist supported by a beam needs to be calculated and entered into the beam span table to determine beam size. In the simplest case, this can usually be figured as halfway to the ledger plus any cantilever, or as halfway to the next support in both directions plus any cantilever.

Cantilevered Joists over Beam

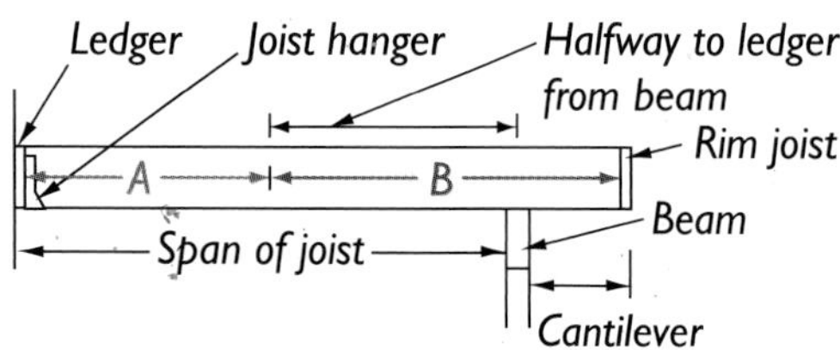

A. Joist length supported by ledger = ½ total span between supports

B. Joist length supported by beam = ½ total span between supports plus cantilever

C. Joist length supported by beam = ½ total span between supports

D. Joist length supported by beam = ½ total span in each direction to next support

Beam in the Same Plane as the Joists

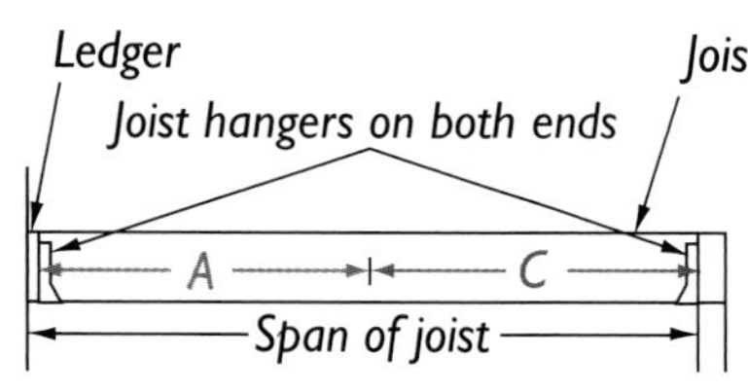

Continuous-post Framing

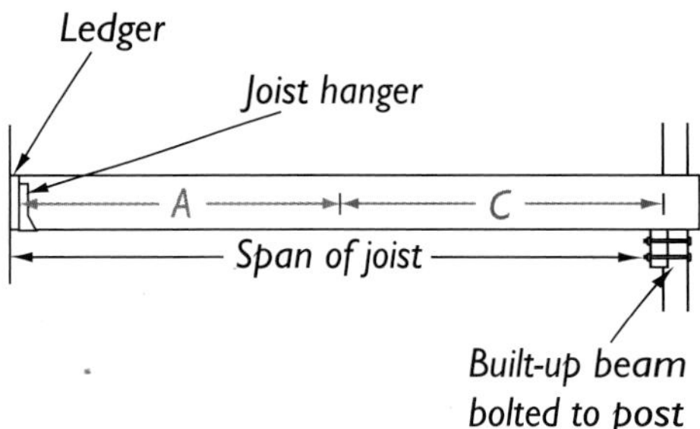

Cantilevered Joists over Multiple Beams

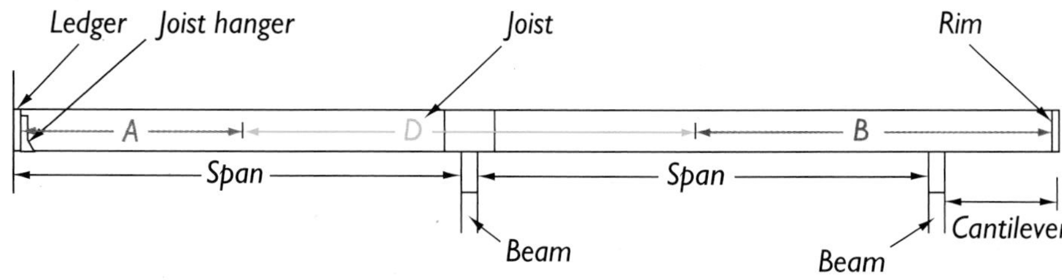

by using two 2×12s in a built-up beam (3×12), or a 4×10 or 6×8 solid timber. I could also use a smaller beam that could only span 7 ft., but this would require adding extra posts. Since I plan to use 4×4 posts, I don't want to use a 6×8 beam, which would be hard to attach using standard connectors.

Because joist size is determined by their maximum span and spacing (see next section on joists), it can be reduced if an extra beam is added midspan. This will certainly add to the labor and material cost for foundation post and beam work, but the extra costs may be justified in the joist savings. Extra beams may even be a necessity in poor soils or on especially large decks.

Beam sizes can be reduced by spreading the load over multiple beams or by using more posts and decreasing the beam spans. I find that one beam is almost always the most cost-effective approach, even if it means using a few extra posts

Maximum Beam Spans between Posts or Supports

Wood Species	Beam Size	Joist Length Supported (in Feet) 4	5	6	7	8	9	10	11	12
Southern yellow pine, Douglas fir	4 × 6	6	6	6						
	3 × 8	9	8	7	6	6	6	6		
	4 × 8	10	9	8	7	7	6	6	6	
	3 × 10	11	10	9	9	8	7	7	7	6
	4 × 10	12	11	10	9	9	8	8	7	7
	3 × 12		12	11	10	9	9	8	8	7
	4 × 12			12	11	11	10	9	9	9
	6 × 10			12	11	10	10	10	9	8
	6 × 12						12	11	11	10
Hem-fir	4 × 6	6	6	6						
	3 × 8	8	8	7	6					
	4 × 8	9	8	7	7	6	6			
	3 × 10	11	10	9	8	8	7	7	6	6
	4 × 10	12	11	10	9	9	8	8	7	7
	3 × 12		12	10	10	9	8	8	8	7
	4 × 12			12	11	10	10	9	9	8
	6 × 10			12	11	10	9	9	9	8
	6 × 12					12	12	11	10	10
Western red cedar, redwood	4 × 6	6	6							
	3 × 8	7	6							
	4 × 8	8	7	6	6					
	3 × 10	9	8	7	6	6	6			
	4 × 10	10	9	8	8	7	7	6	6	6
	3 × 12	11	10	9	8	7	7	7	6	6
	4 × 12	12	11	10	9	9	8	8	7	7
	6 × 10		12	11	10	9	9	8	8	7
	6 × 12			12	12	11	10	10	9	8

Notes: All beams should be #2 or better. 3× beam dimensions assume doubled 2× stock, fully nailed with joints over supports. Spans are for 50 lb./sf. total load (40 live plus 10 dead)

PRO TIP

Beams can be large timbers or made from layers of 2× framing lumber, but the material should be pressure-treated.

IN DETAIL

When you're flashing the ledger area, you'll have to detail the meeting point where the flashing ends and the siding begins. The basic idea is to make a 90-degree bend outward at the end of the flashing to divert water out away from the siding (as shown). For extra insurance, use some silicone caulk to help seal the area, and polyurethane caulk where the flashing bends out over the siding.

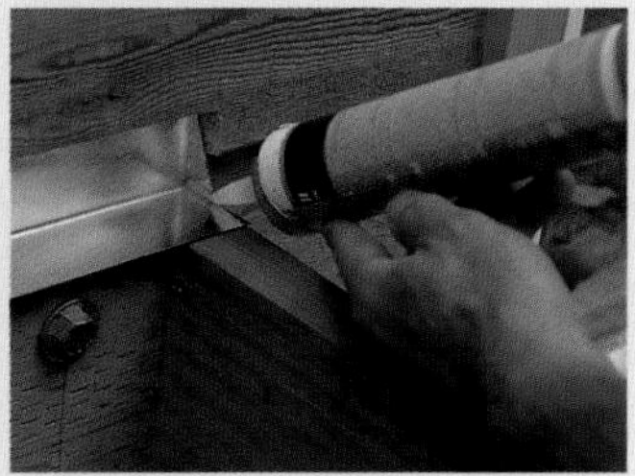

Ends of flashing should be bent in and caulked to keep water from running behind siding.

Using extra beams will lower the joist span and allow the use of smaller-sized components but will also require more foundation work. Extra beams may be needed for long joist spans, unavailability of some treated lumber sizes, or poor soil conditions.

Lifting Big Beams

Lifting beams is heavy work and can be dangerous. If you need to lift a 20-ft. 4×12 solid beam above shoulder height, plan on having three to four people; a 6×12 beam will need four to six people. Sometimes as few as two carpenters can lift heavy beams by using some temporary bracing or scaffolding and lifting one end at a time, but the last move from the scaffolding to the posts is always a little uncertain. Here are some safety tips:

- Don't underestimate the weight or instability of a timber or the damage it will do if you make a mistake.
- Be ready with scraps of 1×4 (called *scabs*) nailed to the posts to help keep the beam in position.
- Never let anyone get directly underneath a beam, and always have an escape route in mind if things go wrong.
- Be aware of the location of your fingers and toes and how they will fare if the beam were to drop unexpectedly.
- Take the time to get set up for a safe move.

to support it, a larger beam, or even larger-sized joists. The final choice will involve considerations on size, span, soil, material and labor costs, and availability of materials in an attempt to find the most efficient combination.

If one end of a beam is supported by a hanger rather than a post, you'll need to apply post and footing load calculations toward sizing the hanger. The hanger must fit the beam and be strong enough to support the load. Also, it's essential that the fasteners that hold the hanger to the house be anchored in solid framing. This may require opening the wall to add blocking directly behind and below the hanger's location. Setting the beam on a new post built into the house wall will eliminate the hanger concerns, but seek advice if the new post is located over a wide window.

Calculating the number and size of posts

To determine the number of posts you'll need, divide the total length of the beam by the maximum beam span for the size of beam you want to use, round up to the next highest number, and add one more for the first post. For a 22-ft.-long beam, if I want to use a double 2×12 beam with a maximum span of 8 ft. with my load conditions, I will need four posts with three spans between (22 ÷ 8 = 2.75, round up to 3 and add 1 to equal 4). The actual span and spacing between post centers is 7 ft. 4 in. (22 ÷ 3 = 7.33 ft., or 7⅓ ft.). Two sections (with three posts) would require a beam span of 11 ft., which would require a larger beam. From experience, I know to usually shoot for less than 10 ft. per span in typical situations.

The next step is to determine the proper post size, which depends on the height of the post and the load that it must bear. Small posts can hold up large loads provided the deck is not very high, but if you have a high deck, you will need a larger post even if the deck is relatively small.

The total load on a post—and therefore, the size of post needed—is based on the load area (in sq. ft.) supported by each post and the deck's design load. In Chapter 2, I explained how to calculate the number of square feet each post supported and then multiply that by the load per sq. ft to get the footing load. In this example, the deck's live load is 40 psf, and I've already calculated that the load area of the interior posts (the posts that support the most area) is 66 sq. ft. (see the drawing on p. 30). Checking my post sizing table (see the chart at right) for the appropriate supported load area (I go up to the next column, or 72) and wood species, I find that I can use 4×4 posts that are up to 9 ft. long.

Maximum Post Heights for 40-lb./sf. Live Load

The maximum length of post allowed depends on its species, size, and the load it carries. To determine the maximum post length, first calculate the supported load area of deck of each post (see the drawing on p. 30) and find this on the top row heading. Then look down the left column for the species and size of post you want to use and read across to the maximum height for this post.

		Supported Load Area in Square Feet									
		36	48	60	72	84	96	108	120	132	144
Wood Species	Nominal Post Size	Maximum Post Height in Feet									
Southern yellow pine, Douglas fir	4×4	10*	10*	10*	10	10	9	9	8	8	7
	4×6	12*	12*	12*	12*	12	11	11	10	10	9
	6×6	12*	12*	12*	12*	12*	12*	12*	12*	12*	12*
Hem-fir	4×4	10*	10*	10	9	9	8	8	7	7	6
	4×6	12*	12*	12*	12	11	10	9	9	9	8
	6×6	12*	12*	12*	12*	12*	12*	12*	12*	12*	12*
Western red cedar, redwood	4×4	10*	10	9	8	7	7	6	6	5	4
	4×6	12*	12*	12	11	10	9	9	8	8	7
	6×6	12*	12*	12*	12*	12*	12*	12			

Note: All Lumber should be #2 grade or better. 10 lb./sf. dead load included. *Taller posts may be allowed, but consult an engineer.

Installing Posts and Beams

After pouring concrete for piers, I reset string lines to reestablish and mark the exact centers of the posts on the top of the piers. Regardless of how carefully the piers were located, they may have moved during the pour or backfill. The strings will also directly (or with the help of a simple measurement) locate the outside of the deck framing, providing the starting point for the main beam and for the layout of the post centers. With the post bases in place (as described in Chapter 2), we can begin to set our posts.

Installing posts

It's likely that footings will be at differing heights, especially on hillsides, and so posts will all be different lengths. I determine the length of each post one at a time, using the ledger as a reference to establish the elevation of the bottom of the main beam (or beams), which I then mark right on the posts. If the ledger hasn't been installed during the layout of the foundation, now is the time to do it.

PRO TIP

Whether installing beams or joists, put the crown facing up. It will flatten under the weight of the deck. The crown facing down could create sag.

TRADE SECRET

You can check board's moisture content with a moisture meter, or you can carefully weigh a few wet samples, dry them in an oven at 200 degrees for 24 hours, and then reweigh them. Divide the difference between the wet weight and the dry weight by the dry weight and multiply by 100. You can also take a nonscientific approach. Pick up a board and qualitatively judge its weight (it will lose about a fourth or more of its wet weight as it dries), then try cutting a piece. If it still sprays you with water and wet sawdust, it needs more drying.

IN DETAIL

Air-drying is a simple (but time-consuming) process. Just stack the boards someplace dry with 1× or larger stickers between the layers to promote good air circulation. The pile should be covered with scrap plywood to keep off the rain. Direct sunlight may cause warping, so lean a piece of plywood against the sunniest side for protection. And stack some heavy concrete blocks on top of the pile to help minimize cupping or warping as the boards dry.

Once the ledger is in place, its bottom edge can be used as a benchmark to find the height of posts, in this case with a builder's level.

Next, the level is pivoted to the post location and the tape measure is adjusted up and down until the level reads the same mark on the tape measure. Then the bottom elevation of the ledger is marked on the post.

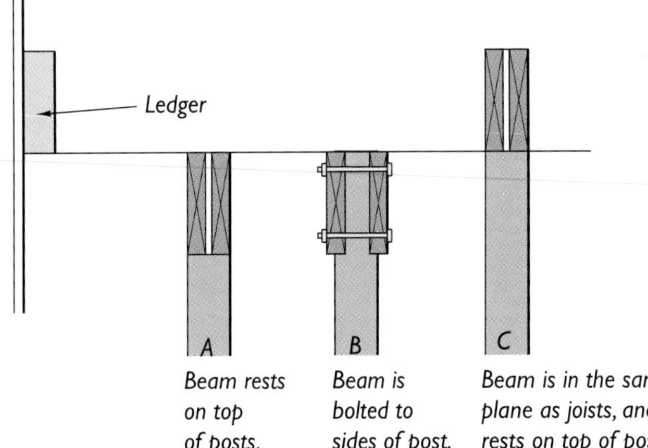

Finding Top-of-Post Elevation

Shown are post heights for three different types of beam; all depend on the position of the ledger. To find the top of post elevation:

A: Post height = elevation of bottom of ledger minus height of beam

B: Post height = elevation of bottom of ledger. Posts are notched slightly to support beam.

C: Post height = elevation of bottom of ledger

(Drop beam slightly by shortening post length to insure drainage.)

(See pp. 54–59 for information on installing the ledger.)

To ensure good drainage, I like to drop the beam a little bit from level with the ledger so that the joists fall slightly downhill away from the house. On a perfectly level deck, small variations in framing (such a joist crowns) can cause some areas to slope toward the house, and water will drain in the wrong direction. Dropping the beam is easily accomplished by lowering the beam mark on the post by about ½ in. This slight tilt will not be noticeable on most decks, but decrease the amount of drop if your joists are less than 8 ft. long.

To transfer the ledger elevation over from the wall, set a post in place and brace it temporarily (or have a helper hold it in place). Then, using a water level, builder's level, or simply a long straight board with a 4-ft. level on top, transfer this mark to the post. To get the actual height of the post if the beam sits on top of the posts, subtract the beam height from the ledger elevation marked on each post. The bottom of the beam will be the height at which the posts are cut. If the beam is attached to the side of the post rather than set on top, the bottom-of-ledger mark transferred from the wall would indicate the top of the beam and the post. If the joists are in the plane of the beam, the transferred ledger mark is the bottom of the beam and the top of the post.

Although you can cut a post to length in place, I find it easier and safer to take the post down and work off a set of sawhorses. First, I extend the cutline around all four sides of the post with a speed square. Next, I use a circular saw to cut the post to length, rotating the post as necessary to complete the cut. Of course, this cut can also be made with a large chopsaw if one is available, which makes a quick, smooth, and accurate cut. After making the cut, I field-treat the end grain of the cut post ends with preservative. Then I set the post in place on its foundation, using temporary bracing to hold it while I check for plumb.

Measure down the height of the beam from the ledger elevation to get the cutline for the top of the post.

Once all the posts are cut to length, plumbed, and securely braced, they're ready for beam placement.

If the posts are to be continuous and part of the deck railing, transfer your mark over from the ledger to get your beam location but leave the posts long for now. Later, after the joists and decking are in place, the tops of all the posts will be cut to the same length at the same time. If the

+ SAFETY FIRST

When a spinning circular saw blade gets pinched in the middle of a cut, or when the operator tries to back the saw up, kickback can occur. The saw instantly climbs out of the slot and cuts anything that is behind it. You can minimize the chance of kickback by keeping a firm grip on the saw, supporting the work so that it won't bind the blade, and having only as much blade exposed as necessary. It's good practice to set the blade depth so that only about ¼ in. is exposed on the underside of the cut.

PRO TIP

If you need to drill more than a couple of holes larger than ¼ in. in concrete, you'll want to rent a rotary hammer drill made for the job.

TRADE SECRET

Thresholds need to be carefully flashed to prevent them from leaking. If you're adding a new door to the house, make a custom flashing that covers the subfloor, extends down the wall, and continues out over the ledger flashing. Set the new door on the flashing in a generous bead of caulk. If there is an existing door, see if you can wiggle a separate piece of L-flashing up under the threshold and have it lap over the ledger flashing. If not, you'll just have to carefully cut the new ledger flashing to fit snugly up to the bottom of the threshold. In either case, caulk generously to seal the joint between flashing and threshold.

When cutting with a circular saw, mark all four sides of the post before cutting.

Cut by following marked lines around the post.

Cutting posts with a power miter box is quick, accurate, and needs only one side marked for cutting.

Cutting posts exposes untreated wood, which benefits from a brushing with preservative.

Check posts for plumb while bracing. Screwing makes it easier.

These posts, braced in both directions for stability, are ready for a beam.

post is to be notched for a beam bolted to the side of it, it will be easiest to cut this notch as the post is lying on the ground, before you stand the post up and brace it.

Installing the beam

Once the posts have been cut, attached to their foundations, and braced, the beam can be lifted into place. You'll probably need to slide the beam laterally to its exact location, which you can find by hanging a plumb bob from the end of the beam down to a foundation stringline (a level will work for low beams). After the beam is in position, secure it to the post with a metal post cap, but don't completely nail off the connector until after some joists have been installed and you've made sure that the positioning is correct. If you are bolting a beam to the side of a post, clamp some temporary support blocks to the post to rest the beam on and then use several more clamps to hold the beam itself to the post.

If you're lucky enough to have a beam that's longer than necessary, you may want to install it with a little extra length at each end, leaving it uncut at the outside ends until the joists are installed. This is easier than trying to move a long and heavy beam back and forth a little bit into alignment; it also ensures against error introduced by bumped batter boards when you are plumbing up from layout strings, or any uncertainty about the beam's location. If you are working up high, remember to use caution and carefully check your footing and ladder position. Cutting the beam after it's set on posts is more dangerous than cutting it while it's lying on the ground.

Built-up beams. If they are small (no more than 16 ft. to 20 ft. long), built-up beams are most easily built on the ground and lifted in one piece. If the beams are longer than this or more than two layers thick, they can be built and lifted in sections. When beams are low to the ground and easy to work on, they can also be built in place, one board at a time, on the post tops. This is easier on the back, and often this spot is the only flat and even place for you to work.

PRO TIP

Even when the beam is supported by a notch, properly sized bolts should always be used to secure the connection.

TRADE SECRET

You'll need to use a beam sizing table specific to the species of wood your using, as well as the design load you have chosen for your deck. Also, these tables won't work for particularly heavy loads that include hot tubs or big planters; for those, you should consult an engineer. And while standard tables like these tend to be conservative, it's always better to be a little overbuilt. Your local building inspector should be able to confirm if there is any reason that these tables are not appropriate for your area.

IN DETAIL

Nothing more than a water-filled reservoir and clear plastic tubing, this handy and inexpensive level can read around corners and go up, down and around obstacles. While I've found water levels to be a little messy (lay it down incorrectly and the water can leak out), they're cheap and accurate.

A built-up beam is attached to the posts with metal connectors. Using a small level to make sure the beam is plumb will make it easier to cut and hang joists later on.

1. To build on the ground, lay the first layer of cut-to-length 2Xs on a flat surface, remembering to crown all the boards in the same direction. If spacers are used, tack these in place every 2 ft.

2. Place the second layer on and nail the boards together through the spacers, taking care to align the tops and bottoms of both boards (a combination square set across the top of the beam works well for this) so the completed beam will set straight. Built-up beams need to be nailed together well to be most effective, and each layer should be nailed to the next layer at least every 6 in., with nails in a zigzag pattern, alternating top and bottom. When plywood spacers are used between layers, the nailing is only effective when done through the spacer area, and it will be necessary to condense the same amount of nails into this smaller area.

3. Joints in long beams should break over posts and have a spacer at the joint if spacers are used in the rest of the beam.

One way to build a longer beam on the ground is to build it in sections joined by slip joints located over posts. Build each section of the beam conventionally, but let a spacer protrude halfway out of the joint at the end of each beam section. Also, create a slot by leaving off the first spacer at the beginning of the next section. The nailed spacer slips between the next beam's slot when it is put in place. After the beam is assembled, completely nail off all the slip joints.

Building a layered beam in place works well if you can do your nailing without ladders. Just put

A heavy beam that is not built in place should be lifted by several people to ease the load and aid stability.

Deck Fasteners

Deck framing is held together with nails, bolts, and screws. These can be made of mild steel that's hot-dipped galvanized with zinc, or electroplated with zinc or cadmium, or made entirely of stainless steel.

Stainless-steel fasteners cost the most and will last the longest; they're essential in salty coastal environments. Contrary to common belief, stainless is softer than mild steel, so nails bend more easily, screws can snap, and bolt heads can get bunged up too. Using all stainless fasteners on a deck could easily increase cost by several hundred dollars, even on a small deck. Stainless bolts are often specified as 18/8 (18% chromium and 8% nickel) and screws and nails by a number in the 300 series (which has a composition very close to 18/8 bolts). The basic grades adequate for most exterior work are 304 and 305, while 316-grade stainless fasteners provide added corrosion resistance (at a price) for fasteners and metal connectors used in marine conditions. (See Resources, pp. 179–181.)

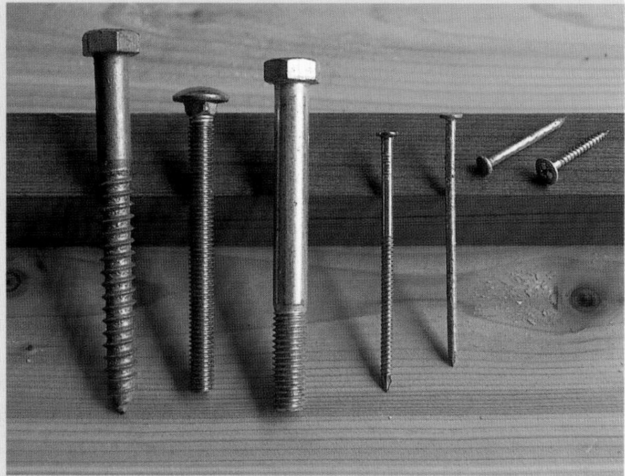

An assortment of fasteners is necessary for deck framing. Shown here (from left to right): hot-galvanized (hg) lag bolt, stainless-steel (ss) carriage bolt, zinc-plated (zp) machine bolt, ss box nail, hg box nail, hg joist hanger nail, and zp joist hanger screw.

Hot-dipped galvanized nails are my choice for most situations. They're dull gray in color, with a rough to semismooth coating. They're readily available, competitively priced, and hold up well. Tumble-coated galvanized nails are not as uniformly coated, and their protective coating seems to chip off more readily.

Electroplated galvanized fasteners have a thinner coating that is typically shiny and smooth. Because this coating doesn't seem to last as long, I steer clear of these fasteners. Most nailer nails have this coating, and although some are thicker and better than others, to avoid problems, I always nail my deck framing by hand. Zinc or cadmium electroplated bolts are the most readily available, and while I admit to using them occasionally, it is always with reluctance.

PRO TIP

Because the tops of freshly cut posts are particularly exposed to weather, add protection by flashing them with metal or sealing them with roof asphalt.

TRADE SECRET

One trick that makes locating end posts easier is to cantilever the beam over them. This makes positioning them a little less fussy and gives you the flexibility to move the beam one way or the other if need be to get it in the right spot. However, the beam shouldn't be cantilevered more than a few inches, and never more than the height of the beam. For example, a 4×10 timber shouldn't cantilever more than 10 in.

Clipping the corner of a cantilevered beam at a 45-degree angle gives it a finished look and makes it safer.

A protruding plywood spacer creates a tongue at the end of a multi-sectioned beam.

The tongue of one beam section slides into a slot left in an adjacent section of beam.

up one piece at a time, attach post connectors as soon as possible to aid stability, and keep adding spacers and layers until completed. This method also offers the advantage of staggered, or "railroaded," joints, in which only one layer of the beam is broken at each post instead of both. This adds integrity and stability to the beam.

Regardless of whether you're using timbers or built-up beams, all joints must fall over posts. After the sections are set up on the posts, the beams will need to be tied together on the sides or top with metal strapping or plywood gussets.

Beams bolted to the side of posts. Sometimes a beam is bolted to the side of a post, whether for stylistic reasons or to help stabilize other beams that are tall for their width (like a 3×12) and hard to restrain as they dry. Bolting the beam is necessary if the posts continue up through the beam to become part of the railing system. However, a beam that is bolted only to a post relies on the strength of the bolt and the ability of the wood not to split, so it has some severe structural limitations. In all but light-load situations, I recommend adding a notch to increase the carrying capacity of the joint. The notch should not significantly weaken the post, and its depth should consider the size of beam, post, and load situation. Don't forget to brush any untreated wood in the notch with preservative.

Use 2× lumber—one layer on each side of the post—to build bolted beams. When bolting on two 2×6s or 2×8s, use two ½-in.-diameter bolts at each connection. When bolting on two 2×10s or 2×12s, use three ½-in.-diameter bolts. Using more bolts than this will tend to weaken the joint instead of adding strength.

Bear in mind that the unnotched connection can support only a limited deck area, which will depend on the size of the beam, the number of bolts, the species of wood, and the quality of the wood in the vicinity of the bolts. As a general guideline, each unnotched 2×6 or 2×8 connection will support only about a 4×6-ft. area of deck in weaker species like cedar, and about a 4×8-ft. area in woods with higher strength like fir or yellow pine. A 2×10 or 2×12 connection will support about a 4×8-ft. area in weaker woods and about a 4×10 foot area in stronger ones. Larger-diameter bolts can increase the amount of area that can be supported by larger beams.

If the posts don't continue up to form the railing, I prefer to set the 2× layers of my built-up beam into ¾-in.-deep notches on each side of a 4×4 post, then bolt through the layers and the remaining 2-in. tenon with several ⅜-in.-diameter (minimum) bolts. If you need to keep both layers of the beam on the same side of the post, you can increase the depth of the notch to 1½ in. and still leave a 2-in. tenon for bolting. Remember, though, that in this case the outside beam layer relies on bolting alone. Notched or not, bolting a layer of 2× to each side of a post works best when the joists are cantilevered over the whole beam so that both layers share the load. If the joists are hung with joist hangers off one side of a layered beam, then the layers will need additional bolts and extra blocking to help tie the two layers into a single load-bearing unit.

A 4× or larger timber can be bolted to the side of a notched 6×6 post, and the notch should

A long built-up beam can be built in place right on top of the posts. Be sure that all joints are supported by posts.

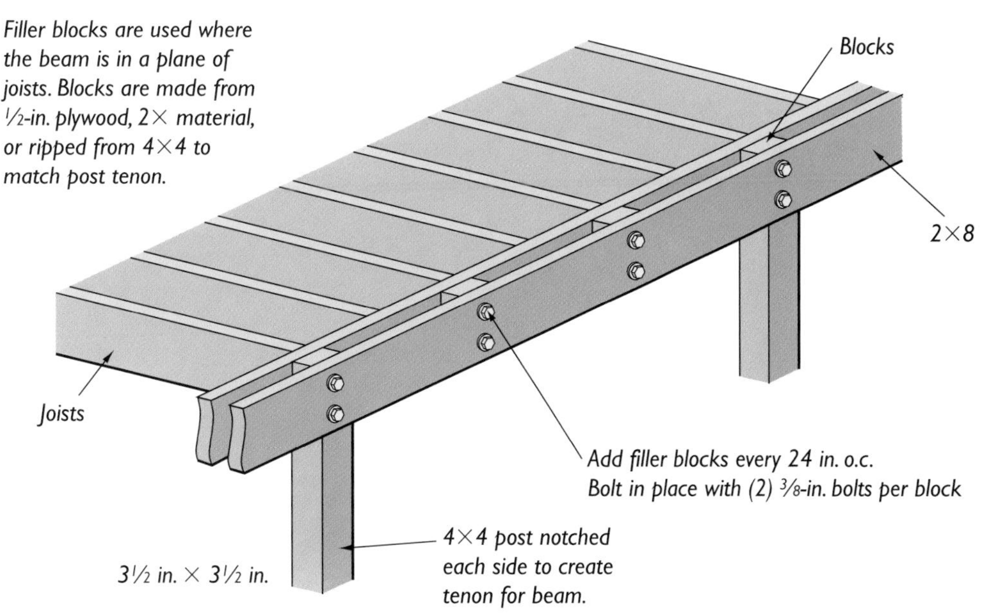

Building a Stronger Built-up Beam

When joists are hung from a built-up beam, only the inside layer supports the load unless both layers are well connected. Use spacer blocks to match the thickness of the post tenons, space them 24 in. o.c., and bolt the sections together securely through the spacer blocks as shown.

PRO TIP

Whenever possible, I use a square post that is the same width as the beam, even if the post sizing tables will allow something smaller.

IN DETAIL

When joists rest on beam:

- Posts are simpler to lay out.
- Cantilever design simplifies joist framing.
- Beam location doesn't need to be exact.
- Method doesn't require joist hangers.

When joists are hung from beam:

- There's usually not enough room underneath a low deck to stack the joists on top.
- Access (and headroom) below the deck is increased.
- The beam can be disguised by making it part of the joist system, which imparts a lighter feel to the deck framing.

IN DETAIL

Metal post caps are available in different configurations. Two-piece post caps can be attached after framing; one-piece post caps need to be attached to the top of the post before the beam is put in place. While most post caps can be field-modified to fit posts on the end of a beam, there are also specific, less-obtrusive caps designed for end posts.

Three Ways of Bolting Beams to Posts

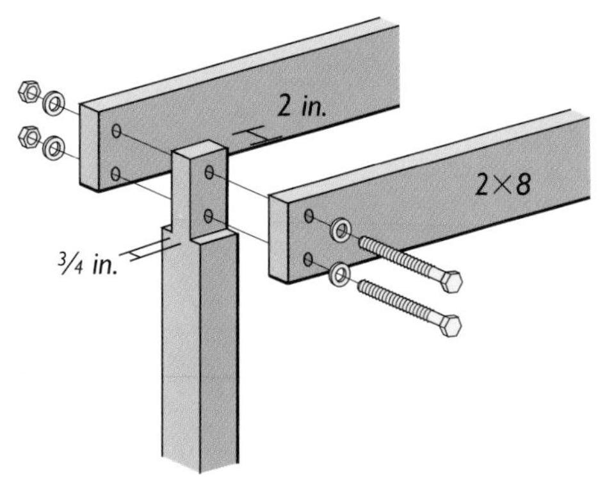

1. A notched post offers a strong connection.

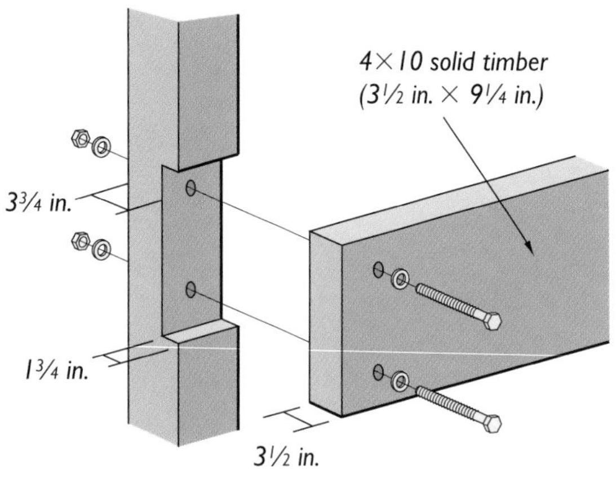

2. A continuous 6×6 post can be notched to receive a solid timber. The notch is no more than ½ the timber thickness to leave plenty of post to support railing.

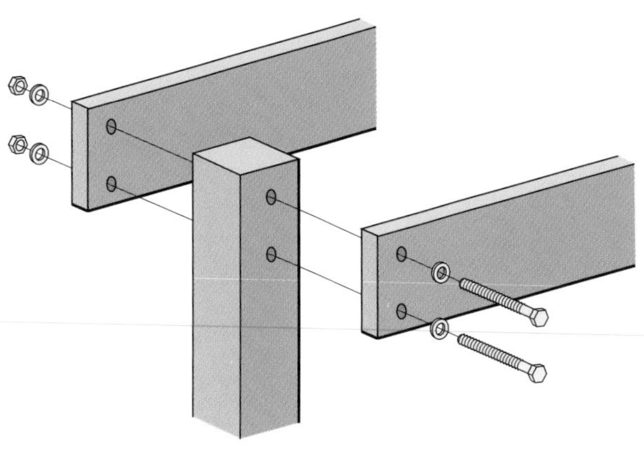

3. No-notch connection relies on bolts only, and the strength of this joint is limited more by wood splitting failure than the bolts.

be about 1¾-in. deep (half the thickness of the timber). The timber can then be bolted using several ½-in. bolts and washers at each post connection. When 4×4 posts continue up to become part of the railing system, keep notching to a minimum, as 2 in. of post is not strong enough for a railing. Instead use 4×6s or 6×6s and leave at least 3½ in. of solid wood in the unnotched area.

Here is one half of a two-piece post cap. Caps made for posts near the end of the beam have a flange in one direction only.

Post-to-beam connectors

Metal post caps are the most common connector for beams that sit on top of posts. Although very functional, post caps aren't very attractive, though they can be painted with proper preparation. Sometime on smaller, low decks, I will use only one half of a two-piece connector on the back side of the connection, where it isn't quite so visible. Like all metal connectors, post caps should be fastened per manufacturer's specifications, which usually means filling every hole with the correct fastener.

As an alternative, you could make treated plywood or solid wood gussets. While these tend to look bulky, they'll work as long as they are thoroughly nailed. Also, wherever there are butt joints in a beam over a post, I always nail a metal strap across the top of the joint for added security.

✚ SAFETY FIRST

In order to keep up the manufacturer's warranty on treated lumber, you're supposed to brush preservative (available in quarts as *end cut solution* from your lumber supplier) on cuts that expose untreated wood. I keep the can in a plastic dish tub to contain the spill if it should get knocked over. I also keep a separate plastic container in the tub to hold the dedicated and never-washed brush, as well as a pair of solvent-resistant gloves that I *always* wear when applying this toxic stuff.

PRO TIP

Step up to a larger joist whenever you come close to the maximum span acceptable. I usually use a 2×8, except on landings and other small areas.

IN DETAIL

"On center" —or *o.c.*—is a term commonly used by carpenters to describe the distance from the center of one joist to the next. But joists are seldom laid out that way. Instead, measure "centers" using either the same left- or right-hand face for all the joists except the end ones.

IN DETAIL

Douglas fir deck joists span 12 ft. from the ledger to the beam, then cantilever another 3 ft. If I hope to use 2×6 Western red cedar for decking, I know my joists could be 24 in. o.c., according to the decking span tables (see the chart on p. 103). From the joist span table (see the chart on the facing page) in the live load column (under 40 psf with #2 Douglas fir joists 24 in. o.c.), I find that 2×10 joists can span up to 12 ft. 7 in. I could also use 2×8 joists with a maximum span of 12 ft. 5 in. if the joist spacing were 16 in. o.c. Using 2×8s would require five extra joists, which may cost $20 more than using 2×10s but would be easier to install. In addition, closer joist spacing tends to give a deck a sturdier feel.

Laying Out and Installing Joists

On most decks, the joists are attached to the ledger at one end, extend away from the house, and are capped at the other end with either a beam or a single board called a rim joist. Other parts of the joist system include headers (short beams made of doubled joist material that span framing discontinuities and support cut joists) and blocking (short pieces of joist material installed perpendicular to regular joists to help stabilize the system or reinforce particular areas such as railing attachment points.

Joists need to be sized and spaced with considerations for loading, span, wood type, and decking material. Like all other deck framing, joists are subject to rot and should be made from treated or rot-resistant wood. Sometimes joist framing is covered around the perimeter with a finish material called a skirt or fascia.

Sizing joists

With cost in mind, I initially choose the smallest and least number of joists that will do the job properly from the span table. In this case, the live load for this deck is 40 psf, but remember that live loads vary according to use. Wood species is also an important factor, as some woods are definitely stronger than others. Again, this difference is taken into account in the various span tables.

Although span tables are conservative, I prefer to step up to a larger joist whenever I come anywhere close to the maximum span acceptable; very seldom do I use anything smaller than a 2×8, except on small areas like landings. Overbuilding may cost a bit more, but it will give you a deck that feels solid.

Spacing joists closer will increase their span, because the load will be spread over more joists. If you are close to the maximum span, you will have to evaluate the economic advantages of choosing more closely spaced, smaller joists or choosing to use larger-sized joists that are spaced further apart. The type of decking that you are using will also influence your joist spacing. Decking such as 1½-in. thick cedar or pressure-treated wood is strong enough to span joists that are 24 in. o.c., while some of the newer composite decking materials require joist spacing to be 16 in. or even 12 in. o.c. (see the chart on the facing page). If your decking choice requires you to place joists closer together than the span tables call for, you might be able to reduce the size of the joists.

Deck joists are installed and ready for finishing framing details such as blocking and bracing.

Joist layout

Sizing the joists also helps determine the spacing between them. Usually they are placed 16 in. or 24 in. o.c., so this spacing—called the layout—needs to be marked on the ledger for one end of the joist and either the beam or rim joist at the other.

Layout isn't complicated, but it does require a consistent approach. Make sure that your starting point on the ledger and rim joist is referenced off of a joist common to both. On a simple rectangle, this is usually the outside joist, but on more complicated decks with angles, it may need to be an interior joist that is uncut and perpendicular to both rim and ledger.

Choosing the exact location to begin your layout will depend on such considerations as what

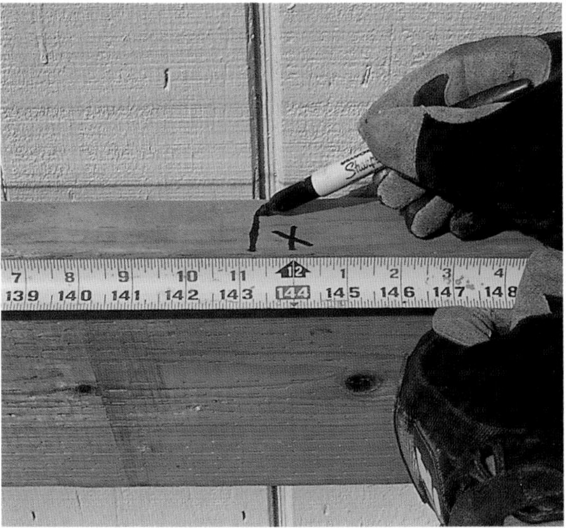

Mark ¾ in. to one side of a joist center for the edge of the joist and hanger. Place an "X" to the joist side of the mark to avoid confusion.

From the layout mark, use a square to draw a line across the ledger face to help align the joist hanger.

Span Table for Joists

Species	Joist Size	Maximum Span between Posts or Supports 12 in. o.c.	16 in. o.c.	24 in. o.c.
Douglas Fir, Southern Yellow Pine	2×6	10 ft. 4 in.	9 ft. 3 in.	7 ft. 6 in.
	2×8	13 ft. 7 in.	12 ft. 4 in.	10 ft. 5 in.
	2×10	17 ft. 4 in.	15 ft. 7 in.	12 ft. 9 in.
	2×12	20 ft.	18 ft. 1 in.	14 ft. 9 in.
Hem-fir	2×6	9 ft. 8 in.	8 ft. 10 in.	7 ft. 4 in.
	2×8	12 ft. 9 in.	11 ft. 7 in.	10 ft. 2 in.
	2×10	16 ft. 3 in.	14 ft. 9 in.	12 ft. 4 in.
	2×12	19 ft. 10 in.	17 ft. 7 in.	14 ft. 4 in.
Redwood, Western Red Cedar	2×6	8 ft. 10 in.	7 ft. 3 in.	6 ft.
	2×8	11 ft. 7 in.	10 ft. 5 in.	8 ft. 6 in.
	2×10	14 ft. 9 in.	12 ft. 9 in.	10 ft. 5 in.
	2×12	17 ft. 1 in.	14 ft. 9 in.	13 ft. 6 in.

All joists should be #2 grade or better. These values assume 40 lb./sf. live load (10 lb./sf. dead load included). They permit a deflection of 1/360 of the joist's maximum span when fully loaded.

Lay out joist locations on the beam, starting at a point analogous with the ledger starting point so layout marks will correspond.

PRO TIP

Layout requires a consistent approach. Make sure that your starting point on the ledger and rim joist is referenced off a joist common to both.

IN DETAIL

Joist hangers are U-shaped metal brackets that make butt connections between two boards easy and secure. Hangers are available in different sizes for different size joists, for doubled joists, and for beams, and come in different strengths for regular and heavy-duty loads. All hangers used on deck construction should be galvanized; stainless-steel hangers should be considered for severe or coastal environments. Fasteners used with joist hangers should be of the same material, and properly sized for the hanger.

Cantilevering Joists

Cantilevering is an effective technique that I use on almost all of my decks. It allows me to add several feet to the width of a deck without exceeding the maximum span rating for the joists; it sometimes allows me to use a smaller size joist by decreasing the span between ledger and beam. And cantilevering lets me be less fussy when locating the posts, beams, and foundation work. However, there are a few guidelines that limit the distance that a joist can extend unsupported past the beam, and these assume there will be no unusual loading out at the end other than occupants.

Under the right conditions, it's technically okay for joists to cantilever up to about 40% of the distance they are spanning between supports, as long as the cantilever doesn't exceed four times the joist depth. For example, a joist spanning 10 ft. between supports could theoretically cantilever another 4 ft. past the supporting beam, for a total joist length of about 14 ft. But if the joists are 2×10s (with an actual width of 9.5 in.), then your cantilever would be limited to 38 in. (4×9.5 = 38).

Unless you like bouncy construction, I would limit the cantilever to about 25% of supported joist length. In fact, I never exceed three feet of cantilever. This makes the deck feel solid even when you are standing out over the cantilevered ends. If you want to cantilever more than three feet, I suggest stepping up to the next larger size joist, even if it exceeds requirements.

Large cantilevers require joists to be well anchored at the opposite end.

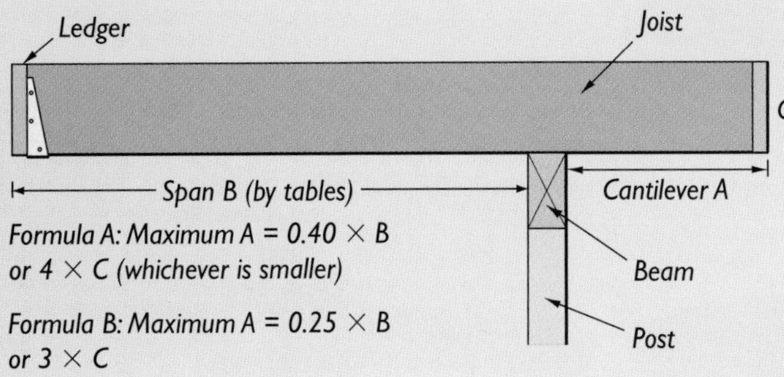

Cantilevers
The maximum length of a cantilever is based on the length of joist that is supported and the width of the joist. Technically joists can be cantilevered up to 40% of the amount that's supported but not more than four times the joist width (formula A). To avoid callbacks about bouncy decks, I prefer a more conservative figure of 25% the amount supported or three times the joist width (formula B).

railing style you choose and whether the ends of the decking are to be covered with a fascia board or left overhanging the end joist. Don't forget that your end joist may not be installed on the ledger yet, so you may need to add an additional 1½ in. for this. Then find the mark at 12 in., 16 in., or 24 in. (depending on the span tables) for the first joist inside the end joist.

When I start my layout, I don't mark the center of the joist, but rather one side or the other by adding or subtracting ¾ in. (half the width of a 2× joist). I make my layout mark here, and indicate which side of the mark the joist falls on with an "X." On the layout mark, I use a square to draw a perpendicular line across the ledger face to help align the joist hanger. Then I continue the layout all the way to the end, always marking the same face of all the joists. Once the ledger is laid out, I go ahead and lay out the beam the same way, starting with the same joist and making sure that my layout marks correspond with those on the ledger.

Installing joists

After layout is complete, I install metal joist hangers to support the joists at the ledger and at all other square butt connections. Although some carpenters prefer to install the hangers after the joists have been temporarily toenailed in place, I think that preinstalling the hangers is faster. First, I slip a small scrap of joist material into the hanger as a guide and hold one edge of the block on the layout line and flush with the top of the ledger. This block not only helps with alignment, but also keeps me from nailing the two legs of the hanger too close together. After putting in a couple of nails to hold the hanger in place, I then remove the block and finish nailing. This method works best if all the joists are close to the same width.

With the joist hangers in place, the joists can be measured, cut to length, and nailed in the hangers; remember to install them with their crowns facing up. Cutting all the joists before installation is a necessity when the joists are hung from hangers at both ends. But keep in mind that when joists are hung only at the ledger end and cantilevered over a beam at the other, their ends will only be aligned if the ledger is straight. I find it quicker and more accurate to first install all the joists with one square end in the hangers, but to leave the other ends "wild" and uncut to final length.

Setting the first joist accurately is important because it can serve as a reference for joist layout, particularly when joists are cantilevered over a supporting beam. One way to make sure that the joist is square to the ledger is to align it parallel to the layout string (set during foundation layout; see pp. 34–35) that runs parallel to the house and out to a batter board. Another method I use to square the joist up with the ledger is to use a big, commercially available aluminum square. After setting

Here a scrap of joist is used to help set the hanger height and keep the side flanges the correct distance apart. Attach the hangers with 1 ½-in. long galvanized nails made specifically for metal connectors.

Hanger installed and ready for joist.

PRO TIP

Even though 8d nails may be handy and seem to fit, don't use them to fasten metal joist hangers—they just aren't strong enough.

TRADE SECRET

Take a look at most tape measures and you'll notice that the numbers are highlighted every 16 in., usually in red and with little double-headed arrows. This is to help you avoid addition mistakes when laying out 16-in. joist centers. However, 24-in. centers are easier to keep track of, so your tape may only have an arrow to indicate these.

IN DETAIL

If you're installing your decking at a 45-degree angle, the decking will be spanning more distance than if measured perpendicular to the joists. You will need to space the joists closer together to reduce this longer span and meet the table recommendations. A good rule of thumb is to reduce the maximum joist spacing for a particular decking installed on the perpendicular by about one step when laying it on the diagonal. For example, if the recommended spacing is 24 in. o.c., reduce it to 16 in. o.c. for diagonal decking (or go from 16 in. o.c. to 12 in. o.c.)

Set the first joist square to the ledger, using a foundation layout string for reference.

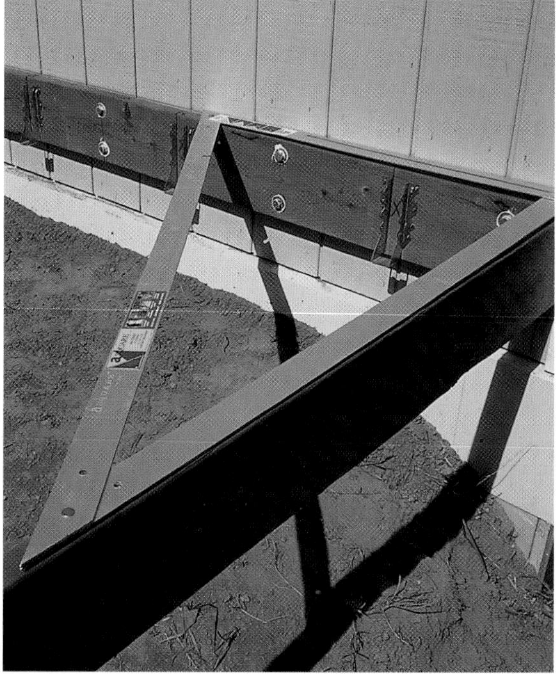

Checking for a square corner between the first joist and ledger is simplified when using this commercially available, folding aluminum square.

the first end joist with a string or a square, I set the opposite side parallel to the first by measuring out along both the beam and the ledger. To quickly double-check that everything is square, I measure the diagonals from corner to corner to make sure they are the same. If they are not, then I adjust the joist before laying out the rest.

Once all (or most) of the joists are in place (but not yet fastened to the supporting beam), I can measure their length from the ledger, mark the ends of my two outside joists, and snap a straight chalkline between them to mark the length across the top of the rest of the joists. Then I draw a square cutline on the face of each joist (using the

After setting the outside joists, check the diagonals to make sure they are equal.

snapped line for reference) and cut all the joists at one time.

On most decks that I build, the last joist on each end laps over the ends of the ledger rather than butting into it like the rest. This hides the end grain of the ledger, while the ledger provides good nailing for securing the end joist. I use 16d galvanized nails, predrilling the holes so that I don't split the ends. For additional support, I clip a regular joist hanger in half and use it on the inside of the connection.

If the rim and end joists are going to be exposed on the finished deck, I miter the outside corners because I think that it looks better than a butt joint. You should stitch mitered corners together with nails or screws from both sides, predrilling and keeping the holes as far back from the ends as possible to avoid splits.

After joists are fastened to the ledger and cantilevered over the beam, they need to be trimmed evenly for the rim. Joists on opposite sides are measured for length and marked, and the marks connected with a snapped line.

Joist Details

Getting all the joists attached to the ledger is a big step forward, but many details must still be finished before decking can begin. Lapping a second row of joists, adding a rim, and putting in midspan blocking are all details that require time. Once all the major pieces are finally in place, the whole unit can be squared up, permanently attached to the beam, and solidly braced to the posts.

Lapping joists

Large decks may require a second set of joists and an intermediate beam. If the beams are in the same plane as the joists, they will all rest on their own set of hangers. If the beams are underneath, however, it's likely that the joists will lap each other over the top of the beam. The joists should overlap each other by at least 12 in. and be well nailed with at least a half dozen 16d nails. If joist lengths are too short to allow lapping, inner joists can be butted and reinforced with 16-in. to 18-in. blocks nailed over the joint.

A square cutline is extended down the face of the joist from the chalkline on top.

PRO TIP

Square the joist to the ledger, aligning it parallel to the layout string that runs parallel to the house and out to a batter board.

WHAT CAN GO WRONG

Before metal hangers were readily available, an old technique for supporting joists involved nailing a smaller second ledger (a 2×3, for example) parallel and even with the bottom of the main ledger. All the joists were then notched over this second ledger, with the whole business secured with a massive dose of toenails. I can't recommend this method, however. Besides creating a shelf for water to collect on, it weakens the joist and provides a starting point for a split along the board. Use joist hangers instead.

IN DETAIL

Some connector companies make special 1½-in. and 3-in. screws as a substitute for hanger nails. These are great for situations in which splitting is likely to occur or a more finished appearance is desired. Unfortunately, these screws have a lower strength rating than nails, so you must check the manufacturers' charts for your application. Because the screws are usually electroplated, they should definitely not be used in constantly wet or marine environments.

Joists ends are trimmed to the line. Set the saw blade so it cuts only one tooth deeper than the board thickness.

Lap the end joist over the ledger, face-nailing it with several 16d galvanized nails.

Lapped joists can cause some confusion with layout and decking. For an even appearance and overhang, don't lap the end joists. Instead, butt them into each other over the beam and reinforce them on the back side with a short section of joist stock. Before securing doubled joists (especially the end joists) to the beam, check by eye or with a stringline to be sure joists are reasonably straight from end to end.

Rim joist

Laying out the rim joist is a lot like laying out the ledger. Remember, though, that adding a miter where your rim joist meets the end joist has an effect on the layout. Although you need to account for a missing end joist when laying out the ledger by adding an extra 1½ in., don't add this extra amount when laying out a mitered rim. The point of the rim joist miter is already even with the outside of the end joist. You can put layout marks on the top of the rim joist and then use a square to add full-width marks across the inside face of the rim joist to keep the joists aligned.

Reinforcing the lapped connection between the end joist and ledger can be done with an angle clip or a joist hanger that has been snipped in half.

Exposed exterior corners will look neater if they are joined by a miter instead of a simple butt joint.

If joist length permits, lapping over beams is the simplest way to connect a second row of joists. Both joists should rest on the beam, and the lap should be at least 12 in.

First, hold the rim board in place and nail the mitered end to the miter on the end joist. Then move down the line of joists, one at a time, with one person aligning the top of the rim joist with the top of each joist while the other person drives several nails to hold it in place. Continue along until each of the joists has been nailed with three or four equally spaced 16d galvanized nails. This may feel like framing, but it's also finish work: Try to be neat and accurate when hammering the nails home. Misses will be very visible for a long time afterward, a testament to your carpentry skills (or lack thereof).

Some joists will be twisted and will need to be straightened as you nail them. To do this, I usually

Instead of lapping joists over a beam, you can butt them end to end, temporarily toenailing at the top.

+ SAFETY FIRST

In order to achieve the full rated strength of any particular metal connector, be sure to follow the manufacturer's nailing recommendations. Use the correct size galvanized or stainless-steel fastener, and be sure to fill every hole with a nail.

Then reinforce with a splice plate made of scrap joist material nailed over the butt joint.

PRO TIP

The easiest way to install blocking is to stagger the blocks on either side of a line snapped on top of the joists.

IN DETAIL

If your deck requires more than one board to make up the rim joist, you'll need to put the break over a joist. Although you could make a simple butt joint, mitered lap joints look better and tend to stay that way even as the boards dry out and move. I cut lap joints with a circular saw set at slightly less than a 45-degree angle to insure a tight fit. The long point of the first mitered rim joist end completely covers the backing joist, and the second rim joist's miter laps over the first. This gives both of them solid nailing.

Rim joist installation is a lot easier with two people. Start at one end and nail while adjusting and aligning the rim for each joist.

put the first nail near the top to hold the rim flush with the top of the joist; then I have my helper untwist the problem joist while I quickly finish nailing it in place.

Squaring up the frame and securing it to the beam

After all the joists and rim are installed, I make one final check and compare diagonals to be sure the whole structure is square. Ideally, the joist framing should line up with the beam ends, which were located using the squared foundation layout. If your joists are cantilevered and you were able to leave your beam ends long, you can now adjust the joist framing as a unit to be square, and then cut the beam ends flush with the outside of the end joists. However, if you've cut your beam ends before framing your joists, you won't have much latitude to adjust the joist framing. Don't worry too much if things are a little out of square. This won't cause problems with decking installation and probably won't ever be noticed. If there's a large mistake and the framing doesn't line up with your beam work, go back and check your foundation layout.

Each joist should be securely nailed to the rim with three or four nails. This rim will be covered with a finish skirt, but avoid hammer dents like these if your rim is a finished surface.

Once everything is aligned and checked, fix the joists to the beam using metal connectors. I usually use hurricane clips from Simpson® (H2.5), a twisted metal connector that I nail to the back side of the beam and to the joist. These connectors are required by some codes, but simply toenailing with 10d to 12d galvanized nails may be allowed if you can do it without splitting the joists.

Twisted joists are easily straightened before nailing with a forked framing tool called a Stud Tuner.

Metal twist clips securely connect joists to the supporting beam.

Although metal clips offer a more secure connection, some building codes may allow you to carefully toenail joists to the beam.

With joists running parallel to the house and no well-anchored ledger with joist hangers, blocking adds important stability. Block between joists over beams at least middeck or every 12 ft. on larger decks.

Blocking is easier to install by alternating on either side of a snapped line.

PRO TIP

If special framing techniques are needed, make those decisions at the design stage.

WHAT CAN GO WRONG

Joist widths can vary by as much as ½ in. and more, a seemingly small problem until you go to hang the joist in a joist hanger. If you set your joist hangers using a narrower joist offcut, the tops of some of the wider joists will be higher than the top of the ledger, making flashing and deck installation difficult. To avoid this situation, be sure to use a block representing the widest of the joists. While this may be too low for some narrower joists, those can easily be shimmed to the proper height, a better solution than notching the wider joists. Another solution is to first toenail all the joists to the ledger and then come back and install the hangers. This method is slower, but it eliminates the shimming.

IN DETAIL

A large, accurate square can be a very useful tool when you are building a deck. I own a foldable aluminum version called an A-Square (see Resources, pp. 179–181), but you can make your own by screwing three pieces of 1×4 together. Use the ratio of 3-4-5 for the outside lengths of the three sides to get a 90-degree angle.

Bracing between posts and beams can be diagonal 2×4s or 2×6s firmly attached to the back side with ⅜-in. lags. The ends should be cut vertically and sealed to shed water.

Using 4×4s for diagonal bracing completes the look when chunky posts or beams are used. The braces are given a 45-degree cut at each end and then attached using ⅜-in. or ½-in. lag bolts. Here the bottom is also mortised into the post, and the top fits between layers of a built-up beam.

For low decks with simple bracing requirements, instead of bracing between posts and beams I add long diagonals across the bottoms of the joists and they work like diagonal decking. These 2×4 or 2×6 braces run at a 45-degree angle from the ledger out to the beam and are secured at each joist with two screws. Two braces, running towards each other, are adequate on smaller decks.

Blocking and bracing

Although there is some debate about the effectiveness of midspan blocking, it is still required by some codes. Short sections of joist material installed perpendicular to the joists not only help distribute loads over several joists, but also help stabilize the framing system against sideways collapse under extreme stress. Blocking is generally only used every 8 ft. on spans of more than 12 ft., and then only on taller joists, such as 2×10s or 2×12s; as always, check your local code requirements.

There's no quick way to install blocking, so it's not a favorite of any carpenter. The easiest way is to stagger the blocks on either side of a line snapped on top of the joists. Then you can nail the blocks through the joist into the end of the block without relying on toenails. It works best to cut the blocks about 1/16 in. shorter than a perfect fit, because cupped joists tend to make them too tight. You may find it necessary to cut an occasional block even shorter to avoid pushing joists out of layout.

Blocking also needs to be installed between the last two joists at each end of the deck where there is a railing. A railing post attached to a single end joist can easily lever that joist and result in a flimsy railing system. I'll go into this in more detail when I discuss railings in Chapter 5.

Bracing

The simple connections between joists, posts, and beams aren't stiff enough to keep a deck from flexing laterally, even after the decking is applied. To eliminate this sway, you'll need to add bracing to create inflexible triangles that stiffen the whole structure. In some cases, the style of the deck may have built-in bracing, as with decking that runs at a 45-degree angle to the joists or a deck that is buttressed on one or both sides by another deck. Codes require bracing, especially on high decks or on decks in seismically active areas, and it can be accomplished in different ways, depending on your particular situation.

Special Framing Techniques

If your deck is a little more complicated than a flat rectangle, you'll need a few more framing techniques. Some of the special features that make decks more interesting require only modifying joist positions, but others must be tackled from the foundation up. To minimize extra work and building errors, decisions are best made at the design stage.

Framing Deck Openings

Occasionally a deck is built around an object—a tree, a rock, a hot tub. Whether the decking will butt closely to the object (as with a hot tub) or leave room for expansion (a good idea if the object is a tree), the framing can usually be built with only square and 45-degree angles. The decking is then cantilevered over the framing to provide the appearance of a differently shaped hole.

First, cut out joist sections that would pass through the opening and add a supporting header running perpendicular to the remaining continuous joists. Although a single header thickness is adequate if there is only one cut joist, it should be doubled if it supports two or more. Likewise, if the unbroken joists that support the header are close to maximum span or if the header is longer than a few feet, the supporting joists should also be doubled.

The resulting square opening will probably be too large, but the corners can be filled in with short diagonal boards to create an octagon. This octagonal opening should be sized as closely as possible to the size of the finished hole to minimize the cantilever of the decking.

When laying the decking, run it long over the joists, draw the correct shape on top, and cut the hole to the finish shape with a jigsaw. If the rock or hot tub is already in place, each decking board will need to be scribed and cut to the right shape as it's installed. A 2×6 decking board can cantilever a foot or so in low traffic areas without a problem as long as the board is well fastened and isn't a short piece.

Framing for a Hole in the Deck

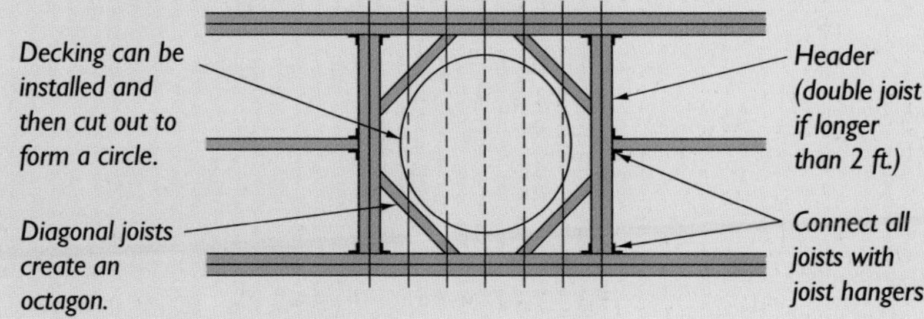

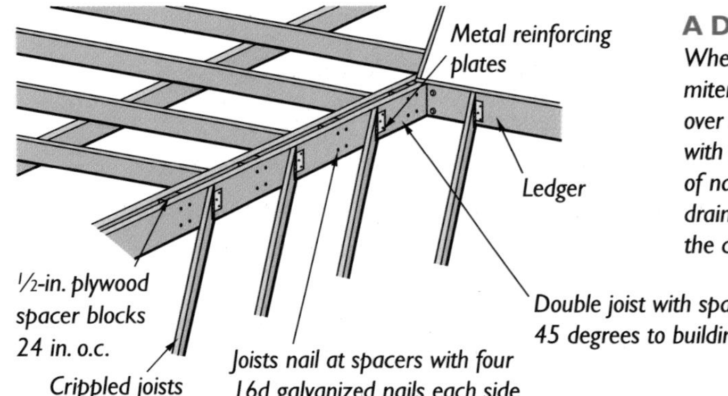

A Doubled Diagonal Joist
When turning a corner with mitered decking, break the miters over a pair of joists separated with spacers. This will give plenty of nailing surface and aid drainage directly underneath the decking joints.

PRO TIP

It works best to cut blocks about $^1/_{16}$ in. shorter than a perfect fit, because cupped joists tend to make them too tight.

TRADE SECRET

I save my straightest and longest joist stock for my rim joist. This makes installing it easier and results in a better-looking deck. Order the longest boards you can for the rim in order to cut down on joints, and have someone help you install it.

IN DETAIL

When decking runs perpendicular to the house, the joists run parallel to the wall and supporting beams are perpendicular. This means that the ledger is really a simple end joist. On high and heavily loaded decks, decks in areas with seismic activity, or decks where the beams are freestanding at the house end, bolting this end joist like a regular ledger will help reinforce the deck's attachment to the house. (See the photo on p. 89.)

TRADE SECRET

One simple test to determine if a deck is adequately braced is to get up on the finished deck and do a sudden stop from a run. If you feel motion, then the deck needs more bracing.

Here an upper level deck laps onto the beam structure of a lower deck, and this saves adding an extra footing at the level change. The upper level was a design addition made after the footings were installed for a one-level deck.

Snapping a chalkline to mark the cuts for a clipped deck corner. Note that the beam has been angled to support this moderately sized corner angle.

Level changes

Besides being a great way to spice up an otherwise humdrum project, a deck with two or more levels is often a necessity on sloped sites. Framing for elevation changes can be done in several different ways, depending on the size of the area involved and the style of framing being used on the rest of the deck.

The simplest way to introduce an elevation change is to simply build another deck entirely on top of the first. This is most practical if the upper level is relatively small, such as a landing under a door. Although some joists may be duplicated, this is a small price to pay for the elimination of extra foundation work. The new joists and decking thickness will dictate the elevation difference, so they don't need to be very wide, usually no more than 2×6s.

A second way to accomplish a level change is to essentially build two separate decks, each with its own foundation and framing. The decks can be bolted together at the point where they touch, or if the elevation difference is large, left independent and connected only by a stairway.

The third option, and the one that I use most frequently, requires that the upper level overlaps and rests on part of the lower level framing. Usually this requires only one footing at the overlap for both levels, but the exact configuration will vary from deck to deck, depending on the framing direction of the beam and joists. Elevation differences will dictate whether the two decks touch directly, one on top of the other, or whether they are separated by a supporting vertical frame wall.

When you're planning on two deck levels sharing the same supporting structure, it's important to size the foundation, posts, and beams to carry both levels. Make sure that the upper level has adequate bearing on the lower level, and reinforce the connection between the two levels using metal anchors, strapping, or wood blocking and bolts.

Turning corners

Lots of decks wrap around a corner of the house, and one of the main decisions to be made about this type of deck is how to handle the decking pattern. The joist framing plan will be determined by this decision.

When the outside corner of the deck is going to be square, I think the most attractive option is to create a mitered corner with the ends of the mitered decking boards breaking over a doubled joist. This doubled joist runs out diagonally from the house corner to the outside deck corner at 45 degrees and rests on the intersecting beams supporting the other joists. Successively shorter "cripple" joists run from the rim to the doubled joist and fill in the framing. Position this diagonal as close to 45 degrees as possible, or the decking will need unequal miters to keep the boards lined up. This in turn will require larger gaps between the decking boards on one side of the deck than the other.

A second option is to keep all the boards running the same direction continuously on both sides of the corner. This requires that the joists run perpendicular to the house on one side and parallel to the house on the other. To do this, beams will need to run parallel to the house on one side, and perpendicular to the house on the other.

Decking Patterns and Framing for Turning Corners

A deck that goes around the corner of a building usually follows one of three basic decking patterns. (A) This pattern creates an unattractive line of butt joints across the deck but avoids time-consuming miters. (B) The pattern used here keeps decking running parallel on the whole deck but requires a major shift in joist direction. (C) My most frequent choice uses mitered decking at the corner but requires a doubled joist and "crippled" joists.

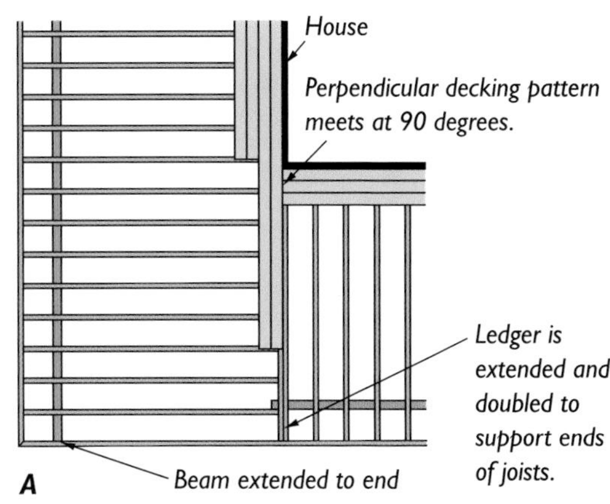

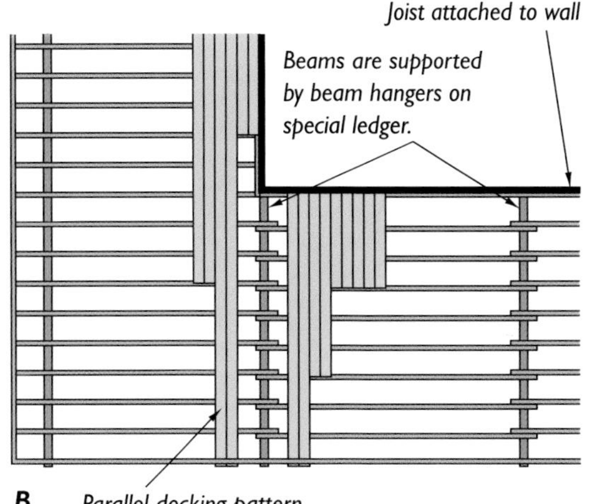

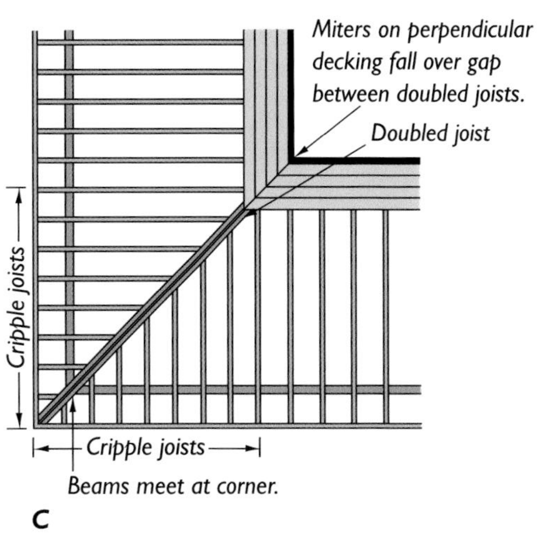

PRO TIP

When the outside corner of the deck is going to be square, create a mitered corner with the ends of the mitered decking boards breaking over a doubled joist.

Turning a Corner with a 45-Degree Angle

When a deck turns around the corner of a building, I find it more interesting to frame a 45-degree angle on the outside corner of the deck instead of the usual square. This will require two doubled diagonal joists (to support crippled joists and decking ends) instead of one doubled joist. (A) Sometimes the doubled joists are placed at right angles to each other, but this results in a narrowed deck and misalignment of the decking pattern. (B) A better solution places the doubled joists 45 degrees apart, which maintains the full width of the deck and keeps decking board miters and spacing all the same.

Turning a Corner with a 45-Degree Angle

(A) A Poor Design—
The width at the corner is narrower than the width of the rest of the deck.

(A)
90 degrees
Double joists

(B) A Better Design—
The width at the corner is the same as the width of the rest of the deck.

(B)
45 degrees
Double joists

TRADE SECRET

Normal joist hangers work only when joists meet the ledger at right angles. You can buy hangers made for 45-degree intersections, as well as adjustable ones that work for a range of angles. These special hangers require only a simple square cut on the end of the joist, but they have to be special-ordered, a process that is expensive and not always timely. Instead, I first cut the joist to the proper angle and simply nail it in place, using plenty of 12d or 16d nails. For insurance, I add a reinforcing angle plate (like a Simpson LS) to tie the two joists together.

Angles on decks often have joists with ends butting into a support member at an angle. Depending on the length of joist supported, this connection can usually be nailed with four or five 16d nails and reinforced with a metal plate, if necessary.

Mixing framing systems is a lot more work but may be worth it to get the look you want for your deck.

I think that the least-attractive option is to have the decking of one section meet the decking of the other section at a 90-degree angle along a line extending out from the house corner. Here the beam, ledger, and joist framing of the first section simply extends out past the corner to the end of the deck. The ledger is extended and becomes a supporting beam that will need to be sized to carry the ends of the joists. A second beam positioned 90 degrees to the first picks up the end of the ledger extension and the extra joists necessary to support the decking around the corner.

Angles

Angles add a interest to a boxy deck. Clipping off the outside corners of a deck by a few feet is an easy style change that doesn't require a lot of planning. Larger angled areas provide more impact but require extra effort and planning from the foundation stage all the way through railing installation. No matter what size angled area I choose, I try to use only 45-degree angles, which keeps planning and construction much simpler.

A simple way to add a small 45-degree angle to the outside corners of a deck with cantilevered joists is to progressively shorten the last couple of joists and cap them with a small angled rim. This won't require any foundation changes if you only shorten the cantilevered part of the joist, and may be a reason to use a larger cantilever to maximize the amount of corner you can angle. But keep in mind that adding even a small angle like this will double the amount of railing work needed at each corner.

After the cuts have been marked, make 22½-degree cuts for the mitered rim and 45-degree cuts in intermediate joists.

Nailing the new rim joist to the deck corner.

A 45-degree mitered corner should be nailed through the face from both directions with 16d nails.

To add medium-sized angled corners, I find it simplest (although slightly wasteful) to frame a regular square corner on the deck first. Then I measure back along the end joist and the rim joist an equal distance from the outside corner to the point where I want my angle to begin and end. Here, I will cut a 22½-degree miter to accept a new piece of rim mitered to match. Next, I snap a chalkline between these inside heel corner points of the miter across the top of any intermediate joists, which also will need to be trimmed back at a 45-degree angle. The chalkline represents the back side of the angled rim. After cutting the rim joist, end joist, and intermediate joists, I measure and cut the new diagonal rim piece with a 22½-degree miter at both ends. I neatly nail or screw each miter on the outside from both directions, then fasten the intermediate joists to the back of the angled rim.

Curves

Architectural curves are elegant, but they're also labor-intensive and expensive. The easiest way to add a curve to your decking surface is by wrapping a finished curved rim over cut and blocked joists that serve as a giant form. For some finish materials, adding three layers of ½-in. treated plywood to match the thickness of the solid wood rim over the blocking may be necessary to provide solid backing for the final layers of finish material. The finish rim can be formed by glue-laminating thin boards together, or kerfing the back side of a single board, or using a wood–plastic composite or other material that is flexible enough to be bent without any extra work. When choosing the radius for your curve, experiment first with the flexibility of the finish material because some won't take tight bends gracefully.

Joist and beam framing for curves will be different for each situation, but the basic idea is to sup-

PRO TIP

The easiest way to add a curve to your decking surface is by wrapping a finished curved rim over cut and blocked joists that serve as a giant form.

TRADE SECRET

Lay out and mark the joists on a curved deck with a simple trammel made from a 1×2 board. First, tack a piece of plywood onto the joists near where the center of the circle would be (typically a corner). You can lay out and mark the exact center of the curve on the plywood by measuring from references such as the rim or other joists. Then put an 8d nail through one end of a 1×2 that is longer than the radius of the curve. Tap the nail into the center point of the circle on the plywood, cut the far end of the 1×2 to the exact length of the radius, and scribe the circle on top of the joists.

Carpenter's pencil scribes against cut end of trammel as it moves.

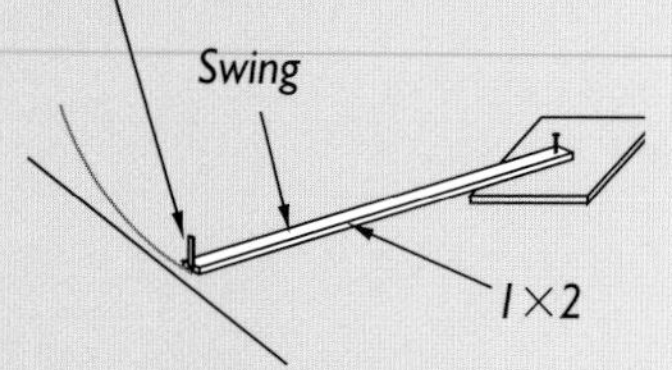

Add nail, then cut 1×2 to length of desired radius.

Finish fascia of composite decking is screwed to plywood rim. Note the scrap deck boards used to set the top of fascia.

port cantilevered joist ends over simple straight beams. You may need to be creative and add a few unusual joists or sections of joist in order to provide the support needed. For example, framing for a curved corner is basically the same as framing for an angled section. In most cases, you'll only need to add an angled beam near the curved section. To radius curve the outside rim as a deck goes around the corner of a building, you may need to provide (as on an angled deck corner) a doubled diagonal joist or two to support the cripples and a second perpendicular beam. Adding a freestanding semicircle or full circle to a deck will require a couple of beams to minimize the amount of cantilevered joist. A scaled drawing of all beams and joists is an essential tool for curved installations.

After all of the posts and beams are in place, the next step is to install all the joists and cripples, leaving them extra long for the time being. Then swing an arc across the top of the uncut joists, using a pencil tied to a string or a trammel. This scribed line indicates where you will eventually cut your joists, so it should represent a radius that is shorter that the final outside curve by the thickness of the finish material (plus another 1½ in. if you add the three layers of treated plywood rim joist).

Before cutting the joists, add some extra blocking between the ends of the cantilevered joists. Use the scribed circle to help locate the blocking—(use leftover joist cutoffs)—and install them on the flat, flush with the top of the joists, so that the curve will fall entirely on them. Rescribe the circle on the blocking, and make your cuts with either a jigsaw or circular saw. Finish cutting off the joist ends, and scribe and cut a second set of matching blocks for the bottom edge of the joists.

Finishing curves

The final step is to add the three layers of ½-in. treated plywood, one layer at a time. Rip the layers to the same width as the joists, and be sure to nail them thoroughly as they are assembled. Use construction adhesive between layers, and stagger the joints. These layers can trap moisture, so it's a good idea to flash the top of the plywood sandwich with a bituminous tape.

Opinions differ about the best method of adding a finished curved rim joist. One way is to laminate together multiple layers of thin material that matches the skirt on the rest of the rim and end joists (usually knot-free and rot-resistant redwood or cedar). Depending on the radius of the

Top and bottom blocking for curved rim backing is fastened between joists, then scribed to the curve and cut with a circular saw or jigsaw. Next, joists are trimmed to final length.

curve, the layers will probably need to be between ⅛ in. and ¼ in. thick, thin enough to accept the curve without breaking. Apply one layer at a time, nailing each thoroughly, staggering joints, and setting each layer into a generous coating of waterproof glue; typically, the final layer is clamped only to eliminate exposed nails.

If you are using one of the new plastic, composite, or recycled decking materials, it may be flexible enough to be used as finish skirt material on a curved section. Although it would still need to be applied over a supporting layer of plywood, it could then be extended seamlessly to cover the rest of the deck framing.

Adding a layered plywood backing, secured with screws or nails and construction adhesive, provides extra support when flexible composite decking is used for finish fascia on a curved deck.

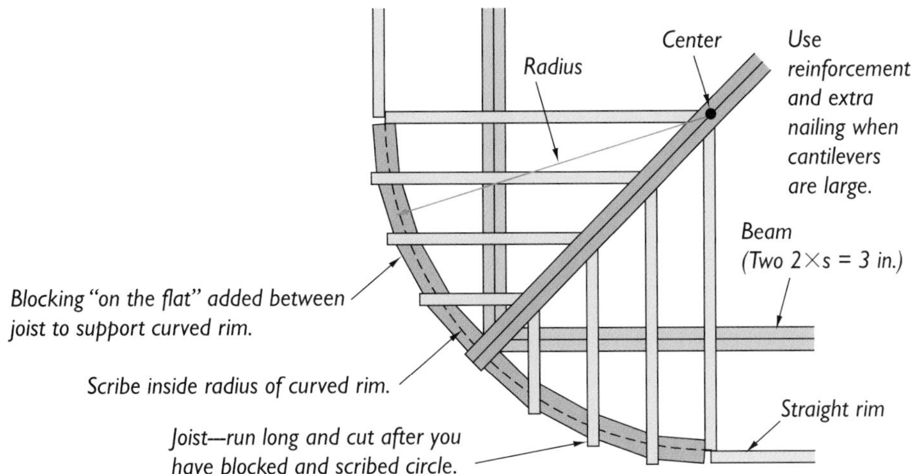

Framing for Curved Corners

Framing for a curved corner is very similar to a square corner with mitered decking. After a doubled joist and "cripples" are installed, blocking is added and a curve scribed for cutting.

Decking

CHAPTER FIVE

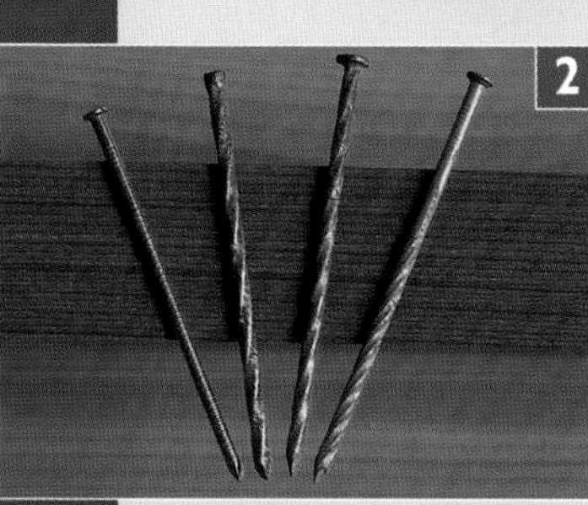

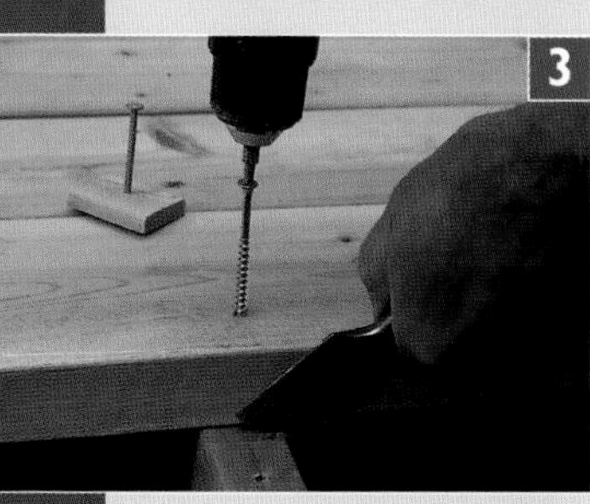

My favorite part of building a deck is putting down the decking. Laying decking involves a lot of kneeling, but it also means I'm off the ground and done with ladder work for a while. As the boards go down, I get to rest occasionally and enjoy the view. And since most of the brainwork has already been done, I can develop a comfortable working rhythm and enjoy being a carpenter.

But soon after it's laid, the decking becomes a part of the background. It still contributes to the overall impact of the deck, but in a less noticeable way than railings, planters, and hot tubs do. In fact, the decking typically gets noticed only when problems develop, usually through neglect. In this chapter, I'll discuss how to choose high-quality deck materials and fasteners, and how to install them correctly so that your deck will be largely trouble-free and a place to enjoy.

PRO TIP

Decking is often supplied in "random lengths," which means that you'll get a mix of lengths. But you can pay a little more and get all longer lengths.

IN DETAIL

Decking is usually available in both nominal 4-in. and 6-in. widths, but I prefer wider decking. Assuming that both sizes use the same number of fasteners, you can finish a deck faster using 6-in.-wide boards. The wider board also makes it easier to place two fasteners per joist without encountering a tough knot, thus reducing your chances of splitting the board.

IN DETAIL

Heartwood is the nonliving center of the tree. In cedars and redwoods, it is the darker wood that is full of the naturally occurring chemicals that deter insects. The light-colored living sapwood outside the heartwood doesn't have these chemicals and isn't resistant to rot and insect damage unless treated.

Cedar and other naturally rot-resistant woods may cost more but are beautiful, easy to work with, and don't involve the use of chemicals. They should be chosen with consideration for their renewability and harvesting consequences.

Choosing Decking

Most decking is done with naturally rot-resistant or treated wood. In the west, the woods used are primarily varieties of fir and hemlock; in the east, southern pine is more common. Cedars and redwoods are used throughout the country. When conditions and supplies change, however, other woods become economically feasible to use—imports like ipe and meranti as well as such underutilized domestic species as yellow cedar and cypress. Factors that affect your choice of decking materials include the wood's color and style, performance, price, availability, and your regional preference. In addition, environmentalism plays an increasingly important role in the decision of which material to use, and has contributed to the growing use of decking made from recycled materials. In the past few years, I have found more people wanting a truly "no maintenance" deck, a quality promised by some of the new synthetic decking materials.

Naturally rot-resistant woods

Western red cedar. The wood I use most often is western red cedar, an abundant species on the West Coast and further inland in the United States and Canada. A cinnamon-brown color when new, western red cedar turns silver gray if left unfinished. The heartwood is very rot-resistant and dimensionally stable, even with repeated drying and soaking. Of the woods commonly used for decking, western red cedar and redwood are the softest, a characteristic that makes them easy to work; they're primarily used only for residential decks. Although western red cedar smells good, I find its dust irritating (just like that of other cedars and redwood). If you are cutting very much of these woods, use a dust mask, especially if the boards are dry.

The grading of cedar decking differs from that of other softwoods like fir and yellow pine. As always, the best and most expensive lumber is clear, vertical grain, all heartwood. Imperfect clear boards containing some flat grain, sapwood, or small knots are called B, C, and D grades but frequently are tagged with a supplier's own trade name.

Knotty grades of decking range through Select, Quality, and Standard, and these may often use a supplier's own trade name grade as well. Red cedar for decking is usually sold green, but is available kiln-dried except in the lowest grades. Remember that grades represent only minimum standards, so the actual quality of the board varies according to the different manufacturers. When you order wood, your best bet is to examine the boards yourself or rely on an experienced local retailer. Red cedar is available in all thicknesses, with 5/4 material often milled for decking use.

Alaska yellow cedar (see the photo on the facing page). Pacific coast cypress, commonly known as Alaska yellow cedar, is a cream-colored wood that is being used more frequently as it becomes more available. It is much harder, stronger, and denser than red cedar and also very rot-resistant. Alaska yellow cedar is not the same wood as southern cypress, which is also rot-resistant but not widely available. Yellow cedar grows above 1,000-ft. elevations on the West Coast and so develops more internal stresses in reaction to the windy environment. This causes the wood to warp and twist as it dries, so most decking-quality yellow cedar is sold kiln-dried to about 14% moisture content. Even so, this wood must be kept out of the sun and neatly stacked before installation, or it can go wild. Yellow cedar turns a nice silver gray when left unfinished and exposed to sunlight and the weather, but it will benefit from an annual dose of waterproofing to minimize checking, especially in hot, dry climates.

The grades of yellow cedar are similar to those of red cedar, with varying qualities in clear and knotty grades. But even more so than with red cedar, the proprietary naming systems of different manufacturers make selecting wood confusing. The quality of the wood I've used in the better knotty grades is very high, but this probably varies with the supplier. Yellow cedar typically is available in all thicknesses.

Other cedars (see the photo on the facing page). Port Orford cedar and northern white cedar share some similar qualities with red and yellow cedars. However, because they aren't harvested in large quantities, they are more likely to be available only locally or as expensive imports for boat building.

Redwood. Redwood has a beautiful reddish brown color and is a very stable wood, but unfortunately, it is also very soft. This makes redwood easy to work but a little brittle, and thinner boards can have a tendency to split when mistreated. Redwood is available in many grades, but the grade typically

Although soft, redwood weathers beautifully and supplies reportedly now come from non-old growth forests. Only the heartwood is naturally resistant to rot and insects, so choose a grade appropriate for decking use.

Using Tropical Hardwoods Responsibly

Although tropical hardwoods offer clear advantages when used as decking material, environmentally they can be quite controversial. Some tropical and domestic wood used for decking is still harvested with too much concern for convenience, popularity, and profit, and not enough concern for long-term sustainability or environmental consequences. Often these woods come from sensitive rainforest areas, where logging practices aren't always well-managed for conservation and reforestation. Fortunately, there is a growing attempt to ensure and certify that these woods have been harvested responsibly.

Certified wood

When you use "certified" wood, you are helping to ensure that the lumber you buy has been harvested with environmental sensitivity. Certified wood comes from forests with audited management plans, and it should be possible to track the lumber through a documented "chain of custody" right up to the final supplier. For more information contact: The Certified Forest Products Council (CFPC, Beaverton, OR, 503-590-6600, www.certifiedwood.org) or the Forest Stewardship Council™ (FSC, Washington, D.C., 877-372-5646, www.fscus.org).

Tropical hardwoods are premium decking material because they are durable, stable, and decay-resistant. However, it can be difficult to determine exactly which species of wood you are choosing. Consider using certified wood to help promote environmentally responsible harvesting.

PRO TIP

You'll want to order about 5% more lumber for waste. Diagonals, wasteful overhangs, mitered corners, stairs, and railing all require more material.

IN DETAIL

Each lineal foot (lf) of nominal 4-in.-wide decking covers about 0.3 sq. ft. (3.5 in. actual width/12). Each lineal foot of 6-in.-wide decking covers about 0.46 sq. ft. (5.5 in. actual width/12). To find the total lineal footage of decking you need, take the total square footage of your deck and divide by the square footage that each lineal foot of decking will cover. For example, a 12-ft. × 20-ft. deck needs 240 sq. ft. of decking. If you are using 6-in.-wide decking, 240 divided by 0.46 = 522 lf of decking. These numbers don't give any coverage allowance for the spacing between boards because wet treated boards are laid tightly, and cedar and redwood tend to measure a little less than the full 5½ in. wide in the first place.

used for decking is called "garden," a lesser grade than the clearest, kiln-dried premium architectural grades used for millwork. Garden grades are divided into two main categories: those with all heartwood and those that allow sapwood. As with cedar, the heartwood is the only part that is resistant to decay. If your climate is dry and rot isn't a problem, some sapwood is OK; otherwise, stick with heartwood. Either category of redwood is available in several grades, each with successively more knots and defects; a good compromise for decking is an all-heartwood B or construction/deck grade. Redwood comes in both 2× and 5/4 material, but availability of either may depend on where you live. Decking boards are usually green, but kiln-dried material is available.

Tropical hardwoods. Tropical hardwoods are some of the most durable and expensive woods available for deck building. They are also heavy and difficult to work, however, and must be predrilled to accept either nails or screws. Using these woods requires a commitment to the craftsmanship required to install them and the long-term maintenance needed to keep them looking good. Tropical hardwoods come from big trees and have few defects. Compared with other woods, they are stiffer, harder, and stronger, which makes them usable in thinner sizes. That being the case, tropical hardwoods are usually sold in ¾-in. and 5/4 thicknesses, and not often in 2×s.

Ipe is a South American wood that is a beautiful brown when fresh, though it is hard to preserve this coloration over time. Cambara, similar to ipe, is a little lighter in color and less durable. Meranti, a mixture of species from Malaysia and the Philippines, is similar to mahogany; depending on which species you end up with, meranti can be either pretty good or soft, prone to warping, and with marginal decay resistance. Before you use any tropical woods, I encourage you to investigate its origin and appropriateness.

Treated wood

Southern pine. Southern pine for decking is usually sold in 5/4 thicknesses and in both standard and premium grades. Southern pine (which could actually be longleaf, shortleaf, slash, or loblolly pine) has a well-deserved reputation for moving a lot as it dries, and it needs to be cared for both before and after installation. A lot of treated pine decks look terrible after several years; they may not rot, but they won't stay nice-looking without regular maintenance. An annual application of water repellent helps significantly reduce the splitting, cupping, and premature aging associated with this type of decking.

Southern pine readily accepts CCA (chromated copper arsenate) chemical treatment, and normally cuts or holes don't require a field application of preservative. Wet boards will need to dry a little after installation, before they will accept some finishes. If it isn't stained, treated southern pine will weather to gray in time, losing its greenish tint.

Because it shrinks a lot when drying, southern pine when green is often put down with no spacing between boards. If wet boards are spaced during installation, the cracks left after drying end up much too large. You'll have more control over the gaps if you use kiln-dried decking or air-dry it yourself, but the boards will be harder and probably require predrilled holes for fasteners.

Treated southern pine offers good value for deck building and can be used on all parts of the deck. Though relatively hard, it is prone to shrinkage, so be prepared to maintain the finish to keep it in good shape.

Hemlock and fir. Western softwoods come in two basic groups: Douglas fir and hem–fir (mostly hemlock but also spurious specifies of fir). These western woods are harder to treat than southern pine, and their treatment usually involves waterborne chemicals such as ACQ (ammoniacal copper quaternary ammonium chloride) or ACZA (ammoniacal copper zinc arsenate) that don't penetrate the entire thickness of a board. This requires the disagreeable task of brushing field preservative on end cuts and holes to prevent untreated areas being exposed and to fulfill some manufacturers' warranties. Frequently these woods are incised or scored with multiple knife cuts to help the chemical penetrate more deeply, but these cuts also make the wood less attractive. When I use this type of decking, I choose 2×4s or 2×6s that are not incised and have been specially selected and graded for visual appearance; a 5/4 thickness is unusual for this decking in lower grades—perhaps because it is weaker and has more defects—but is available in premium grades.

Just like southern pine, western softwoods need to be maintained to avoid splits, cupping, and unattractive degradation. They don't weather gracefully. Some companies add a water repellent to their treatment process, but I haven't found it particularly effective. Annual application of a water repellent is still essential. If wet, these woods will also shrink a lot as they dry and will benefit from some predrying to control gaps.

Abundantly available and relatively inexpensive, treated western softwoods contain a variety of species like hemlock and assorted firs and are often factory-stained brown.

Decking Span Table

The type of decking you use will be based in part on the deck's joist spacing. Weaker species such as cedar and redwood or thinner boards and lower grades of any species need more closely spaced joists. Diagonally applied decking requires closer joist spacing.

Suggested Maximum Decking Spans

	12 in. o.c.	16 in. o.c.	24 in. o.c.
Decking perpendicular to joists	■ Knotty 5/4×6 redwood and cedar ■ Clear 5/4 ×4 radius-edge decking redwood and cedar	■ 5/4×fir, hemlock radius-edge decking (#1 or better) ■ Clear 5/4 ×6 radius-edge decking redwood and cedar	■ 2×6 and 2×4 all species #2 or better ■ 5/4×6 southern yellow pine, radius-edge decking (#1 or better)
Decking diagonal to joists	■ 5/4× fir, hemlock radius-edge decking (#1 or better) ■ Clear 5/4×6 radius-edge decking redwood and cedar	■ 2×6 and 2×4 all species #2 or better ■ 5/4 ×6 southern yellow pine, radius-edge decking (#1 or better)	

Alternatives: composites and plastics

Although everybody likes wood, about half of my customers ask about using one of the newer materials, such as those containing recycled materials and others that use only virgin plastic. Because these new materials won't absorb water and rot (or so it is claimed), annual maintenance is eliminated.

One of these materials, Trex (see Resources), is composed of recycled polyethylene and ground-up waste wood. Because Trex doesn't shrink or swell much, it can be accurately spaced at installation time. It's available in long lengths and in 5/4 and 2× thicknesses. Trex is a little too flexible

PRO TIP

When you order tropical woods, be prepared for some confusion. Grading rules and span tables are impossible to find, and names are often used interchangeably.

IN DETAIL

Decking is usually specified as either 2× (two-by), 5/4 (five-quarter), or 1× (one-by). These numbers refer to the thickness of the rough stock before it is planed down to its finished dimension. For example, 2× material finishes to 1½ in., 5/4 to a full inch, and 1× to ¾ of an inch. If you plan on using 2× decking, your joists can probably be spaced 24 in. o.c.; 5/4 and 1× decking is usually installed on 16-in. o.c. joists. (See the chart on p. 103.)

IN DETAIL

Because 2× is often used for other purposes besides decking, the boards are most commonly sold with "eased" edges, edges that have just the slightest rounding. But 5/4 material often is made specifically for use as decking and frequently will be sold as RED, or radius edge decking. On this type, the top two exposed edges have been given a substantial rounding-over, which minimizes splinters and makes the material more user-friendly throughout its life.

Composite decking is a blend of recycled plastic and wood waste and requires minimal maintenance. While some imitate wood coloration fairly effectively, their ultimate long-term durability has yet to be proven.

for framing, but can be installed as decking on 16-in. o.c. joist framing (for 5/4 stock) and 20-in. o.c. joist framing (for 2× stock). You can use nails, but I recommend installing Trex with screws. It's available in gray and brown, but both age toward a weathered gray. Although it looks pretty slick when new and is indeed maintenance-free, I recently saw a one-year-old Trex deck that felt rougher than new material and looked older than its age. This may be a small price for saving forests and not spending summer weekends renewing the finish on your deck.

Other brands composed of varying amounts of recycled and new plastic and organic materials include Nexwood, TimberTech Engineered Decking Systems, ChoiceDek®, SmartDeck, and WeatherBest™ (see Resources, p. 179). Some of these materials come in a solid plank form, others are hollow in section with reinforcing ribs. A few can be installed just as you would lay wood decking, but others require special fastening systems. Their claims may sound impressive, but none of these materials has been widely used for long; their ultimate performance in demanding climates is yet to be determined.

Decking is also made from extruded plastic (a petroleum-based product) as the main component, though some companies use some recycled material. Although products such as Dream Deck System, Brock Deck, and Carefree® do away with splinters and require no annual maintenance except cleaning, they currently cost more than wood or composites, especially when you factor in fastening systems.

These products come in many different configurations, and some are embossed with a pattern to make them slip-resistant. Most use a proprietary fastening method involving clips or tracks because plastic expands as it heats up in the sun and will crack unless it can move. White or light colors are typical because they help reflect sunlight and thus minimize expansion problems. Other potential problems associated with these products include chalking and fading, which can be countered by the addition of ultraviolet (UV) inhibitors.

Though long-lasting and virtually maintenance-free, vinyl decking has a plastic look that might not be appropriate on some decks. It is relatively expensive compared with common grades of wood decking, and some brands claim to include a percentage of recycled materials.

Fasteners

Nails may be quick and easy to install, but screws are my deck fasteners of choice. They won't pull out over time and are easy to snug up later if the decking shrinks. If you are using a high-end decking, then you may want to consider one of the various types of concealed fasteners now available.

Screws

Screws take about twice as long to install as hand-driven nails (longer still if you predrill all the holes). Screws with a self-cutting tip are less likely to snap off if you don't predrill. Most screws these days have bugle heads and will self-countersink in all but the hardest woods. Don't use regular drywall screws, however; they corrode in short order and tend to be a lot weaker than screws specifically designed as deck fasteners.

Phillips-drive or square-drive screws are designed to be used with screw guns and drills. The Phillips-drive screw works fine most of the time, but the heads can "cam out" or strip when you hit tough spots. Any slipping at all tends to chip away corrosion-resistant coatings, so replace screws that get compromised during installation. Square-drive screws are about impossible to strip, so the coatings don't suffer much. But the screws may snap when the going gets real hard, so use judicious pressure and predrill when necessary.

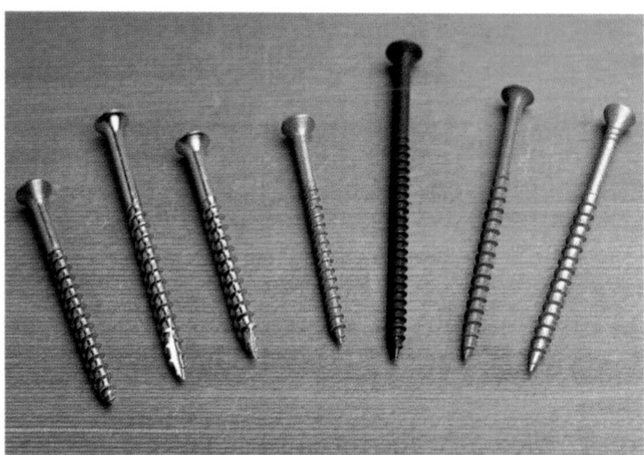

Stainless-steel screws (first three); polymer-coated screws (fourth and sixth); painted (fifth); and hot galvanized (far right).

Stainless-steel screws are good for cedar or redwood decking (especially in clear grades), you'll probably want to use stainless-steel screws. Stainless steel is the most corrosion-resistant type of screw material, and because there are no coatings to chip or wear off, screws made from it should last a lifetime. Stainless-steel screws are recommended for natural finished cedar and redwood, which contain tannins that can turn black when in contact with iron and moisture.

These premium fasteners also make sense for use with long-lasting tropical woods. The standard is 18-8 or 304 or 305 series grade stainless; however, 316 grade, though more expensive, is even more resistant to corrosion and is recommended for all decking woods used in coastal areas (where salt corrodes everything in a hurry). Stainless steel is not as strong as regular steel, so you should use larger size screws and predrill holes in tough wood.

Galvanized steel screws are quite a bit stronger and cheaper than stainless steel and are adequate for use with pressure-treated woods (except in coastal areas). Depending on how the coating is applied and where the screw is used, galvanized steel screws should last between 10 and 15 years. Hot-dipped galvanized screws have a thick, rough surface that makes them harder to drive than other screws, but which offers more corrosion protection. Unfortunately, the Phillips-drive and square-drive recesses can get partially filled when the screws are dipped, so have extra screws on hand. Mechanically coated screws are smoother and don't have this problem, but their thinner zinc coating means they have less corrosion resistance. Electroplated screws have a thin, shiny zinc coating and look like a classic hardware-store screw. These aren't adequate for decks and may fail quickly.

Phillips-head screws (center, right) are a little cheaper and faster to install, but the bit can "cam out" and chip the finish. Square-drive screws (left) aren't quite as widely available, and because the bit is less likely to slip, are more prone to snapping off. I prefer to use them on the harder deck woods.

PRO TIP

If you're using high-quality decking like redwood or cedar, pick the best boards from the decking pile to use for railing components.

IN DETAIL

Some decking and framing lumber can be purchased with a water repellent added during the pressure-treatment process. Some manufacturers (see Resources, p. 179) will guarantee their wood treated with this process for as long as 50 years, while others recommend a biannual topical application of water repellent of some type. Since these factory repellents are usually added to premium grades of wood, the price can be as much as 50% higher than standard pressure-treated wood. These products may give you a longer-lasting and better-looking deck, but I don't think they are essential, provided you keep up with regular maintenance.

TOOLS AND MATERIALS

Plan on using an average of 2.5 fasteners per square foot for 6-in.-wide boards installed on joists 24 in. o.c., 3.5 per sq. ft. for joists 16 in. o.c., and 5 per sq. ft. for 4-in.-wide boards on joists 16 in. o.c. Add an extra 10% for breakage, in addition to the fasteners you'll need for railings, stairs, and accessories.

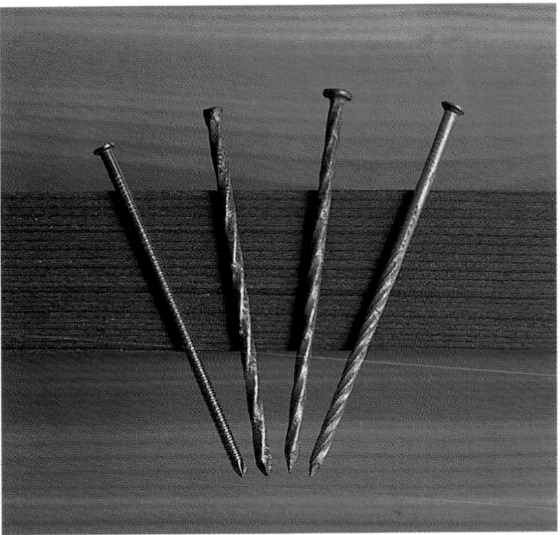

Ring-shank or twisted-shank decking nails with smaller heads can be quickly installed, are relatively inexpensive, and may be adequate fasteners for quality decking in moderate climates, but the nails must be hot-galvanized or made of stainless steel. Casing or finish heads are inadequate for squirmy woods like southern yellow pine. My favorite decking nail (shown at far right) is from Maze Nail Co. and has some unthreaded shank below the head that allows the board to pull tight to the joist.

Premium decking installed with concealed fasteners takes on a furniture-like appearance.

Coated screws: paint, polymers, epoxy, or ceramic. Manufacturers of coated screws claim their screws offer better corrosion resistance than galvanized screws (and sometimes as good as stainless steel) at a fraction of the cost of stainless. I often use coated screws in inland Alaska, but I don't think that I'd use them near the coast. Different manufacturers use different coating materials, and some coatings are a hybrid of materials, but it's difficult to say with certainty which coating works best. Epoxies and ceramics are traditionally tough but may chip, while paint and polymers can be more flexible but may wear more easily. Coated screws are smooth, easy to use, and relatively cheap, but only time will tell which is the most durable.

Nails

While there's no doubt that screws are better, they may not always be necessary. Because decking nails are faster to install and less obvious than screws, I use them on some of my deck jobs and have never experienced any trouble with the fasteners pulling out over time. Of course, I am using decking nails with cedar decking, which is basically free from cupping and warping problems.

At the very least, you'll want to use hot-dipped galvanized nails made for decking use. I avoid electroplated nails (the type of galvanizing usually found on pneumatic gun nails). Manufacturers may claim that their nails are corrosion-resistant, but I prefer to use hot-dipped nails to be sure. Galvanized decking nails have smaller heads and twisted shanks, and may need to be special-ordered. Stainless-steel ring-shank nails with smaller heads for decking are also available by special order. These would be a good choice for cedar and redwood decks, but would probably be unnecessary with treated woods. If I were going to the expense of using stainless-steel fasteners on my deck, I would probably use screws anyway.

Concealed fasteners

If you're using the best clear cedar, redwood, or tropical wood, you may want to install your decking without all those fastener heads showing. There are three different ways to do this.

The first method relies on metal clips. One type of clip is screwed to the joist and uses prongs to hold the deck board down. Another type of clip is screwed to the edge of the decking and jams under the previous board, which has been blind toescrewed. Neither of these clip systems appeals to me, however, because only one edge of the board is held with screws. It seems to me that if the decking were to shrink significantly, the clips could lose their grip.

Another system uses plastic football-shaped "biscuits" that fit into milled slots in the edge of the deck boards. The decking is held down with a screw through the disc. Construction adhesive between the joist and decking is suggested too. While biscuits work great in the right circumstances, I think that eventually shrinkage might make them lose their grip and the screws would be difficult to retighten later. And I'm not a believer in the permanence of construction adhesive in wet situations between woods that might move at different rates. However, for dry cedar and other woods that don't shrink a lot, this system reportedly works fine (though it is tedious to install).

The third system uses a perforated L-shaped metal strip that is screwed first to the side of the joist and then to the decking through the strip from underneath. If enough screws are used, this system could be used with wet lumber and still hold. Installation will take a serious commitment to bending over, even if you use a right-angle drill to install from above; if you're working on a low deck that can't be reached from below, you'll also need some creativity to install the last few boards.

Installing Decking

It's time to get on with the business of laying the decking. While this is a relatively straightforward procedure, there are a few techniques that I use that make the process go easier and result in a better-looking deck.

Getting started

When decking is parallel to the house, I lay my first course right next to the house. To get this course straight (especially on a long deck or where there is waviness in the ledger), I first mark and snap a chalkline on top of the joists. I locate this line away from the flashing (or the existing siding) by the width of one deck board plus an extra ½ in. Then I set the first board in place, align its edge with the chalkline, and fasten it down, working from one end to the other. Using straight boards for the first course makes this process easier.

If I'm installing decking perpendicular to the house, I snap my chalkline so that the first deck board has the proper overhang along the end joist. If I'm decking on the diagonal, I start in the middle and work in both directions instead of starting with the smallest piece in the corner. This

Shown here is the galvanized Dec-Klip®; it provides a hidden fastening system that is quick to install but also has the potential to work loose when decking shrinkage is a big factor. Several manufacturers make clips that are installed much the same way.

Galvanized steel angles attached to joists provide a flange for hidden screws into decking.

Plastic, football-shaped EB-TY® fasteners are inserted into the edge of a decking board after a slot is cut with a biscuit joiner. A stainless-steel screw holds the fastener and board in place. This type of hidden fastener could work loose if the deck board shrinks much, so it is best used where movement is minimal, as with resin composite decking, for example.

PRO TIP

The blade of a circular saw won't be able to cut all the way up next to a house so cut the first courses to their exact length before installing them.

TRADE SECRET

We cut most of our decking with a 7-in. circular saw equipped with a sharp, new, thin-kerf 24-tooth carbide blade. Finer blades than this make smoother cuts, but they aren't essential for outdoor work and have a tendency to burn the wood (especially cedar). Although a chopsaw or compound miter saw is handy for cutting shorter lengths, I don't use it much for longer pieces.

WHAT CAN GO WRONG

One of the places most susceptible to rot is the point at which decking boards butt into each other over a single joist. To prevent this, you can design your decking to break over a gap created by a doubled joist with a ½-in. treated plywood spacer in between. To help make the extra framing economical, choose a decking pattern that requires only a few of these doubled joists. Leave a ⅛-in. gap between the butt ends of the decking boards to provide air circulation.

Letting decking run "wild" over the ends of the framing is faster and allows for boards to be cut all at once in a straight line.

After marking the correct overhang on opposite ends of a row of long deck boards, snap a cutline between the marks.

A circular saw cuts boards quickly and evenly.

Cuts next to a wall must be finished with a handsaw; alternatively, boards can be precut before installation.

makes it easier to align the boards 45 degrees to the joists, and this is where I snap my chalkline.

As I lay the decking, I'm careful to align and fasten all of the butt joints. But I run the ends of the boards that overhang the outside of the framing long for now. Once all the decking is in place, I snap a chalkline and cut all the board ends at once. If I'm cutting the ends flush with the joist, I set the depth of my sawblade to just barely deeper than the decking thickness so that I don't cut into the joist. Near the house, I complete the cuts with a handsaw.

Putting in fasteners

The quickest way to install decking is with nails. For 2× decking, I use 3½-in. galvanized nails, and I use 3-in. nails for 5/4 decking. This gives me about 2 in. of penetration into the joist. The usual pattern is two nails per decking board at each joist, and I keep nails back from the edge about ⅝ in. to ¾ in. to avoid splits.

I drive in the nails so that they're flush with the surface of the decking, then set them with a nailset.

Nails are faster than screws when you are installing decking, but hammer carefully to avoid leaving dents in the boards. Note the spacer, a nail driven into a scrap block of wood.

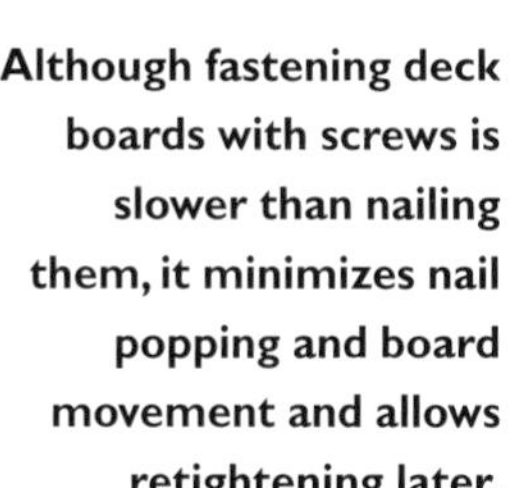

Although fastening deck boards with screws is slower than nailing them, it minimizes nail popping and board movement and allows retightening later.

Southern yellow pine decking that is laid wet and without gaps will shrink in place. Wet decking is easier to screw into place, but gaps may be unpredictable.

Which Side Goes Up?

If you're using expensive vertical-grain wood, it doesn't really matter which side of the decking faces up. But most of us use affordable flat-sawn wood with the annual rings running across the long width of the board, and there's been plenty of debate about which side of that type of board should face up.

Heartwood vs. sapwood

According to one theory, the heartwood side (center) of the tree resists rot better than the sapwood. In fact, heartwood is the *only* rot-resistant part of cedar and redwood; untreated sapwood will rot first, no matter which way it is facing.

You really shouldn't have any untreated sapwood, anyway. Treated sapwood accepts preservative better than heartwood, which may make it slightly more rot-resistant but not enough so that orienting the board one way or the other will make a difference.

Bark side up or down?

One rule says to put the bark side up, so that if the board does swell, it will arch up in the middle and encourage drainage. This may be true for a time if the boards were very dry when laid, but if the boards were laid wet, they might cup the other way as they dry. Put the bark side down and the reverse is true. Initially you may get it right, but after a while, the cycling between wet and dry of boards restrained by nails or screws usually causes the boards to remain in a concave position, especially if the underside of the deck has poor circulation and keeps the bottom of the boards wetter than the top.

Show your best face

The solution? I always use good wood and lay the boards so that the best-looking face is up. Who wants to put a board in with the ugly face up just so it might not rot in 20 years? I'll take my chances. If a few boards cup terribly, just replace them. And remember that keeping your deck maintained with water repellent will do more to keep boards flat and increase their life span than any amount of board flopping.

Using a set that is the same diameter as the nail head helps to minimize chipping of the galvanized coating and exposing of untreated steel. I use a hammer with a smooth face rather than a waffle face to minimize chipping and waffle marks in the deck.

Installing screws is slower going. Since screws can grab the substrate better, I use shorter lengths than I do for nails: 3-in. screws for 2× stock and 2½-in. screws for 5/4 stock. This puts about 1½ in. of thread into the joist.

It isn't necessary to predrill softwoods like cedar, redwood, or hemlock, except near the ends. Wet southern pine or fir can also be installed without predrilling, though it will be necessary if the boards are dry—(this is the reason most southern pine decking is installed wet). Where the screw is close to the end of the board, I predrill at an angle into the joist to avoid splitting. Also, I'm careful to sink all of the screws so the tops are below the surface and not subject to wear by foot traffic.

When it's time to put in a lot of screws, there are a few options but my tool of choice is a cordless drill. It's powerful, portable, and as ubiquitous and useful a carpenter's tool as a hammer. My drill

PRO TIP

If all your butt joints fall over one or two joists, you'll see a regimented pattern. Some like this look, but I think it detracts from the beauty of the wood.

TRADE SECRET

I like to randomize the location of butt joints and spread them around. I try to keep all butt joints at least 4 ft. to 6 ft. away from each other, go three or four rows without a break on the same joist, and never break two adjacent boards on the same joist.

TOOLS AND MATERIALS

A special wrench for applying pressure to uncooperative boards, The BoWrench (see Resources, p. 179) is a hinged affair with a floppy end-piece that pinches the joist, while the longer handle end levers against the offending deck board. The tool is easy and quick to use.

has an adjustable clutch that stops driving the screw at a preset resistance, but I often don't use it because varying wood conditions make for inconsistent results. Instead, I set the clutch almost to the no-slip position to avoid breaking screws, and I stop driving the screw when it looks to be about the right depth.

Spacing the boards

Even after years of deck work, my carpenters always ask what the board spacing will be for a particular deck. This is because the wrong board spacing is apt to cause future problems. Our goal is to end up with a 3⁄16-in. gap between the boards once they've dried and stabilized. So, the real question is: How much will the boards shrink? The answer is easier to predict if you use boards that have been partially dried, either by the manufacturer or yourself. This way, you'll know that the boards won't shrink radically after installation. Wood always seems to shrink after it has baked in the sun for a while, and large gaps caused by shrinking boards are not only unsightly but potential toe-catchers. Remember too that wood will swell again when wet, so you want to leave enough of a gap for adequate drainage. A gap that is too narrow will trap leaves, pine needles, and organic debris.

Deckmate® spacers for laying decking can be purchased (as shown, center), improvised (a speed square, for instance, at right) or homemade (an 8d or 16d nail driven into a block of scrap wood, at left).

If we're working with cedar or redwood boards that have been dried to the average ambient outside humidity, we lay them with our desired finish gap or a little closer. We lay kiln-dried cedar using a carpenter's speed square (which is just under 3⁄16 in. thick) as our spacer. The boards will swell some in wet weather, but they'll shrink again to about the same spacing. If we're using kiln-dried treated lumber that hasn't been site-conditioned, we expect that it will still shrink after installation and install it with only about half the expected finished gap.

But time and budget don't always allow predrying. If we're working with a soaking wet, pressure-treated lumber that shrinks a lot (southern pine or hem–fir, for example), we lay the boards tight without any gaps. When the boards dry, there will be plenty of gapping. Wet cedar and redwood shrinks less, making shrinkage harder to predict. If we're sure the wood is soaked, we lay it tight, but if it has been dried even a little we'll leave a small gap using a 16d nail as a spacer.

Persuading problem boards

No matter how much you've paid for your decking, some of the boards are going to be crooked. Cedar and redwood are seldom cupped, but they may suffer from a bow or curve. Treated woods are likely to have every type of crookedness known to man if not cared for properly. Boards that are badly cupped before being installed should be discarded or ripped for other uses because you'll never get them to flatten out. But bowed boards can usually be coerced into place, while the worst offenders can be sawn into shorter lengths.

You can start a bowed board just as you would any other board and can usually fasten it at several joists before you have to apply more-than-gentle force. Driving a framing chisel down into the joist and using it as a lever can apply enough pressure for moderate bows. Alternatively, a strategically

Driving screws into the edge of decking can help force boards into position.

braced helper can use leg pressure effectively to push a partially fastened board into position. Pipe clamps work well too. Jamb a chisel or thin flat prybar into a crack several boards back to use as an anchor point for one end of the clamp.

The last rows

With about three-fourths of the decking laid, we start thinking about the last row. Using the previously laid decking as a gauge, we try to predict the width of the last row. The edge of the last board usually overhangs the framing, and should have at least twice as much width firmly screwed to the framing as is cantilevered. If we find the last board would end up as a narrow strip (under an inch), sometimes we'll space the remaining boards with a little wider gap so that the decking comes out evenly. Another solution is to buy a wider decking board and rip it down to the required width. If a wider board isn't available, we'll glue up a wide board in the shop using waterproof glue. In lieu of gluing, you can screw a strip to a full-width decking board, then install this wider board with the screw heads facing toward the previous row so they don't show. If we find that the last piece is at least several inches wide (enough to catch the framing but still leaving some concern about its stability), we'll sometimes swap places with the second-to-last row and make the last row full width instead.

First-time deck builders often think they should divide the deck into equal spaces and then adjust the gaps between the boards so they end up with full-width decking. In our imperfect world, this is practical only when you get down to the last few boards. Slight variations in board width and bends and bows cause havoc with your calculations. Just lay the boards and do your worrying when you get there. No one ever notices if the last board or two is a little narrower or wider than the rest.

Alternative decking patterns

On most of my decks, I lay the decking parallel to the wall of the house. I seldom feel the time and material expense of more complicated patterns to be a worthwhile investment. If the budget allows, I would rather add more interest by installing a nicer railing system or adding level changes, planters, or angles. But that doesn't mean you can't run your decking in a different direction. The most common alternative is perpendicular to the house. It's easier to shovel snow off of decking laid this way, and as a bonus, the usually shorter dimensions may allow you to install your decking without any butt joints. But this decision must be made during the design phase, because the joist direction must be rotated 90 degrees.

Another option is to run the decking boards at a 45-degree angle. This is definitely a lot more work, as it takes longer to cut and fit boards this way. It also creates a lot more waste. Diagonal patterns can fit on regular joist framing plans, though doubling joists under butt joints will make it easier. Keep in mind that you may need to space your joists closer together if you're laying decking diagonally, particularly if you are using a 5/4 decking material, because the joist-to-joist span will increase.

Another way to move a curved deck board into position is to tap a chisel firmly into the edge of the joist to get a bite, then pry the board into place as the fastener is installed.

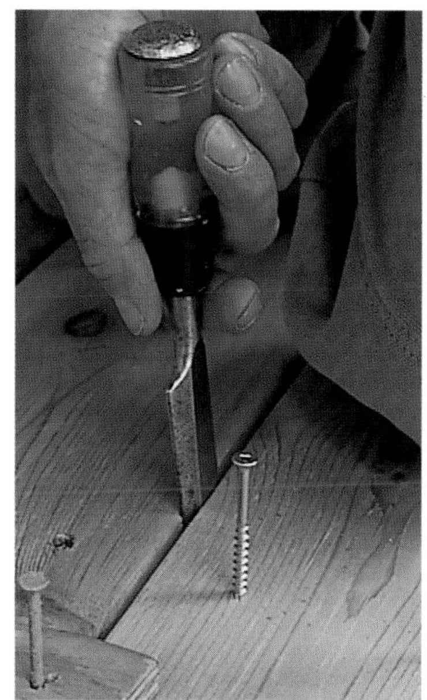

A chisel is also handy for prying apart boards that need a larger gap between them.

PRO TIP

To avoid splitting boards, some people recommend blunting the end of the nail with a hammer blow. Better advice is to predrill instead.

IN DETAIL

Most deck screws have an unthreaded portion of shaft just under the head that allows the board to pull up tight to the joist as the threaded part digs in. If your deck screws are threaded their entire length, you may need to predrill holes in the decking so the screws don't hold the board off the joist. Predrill just enough to facilitate this and don't make the hole too big.

To avoid splitting the end of a board, first predrill at an angle with a bit sized to match the shank of the screw.

WHAT CAN GO WRONG

When two deck boards break over a single joist, their fasteners are going to be close to the end of the board. This can lead to splitting.

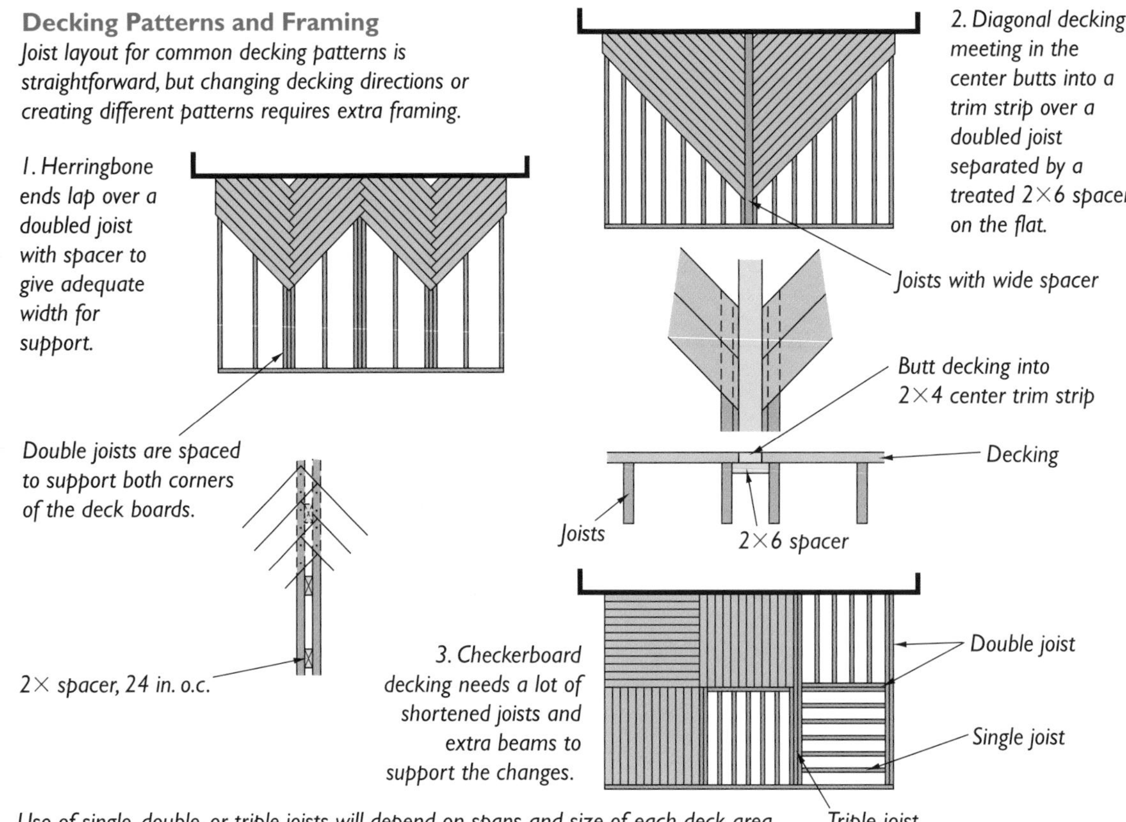

Other patterns include mixtures of parallel, perpendicular, and diagonal decking. All these patterns will require an increase in the framing work beforehand and probably double the time needed for laying the decking itself.

Decking is most often installed parallel with the house, a configuration that simplifies framing and looks good with most houses.

There are some easy tricks that you can use with decking to add interest without much extra work or expense. Try alternating decking board widths between 4 in. and 6 in., or use two boards of one width followed by a one board of a different width. Or change the direction on intermediate steps between level changes. This switch adds a touch of pizzazz and will attract attention to help avoid a stumble.

Finishing the Decking

There are several ways to deal with the exposed edges of the decking. The easiest way is to allow the boards to simply overhang the framing by about 1¼ in. or so. But some people don't like the look of all that end grain, which tends to get rougher over time and requires maintenance with water repellent to avoid splits. In this case, a more formal-looking treatment that covers the ends of the boards might be more appropriate. This can be

Diagonally laid decking gives a unique look and results in a stable platform that may not need additional bracing. Because decking spans are increased, joists may need to be spaced closer together.

Fascia Alternatives

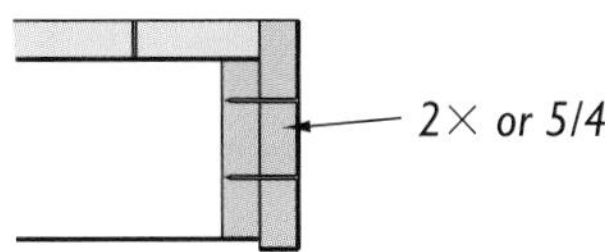

1. A 2× or 5/4 fascia can be attached directly to the framing, flush with the top of the decking after the ends have been cut evenly.

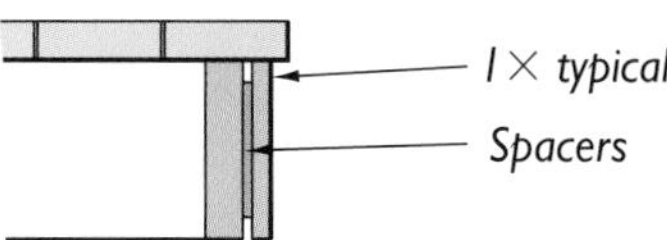

3. A fascia with overhanging decking can be thinner because it's protected from weather.

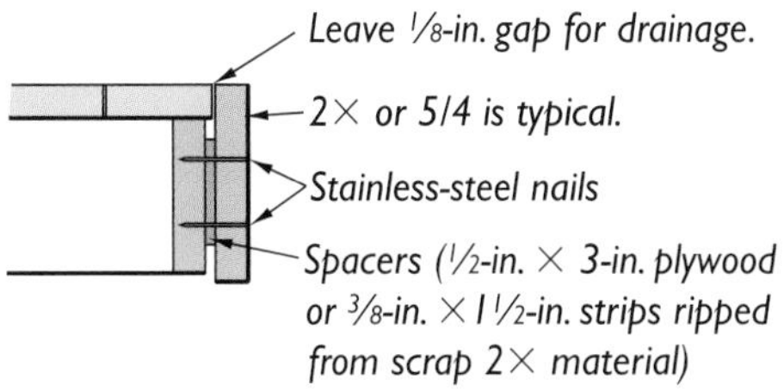

2. Adding a spacer of plywood or wood behind the fascia aids drying. This full-width fascia also has a gap left at the top to help deck board ends dry.

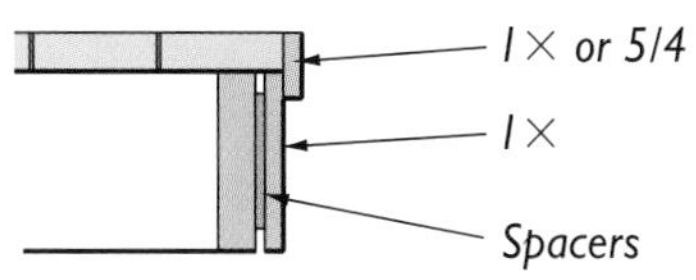

4. When the joists are wide, adding a layered fascia lets you use narrower boards that aren't as likely to split.

A change of direction in the decking can visually alert users to steps or other impediments.

a wide fascia that ends flush with the top of the decking or a separate deck board that caps the ends of the decking. Either way, this look comes at the price of keeping the ends from drying out easily and should be used only if you are committed to touching up untreated ends and maintaining water-repellent finishes.

Installing a fascia

You may want to apply an extra finish layer—called a fascia—to cover your deck's framing, particularly if the framing is treated wood. This layer can simply cover the rim joist, leaving the ends of the decking exposed. Or it can extend up past the cut decking boards, ending flush with the top surface of the deck.

A fascia that covers only the rim joist is usually a 1× board of the same species as the decking and is usually the same width as the rim joist. It's applied with galvanized or stainless siding nails. Ideally, the fascia is separated from the framing by adding 1½-in. by ¼-in. vertical strips ripped from a piece of 2× framing lumber, or strips ripped from ½-in. thick treated plywood. These strips create a gap that facilitates drying and will also need to be added under railing post attachment points. Be sure to allow for the combined thickness of the fascia and spacers when you're calculating your deck board overhang.

To add a wide fascia that covers the ends of the decking, cut the decking boards flush with the outside of the framing. Then nail a 5/4 fascia board to the framing with siding nails, flush with the top of the deck boards. (I've found that ¾-in. boards are too prone to being damaged, while 2× material is harder to restrain from cupping.)

This decking has been installed with an even 1¼-in. overhang.

Adding a matching ¾-in. thick fascia directly to the framing under the decking overhang dresses up a deck.

PRO TIP

Rounding over all the outside edges of the decking with a router eliminates "fuzzies," makes the deck safer, and gives it a more crafted look.

WHAT CAN GO WRONG

If your decking is really wet when you lay it, some fastener heads may be left standing too tall when the decking dries. Going back and resetting the fastener heads six months or a year later should take care of the problem. If you used smooth-shank nails, you may have to do this fix on a regular basis since these nails are easily pulled by the swelling and cupping of wood. Screws and spiral or ring-shank nails should stay below the surface.

IN DETAIL

Routing is usually done from left to right for the smoothest cut, but this also increases the likelihood of tearout, where the bit lifts long splinters of wood deeper than the intended cut. Tearout can be minimized by removing the bulk of the wood by climb-cutting, or going from right to left on the first pass. Hold tight or the router will quickly zoom to your left, creating an obvious safety hazard. This climb-cut pass won't be smooth, so follow it up with a final slow pass from left to right to finish the job.

Spacers ripped from treated scraps or ½-in.-thick treated plywood can be added between the framing and finish fascia to help prevent rot.

Capping the cut ends of decking adds an elegant touch to well-crafted decks. It requires a little extra framing and attention to maintenance to keep captured ends in good shape.

Picture-Frame Decking

A cap around the perimeter of the deck adds a finishing touch, but can keep board ends from drying. The cap needs the support of a double joist with spacer and looks best with mitered corners.

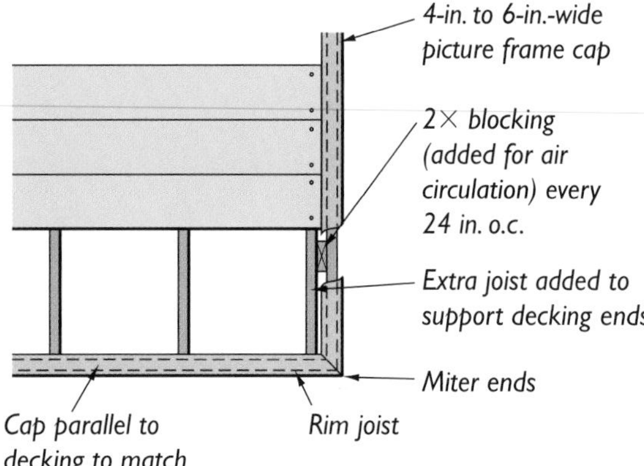

When a fascia needs to be more than 8 in. wide, it's a good idea to layer it to allow the individual boards some movement. To avoid having to notch railing posts to conform to a multilayer fascia, put the top layer on after you've installed all the posts. Another option is to use a 4-in.-wide fascia that covers the deck ends and laps only partway onto the joist. The ends of fascias should be mitered at outside corners.

Another way to add a distinctive look to the deck while covering the decking ends is to add a "picture-frame" edge band to the decking. The band can be the same width as the deck boards and is laid flat, overhanging the rim with the corners mitered. This treatment requires extra joists in the framing and some extra blocking.

Routing edges

After all of the decking has been installed, I like to round over all the outside edges with a router. This eliminates "fuzzies," makes the deck safer, and gives it a more crafted look. For a smoother effect, I use a ¼-in. to ⅜-in. radius roundover bit for 5/4 decking and a ⅜-in. to ½-in. radius bit for 2× decking. If I want a crisper look, I'll use a 45-degree chamfer bit.

It's not always possible to rout right up to walls or corners. This means that the last few inches of decking don't get rounded over, a look that isn't necessarily bad. But if you want to take the edge treatment all the way to the end, consider routing the awkward parts before you install this decking. Another technique that may help in some locations is to turn the router so its base rests on the edge of the board instead of the face, but this requires a steady hand to keep the router balanced and cutting evenly. And finally, hand tools such as sharp chisels, wood rasps, and some coarser-grit sandpaper can usually solve anything the router can't reach.

One of the finishing touches is the removal of saw "fuzzies" with a bevel or roundover bit and a router.

Accessories

A couple of easily constructed deck details can help solve such common problems as storage, cleaning, and water splashing.

Storage. Decks need readily accessible water for cleaning, watering plants, filling fountains, and other functions. The problem is: Where do you store the hose? While you could add an unattractive but functional hose hanger to the wall, a better solution is to store the hose under a hatch cover in the deck surface. The cover is made of several short pieces of decking material with a cleat screwed across the back to hold the pieces together as a unit. This section can be hinged to the fixed portion of the deck, or simply left as a completely removable unit. Drilling a hole in one of the boards creates an inexpensive finger-pull for removing the hatch. Hoses are bulky, but a ventilated underhatch platform can be made as big as necessary by screwing closely spaced strips to the underside of the joist framing and if desired, adding blocking to close the area at the ends. Storage for smaller miscellaneous items such as brushes, soaps and toys can be made by fastening a large wire mesh basket to the joists.

Grates and gutters. In areas with a lot of summer mud and winter snow, people wipe their shoes off just outside the door. This mud and dirt then gets tracked into the house. One solution is to recess a galvanized steel grate into the deck surface. You should be able to rest the grate directly on top of the joists, so just stop the decking halfway on a joist and let the remaining ¾ in. support the grate. You may need to add some cleats for alignment and support if you don't position the grating directly over joists. Although these grates are often located directly in front of a door, you may want to install them in earlier access places and keep the door decking intact. One disadvantage of a grate is that you can see through to the dark, dirty area underneath the deck. If this bothers you, add some widely spaced wood strips screwed to the underside of the joists to help block the view.

Folks often are unpleasantly surprised when their house siding starts turning gray or looking

Attaching a metal basket to the underside of the deck and adding a lid provides a handy, well-ventilated area to store deck tools.

✚ SAFETY FIRST

Routers are the loudest tool on the job, so always wear ear protection. And motors and high-speed bits can throw chips everywhere, so don't skip eye protection either. Use two hands and hang on tight, especially when first turning on a router or doing climb cuts. Powerful motors can make the router jump and knock the spinning bit into the wood before you're ready.

Replacing a small section of decking with a metal bar grate will keep mud from getting tracked into the house.

PRO TIP

There's no such thing as a low-maintenance system for a natural finish. Maintaining a topnotch finish may require an annual recoating.

IN DETAIL

To prevent the wood from absorbing the full blast of the sun's rays, some finishes contain pigments, or suspended particles that reject or disrupt UV degradation. Clear finishes with no pigment use chemicals similar to sunscreens. These chemicals will wear out or wash off in a year or two and must be regularly reapplied. Pigments in tinted clear finishes or semi-transparent stains last longer than chemical blockers do and will make the need for reapplication less frequent. UV rays are responsible for turning wood gray, so don't use a finish with blockers if that weathered gray look is what you want.

IN DETAIL

Wet lumber can be between 30% and 50% moisture content, kiln-dried lumber typically is between 15% and 20%. When lumber is cured in placed, its moisture content may drop down to 12% or less, depending on the climate. Depending on the species of wood, that can amount to a lot of shrinkage.

particularly weathered after they add a deck. This weathering is commonly caused by rainwater dripping off the roof, hitting the deck, and splashing on the wall. This causes premature failure of caulked joints, leaks, and rot where no problem existed before. The best solution is to add gutters and control the water's flow.

If gutters cause aesthetic problems, another solution is to recess a 6-in.-wide strip of deck grating into the deck. Just leave out one or two deck boards in the area directly under the drip line of the roof. Have your steel supplier cut your grating into pieces just wide enough to fill the gap and let the joists support them, breaking the ends over a joist just as you would with decking. Grating will usually stay in place without extra effort if it's cut to a tight fit, but you can use screws and plastic plumbing clips for security if need be.

Finishes

A newly completed deck is a treat for the eyes, but that lumberyard-fresh look will quickly fade unless a finish is applied. Of course, if you like the gray of weathered wood, you could choose to leave deck unfinished, but be aware that you are inviting cupping, warping, and other problems. Most people prefer to apply a finish, both for aesthetic reasons and to prolong the life of the deck.

Both paints and solid-color stains put on a relatively thick film of material to provide protection from the elements but are not recommended on horizontal surfaces. Unfortunately, as wood and fasteners expand and contract, this layer is compromised and the water manages to get in. The trouble comes when it can't get back out, which causes the protective film to peel and blister.

For walking surfaces, I only recommend solid stains when drastic measures are called for (as in the case of an old deck in such dire need of a facelift that you want to completely hide the wood). If you must use a solid stain on decking, choose a product made specifically for decks and make sure it is approved for walking surfaces.

Penetrating finishes. Penetrating finishes help protect your decking against the effects of sun and moisture, and include water repellents, clear and lightly tinted "natural" finishes, oils, and semitransparent stains. While penetrating finishes can be simple water repellents (with or without preservatives), the types I use and recommend—such as Behr®'s Waterproofing Natural Seal Plus—have additional ingredients and are often referred to as "natural," oil, or transparent water repellent finishes. They allow most of the wood's natural color and grain to show through, but they can also be used to enhance and darken an already grayed surface. These finishes are specifically formulated and labeled for deck use.

These "natural" finishes contain water repellents, preservatives, UV blockers, and a good amount of oils and resins. In the "clear" version, the liquid is usually amber, but to increase the effectiveness of this type of finish, manufacturers also produced lightly colored versions that have small amounts of pigment added that provide additional UV protection and even out variations in wood color. Although I usually choose the untinted formulation for new cedar decks, a tinted shade that imitates redwood or cedar adds some visual zip to faded decks. These finishes can even be used to gradually change the color of a treated wood deck that has had enough time for the green color to fade. Under good conditions, this extra pigment may make it possible to go two years before recoating.

Semitransparent deck stains. Semitransparent deck stains are moderately pigmented penetrating finishes that provide a lot more color than the tinted natural finishes but still allow some grain to show through. They leave a surface layer of stain but still allow moisture to escape without damage to that layer. Because the extra pigment provides a lot more UV protection for the wood, this type of finish may not need renewal as often as natural finishes do. This also makes them a good choice for treated woods when you need to hide an ugly brown or green treatment coloration or for older decks that are a little too tired to easily revive to their former glory. You can choose from a huge number of easily mixed colors or even have a can tinted to your specifications. But avoid refinishing semi-transparent stains too often or you can build up a thick layer. Wait until the pigment loss is apparent, or apply a water repellent instead.

Most deck-finishing tools are common brushes, trays, and rollers made for oil-based products. Safety equipment such as gloves, glasses, and an organic cartridge mask are essential for the somewhat messy and smelly application procedure.

Although a little slower than spraying, brushing rail tops and other flat surfaces is less messy and doesn't result in overapplication.

A small hand-pumped sprayer can be used to apply drippy finishes onto balusters and the underside of rails quickly, but put down plastic sheeting to guard against overspray on the house and vegetation. After spraying, use a brush to work finish in.

+ SAFETY FIRST

I know of several spontaneous combustion fires that were caused by improper disposal of rags used to wipe up penetrating oil finishes. Rags with *any* finish on them should be spread to dry on a noncombustible surface out of the sun before they are tossed in the trash. Alternatively, you can put the rags back into the empty metal finish can immediately after using them, fill the can with water, and put the lid back on. Don't leave oil-soaked rags lying around or heaped in a pile.

A $\frac{1}{2}$- or $\frac{3}{4}$-in. nap roller applies penetrating finish quickly to the deck surface and other large flat areas. After applying the first coat, go back and spread the puddles around, adding extra finish, where needed, to ensure good penetration. Any wet spots that remain may need more spreading.

Whether applied by rolling, brushing, or spraying, excess penetrating oil finishes need to be wiped off before too long or the result will be a shiny sticky patch that never dries. Rags soaked with finish or other flammable substances are prone to spontaneous combustion so be sure to dispose of them according to the recommendations on the finish can.

Railings

CHAPTER SIX

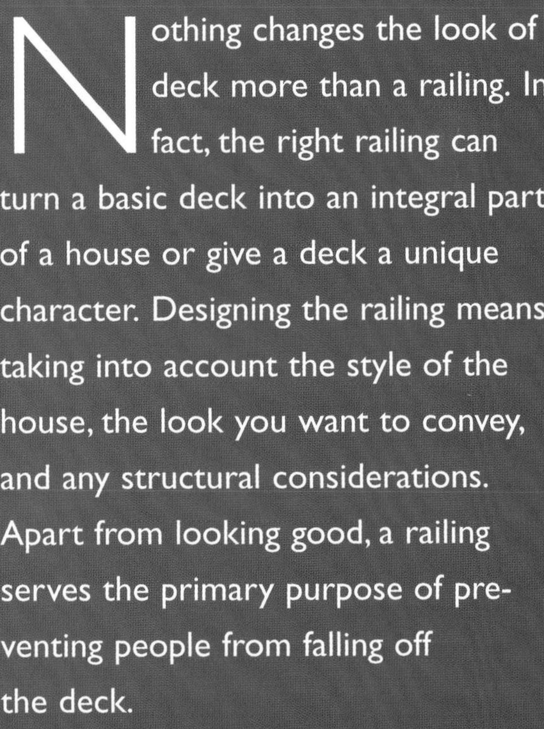

Nothing changes the look of a deck more than a railing. In fact, the right railing can turn a basic deck into an integral part of a house or give a deck a unique character. Designing the railing means taking into account the style of the house, the look you want to convey, and any structural considerations. Apart from looking good, a railing serves the primary purpose of preventing people from falling off the deck.

Because they serve this important safety function, railing systems are subject to a lot of code requirements. In this chapter, I'll explain the basics of building a safe, functional, and attractive railing system. Most of the focus will be on building railings made from wood. But don't overlook the possibilities presented by materials such as steel pipes and cables, glass, composites, and plastics. These materials can give a unique look to an otherwise basic deck.

Designing a Railing System

Traditional railing systems have several components: vertical posts for support, horizontal top and bottom rails that connect the posts, a cap rail at the very top, and a balustrade, usually made up of numerous small, vertical balusters. When designing a railing system, I've found that the most effective ways of varying its look is by manipulating the components' frequency, size, and direction, material choice, and decoration.

Design principles

The spacing of posts or balusters can change the entire look of the railing. Older homes often have balusters spaced much more closely together in the Craftsman style. Until a few years ago, newer homes tended to use a wider, more rustic spacing, a trend that has been reversed by newer code requirements. Extra rails add horizontal elements that affect the design, changing the look from simple to complex, even though these rails may not be needed structurally.

You can vary the visual complexity of your railing system by adding different elements, such as an extra top rail.

The size of the railing elements can emphasize or minimize a sense of mass or lightness. Large posts—either boxed or solid—add punctuation and definition. Narrow balusters help create an open feeling; wider balusters make a space seem more enclosed. Compare, for example, the open

Railing Anatomy and Code Requirements

Railings must meet code requirements for size, spacing between parts, location, and strength.

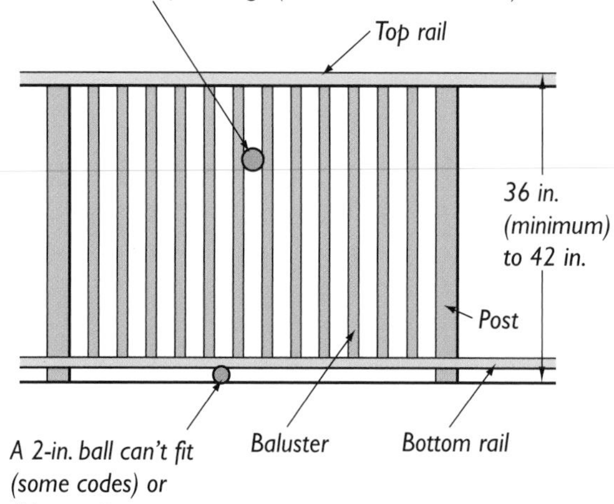

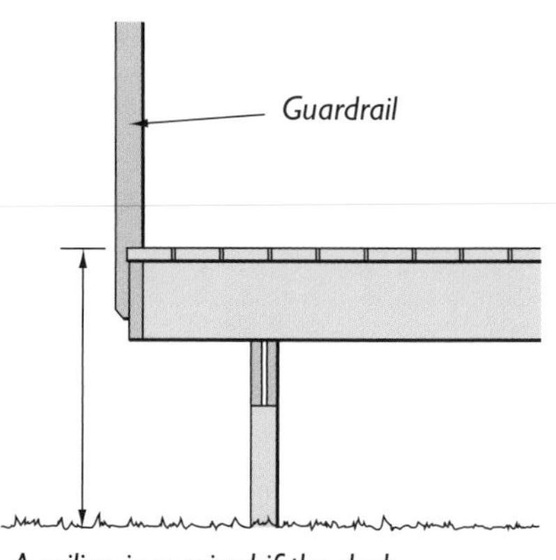

PRO TIP

Posts are usually uniformly sized throughout a railing, but a baluster introduced on a regular basis can spice up an otherwise monotonous design.

IN DETAIL

Posts aren't necessary if strong balusters lap onto the rim joist of the deck instead of a bottom rail, and if the balusters are attached solidly with screws. This is a very simple and repetitious style that isn't appropriate for some houses. Adding an occasional larger baluster breaks the monotony and gives a little extra strength to the system.

Railings without posts offer a different look, but rely on a well-fastened connection between the balusters and rim joist for strength.

WHAT CAN GO WRONG

One thing to remember is that small wood pieces less than ¾ in. thick tend to deteriorate rapidly in an exterior environment unless maintenance is meticulous.

Horizontal metal-tubing balusters through rectangular wooden uprights provide contrast in material shape, texture, and orientation.

feeling of a modern steel-pipe railing with the feel of a traditionally Scandinavian balustrade featuring wide boards with designs such as trees or circles cut into the mating edges of the balusters. And although you may not be able to change the orientation of posts, you can change the orientation of the balusters. Running them horizontally or diagonally instead of vertically will create a whole new look.

While most railings are made of wood, I find that using other materials for posts, rails, or especially, balustrades can add a lot of character. Copper, aluminum, plastic, glass, and galvanized or stainless steel can all be used to give your railings a distinctive look. Regardless of what material you use for your railing, a well-designed system deserves a finishing touch. Chamfering the edges of posts, balusters, or rails adds crispness; rounding them over adds softness. Adding color to all or some of the elements will make them stand out in relation to their neighbors.

✓ According to Code

Building codes recognize a difference between *guardrails,* which prevent people from falling off of raised decks, platforms, and stairways and *handrails,* which people grab for stability as they climb or descend stairs. In this chapter, "railings" usually refers to guardrails, but later in the stair chapter, I'll discuss the requirements for a code-complying handrail.

Posts

The posts connect the railing system to the deck. They must be strong and they must be fastened to the deck in a way that resists the forces applied through leverage. Wood is the most common post material because it is easy to work and is readily available in the 4×4 and 6×6 sizes often used for posts. Sometimes, posts have a central structural core of wood, with an overlay of a different material.

Because metal is much stronger than wood, metal posts can be smaller in section. Metal posts

Posts are often attached to the outside of the rim joist, which adds definition to the railing system. Unnotched posts are harder to attach and can make the railing look less secure, but notching should be done with caution to avoid weakening the rail system.

PRO TIP

If my railing has post caps, I usually leave one of them loose (or removable) and make a hiding spot underneath it for a spare door key.

IN DETAIL

Posts that aren't covered by a continuous top or cap rail should have more than a simple flat cut on top to provide protection against the weather. The post's open end grain will absorb water readily and eventually crack. Manufactured wood caps are available in a variety of decorative styles, from lathe-turned finials to simple pyramids. My favorite caps from Maine Ornamental Woodworkers (See Resources, p. 179) have a copper overlay that ages to a beautiful dark patina. Caps can be glued in place with construction adhesive, nailed, or screwed.

Post caps are a simple (but not inexpensive) way to add interest to a railing. They are easy to install and can introduce shape, color, and material changes all at once.

Posts attached inside the rim move the whole railing system inboard, creating an integrated look but taking up some deck floor space.

can be fabricated at a local welding shop so that they can be bolted to the deck and accept wooden rails. Larger all-metal sections consisting of posts and balustrade can also be fabricated.

Posts are attached to the deck in two basic ways. They are either a continuation of the foundation post system, or they are separate posts attached with bolts to one side or the other of the framing at the edge of the deck. Posts that don't continue up from the foundation provide more options. They can be placed outside the deck's rim joists, partially notched over the rim joist, or set entirely inside the rim joist. And they can be placed more frequently or be a different size than the foundation posts.

On about half my decks, the posts are 4×4s lapped over the outside of the deck's rim joist—(I don't use 6×6s outside the rim because they look too bulky and are hard to attach). When I do install the post, I usually notch it, even though this weakens it. Otherwise, the entire railing system ends up too far outboard of the deck surface, giving it the appearance of a railing that is about to fly away.

The remainder of the decks I build have their posts mounted inboard of the rim joist. This works well for both 4×4 and 6×6 posts, although again, the 6×6s are harder to attach because of their size. This type of installation puts the post completely inside the decking surface, looks solid and well-integrated from the deck, and doesn't disrupt the horizontal continuity of the rim as seen from the outside. Unfortunately, locating the railing system here also uses up part of the deck surface. Occasionally, when I need every square inch of deck surface, I will notch an inboard post to move it out a little bit, but this adds labor and again, weakens the post for only a slight gain. You'll need to plan the locations of posts inside the rim carefully so that they don't land where there's already a joist.

Top and bottom rails

Most railings systems have a horizontal top and bottom rail, although some may have extra intermediate rails. Still other systems have nothing but horizontal rails and no vertical components between the posts. Rails must meet code requirements for strength and be made of good material and well-secured to the posts. The rails add rigidity to the system by interconnecting posts, which keeps one post from absorbing the brunt of any stress loading; rails also support the balustrade. But perhaps equally important, rails give us a place to set a drink or plate at cookouts or our elbows during stargazing sessions.

Often a top rail is composed of two layers; I call the top layer the cap rail because it goes on last and caps the whole affair. Having a doubled top rail has several advantages. Besides being thicker and stronger, it's also less prone to sag over time. And with two top rails, the joints can be staggered if the rails aren't available in one continuous length. The cap rail also can cover the fasteners used to attach the lower top rail to the posts, and in turn can be attached without exposed fasteners by screwing up through the lower top rail into underside of the cap rail.

Alternate Rails and Caps
Railings can be flat or vertical, and caps can be single, doubled, sloped, or missing entirely.

Sloped Top Cap or Typical Flat Railing

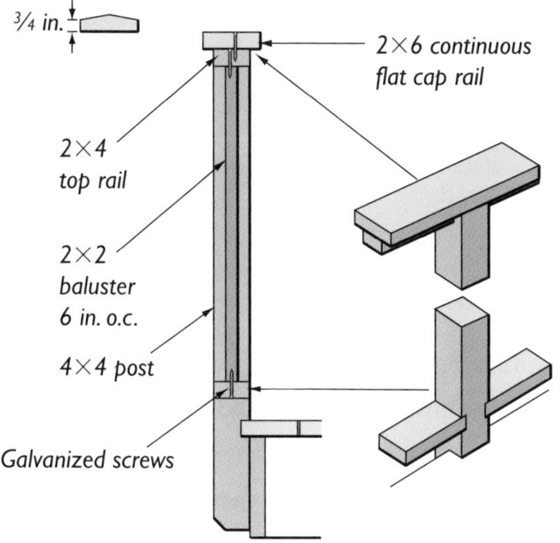

Typical Vertical Rails with Flat 5/4 Cap

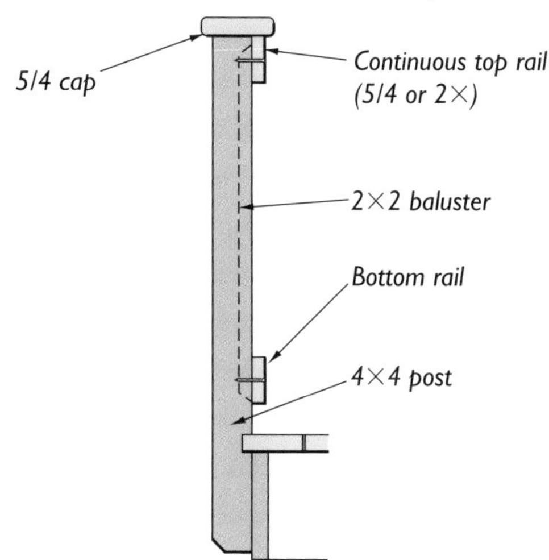

Because of their horizontal orientation, railings are exposed to more rain and sunshine and often show deterioration from lack of maintenance before other components do. Adding some slope to a flat cap rail helps eliminate standing water and gives the railing a more sculpted look. In fact, designers often put a slope on cap rails specifically to keep folks from putting objects on them, which could then inadvertently get knocked off onto passersby down below.

Boxed Posts

Sometimes you may want the look of a post that is larger than normal but without the associated problems (such as splitting and twisting) that come with large, solid-wood posts. The solution is to build a boxed post. This is basically a four-sided sleeve that fits over a conventionally installed treated post. I use this system when the post is inside the edge of a deck; (fitting a sleeve to a post fitted to the outside of the joists would be difficult and time-consuming). I make the inside dimensions of the box slightly larger than the post so that I can adjust it during installation.

The sides can be butted and nailed to each other, but I prefer to use waterproof glue and biscuits to join the edges of the sleeve together. If the post is to have a natural finish, I also miter the long edges by ripping them on the table saw at 45 degrees before I glue them together.

After I assemble the sleeve, I cut it to length, slide it down over the post, wedge it in place at the top and bottom, and hold it in place with screws or nails. The open top of the sleeve will need a cap, which can either be purchased or assembled on site. I sometimes wrap the base and the area directly under the cap with a separate layer of trim or molding to match the style of the building. To encourage air circulation and discourage moisture-related problems, I keep the bottom of the box slightly raised off of the deck surface by setting it on small feet of stainless-steel washers and screws.

Boxed Post Sleeve
A decorative box fits over a treated post that has been attached to the deck framing. Mitered joints, ripped and glued with biscuits, make the box appear as a single timber.

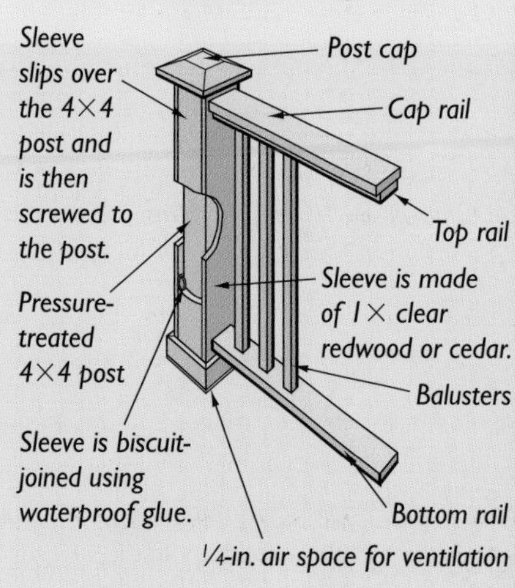

PRO TIP

Inboard posts can be bolted not only to the rim joist but also from a different direction to extra blocking added to the joist framing.

IN DETAIL

Decks must have enough posts to meet code, which is a function not only of the posts' size and how well they are anchored, whether notched or not, but also the strength of the railing system. A continuous post that is part of the foundation system is usually rock-solid, whereas separate posts attached to 2×6 joists aren't easy to strengthen. A second consideration is the span of the rails and the rigidity of the balustrade. Single 2×4 rails will feel springy if they span more than 4 to 5 ft., but adding a cap rail can increase the span to 6 ft. or 7 ft. (about the maximum that I feel comfortable with). I like to be safe and use more posts rather than fewer.

TRADE SECRET

If there are a lot of posts to be cut, I set up a fence with a stop on my miter saw. This is the fastest and most accurate way to make repeat cuts. But if there are only 10 or so posts to cut, then it probably is just as fast to cut one end of each post, mark the length, and cut the other end.

Adding an angled block to the framing at the point where a corner post will be bolted will give the washer and nut a flat landing spot.

flat of the rim. A single post seems as if it would be half the work, but it is a harder installation. For one thing, fastening is awkward because bolts are installed diagonally through both the post and the corner of the deck framing, rather than through a flat face. However, a triangular block on the back side of the framing can help diagonal nuts and washers sit flat. If other posts are notched, a single corner post will require a more difficult mortise-type notch on its inside corner to be in line.

Using two posts per corner lets me use posts that have the same notch-and-bolting configuration as the intermediate posts. To avoid having to put a short balustrade between the two posts, I lay these posts out so that they aren't more than the code-mandated maximum of 4 in. apart. Although this is a simpler installation in some regards, it means that railings will be cantilevered past these posts and rigidity will depend on how well they can be fastened together.

Intermediate posts

Once the location of the corner posts is determined and drawn on the deck, I determine the location of the intermediate posts. I like to have equally sized rail sections, so I divide the total distance between the centers of the corner posts by the number of railing sections, which is a function of the desired span between posts and the total length. This gives me the distance from the center of one post to the center of the next post. Since these represent the centers of the posts, I then add cutlines one-half the post width outside the center marks in both directions to represent the actual

Double corner posts simplify installation but increase visual complexity.

A single corner post is harder to attach to the framing but produces a simpler look.

Here, the decking is marked for cutting a notch for the corner posts.

The notch for the post is cut with a jigsaw.

The finished notch should be flush with the finished surface of the deck framing.

width of the post. When I'm done, the distance between posts should be approximately equal.

I lay out the notches in the decking carefully; they should be snug to help support the posts. If the decking is cut flush with the rim, then I can simply mark the post locations on the ends of the decking and the rim joist.

Once the post locations are marked, I cut the notches in the decking with a jigsaw. If the posts are inboard of the rim, the posts will need a four-sided hole in the decking. Unless there is room in the gap to start the cut, this means I need to drill a couple of starter holes for the jigsaw blade. Because post sizes can vary slightly, I test all the notches with actual posts as I cut them, trimming the sides of the notch as necessary with a sharp chisel if the fit is too tight.

Cutting posts

Next, all the posts need to be cut to length, notched if necessary, and predrilled for bolting. Post length is determined by adding the height of the post above the deck surface to the amount below the deck surface. The height above the deck will depend on the design, but remember that the top rail must be at least 36 in. above the deck to meet code. Generally, the bottom of the post is level with the bottom of the rim or just slightly above.

If the posts run continuously from the foundation up to the railings and were left long, they'll need to be cut to length in place. I measure and mark the height on the end posts, then snap a chalkline between them to mark the intermediate posts. I scribe a line around each post with a square and pencil and then cut it with a circular saw.

After noncontinuous posts are cut to length, they may need to be notched to fit the rim, depending on your design. This is a somewhat tedious process that must be done accurately. First, you need to lay out the notches. Rather than do a lot of measuring and marking, I like to use a small adjustable tri-square with a 1-in.-wide blade. Layout is then simply a matter of laying the square along the side of the post and scribing a cutline. The only dimension that needs to be measured then is the distance from the bottom of the post to the top of the notch. Measure and mark this on the face of the post (making sure that the best face of the post will be the most visible when the post is installed), scribe a square cutline across, and extend this line down to meet the cutlines on both sides.

Then I crosscut at this line with a circular saw set to the notch depth. Next, I rip cuts from both sides with the saw set at full depth and pop out the waste with a chisel. Before setting the post in position, I make sure to clean up the notch with my chisel.

PRO TIP

Post length is determined by adding the height of the post above the deck surface to the amount below the deck surface.

TRADE SECRET

Adding a dado to the post before it's installed is simplified by using a router equipped with a straight-cutting bit and jig. The jig follows the edges of the router. To make the jig, build a "ladder" with two scraps (here I used baluster material) tight and parallel to the post length and screw on two 1× crosspieces. The space between the crosspieces should be the router base width plus the groove width. The first pass with the router will cut a groove in the jig, which you then can align with layout marks on the post.

The blade of an adjustable square works as a guide for layout of a 1-in.-deep notch.

Set the saw blade cutting depth using the layout line.

Crosscut the end of the notch.

The final cuts for the side of the notch are with the grain.

Pop the waste chunk out by prying with a chisel or a small bar.

Using a chisel, clean out the inside of the notch where the saw couldn't reach.

Once the post is cut to length and is square on both ends, a decorative chamfer can be added to the bottom with a miter box before installation.

If the posts lap over the outside of the rim, then their bottoms will be visible. In this case, I like to bevel or chamfer their bottom edges to make them more attractive. You could chamfer one or all three exposed corners; first use a square to scribe a cutline about ¾ in. from the end, and then cut the chamfer on a power miter box or a table saw with the blade set at 45 degrees.

While the posts are on a flat surface and I'm still able to work on them in a comfortable position, I attend to a few more details that are a lot easier to do before post installation. First, if the bottom rail of the balustrade is flat and butts into the post, I like to house it in a dado for extra support. Creating this joint takes a little extra time, but it allows the railing to take the weight of someone who wants to stand on it for a better view. One way to cut this dado is with a router set up with either a ½-in.-diameter or ¾-in.-diameter straight bit. I cut the dado so that it's about ½ in. deep, but I usually make the cut in two ¼-in. deep passes. Another way to cut this dado is with a circular saw set to the depth of the groove. I make multiple passes with the saw, then clean out the waste with a chisel. Although this dado can be cut with either a router or a saw after

Finishing Post Tops

Manufactured caps offer good protection for post ends, but they are expensive. You can decorate the end of your posts yourself inexpensively, using a router and miter box, but keep in mind that a lasting installation must be waterproofed. The simplest decoration is to cut the top in a gentle pyramidal shape, which also helps water to drain off. To cut a pyramid, set your chop saw at about 20 degrees to 30 degrees and cut completely through the post. Then turn the post over and make the second cut to produce a centered ridge. Rotate the piece and add the final two sloping cuts, each time aligning the blade by eye so that you wind up with a four-sided point at the end.

Adding a horizontal routed band beneath this pyramid provides a bit more style and can be done with a V-grooving bit, a cove bit, or a straight cutting bit. Mark the location for the band, and clamp a speed square or framing square to the post to help guide the base of your router and keep it square to the post. Limit the depth of your cut to about ¼ in. per pass and make multiple passes.

PRO TIP

If the posts lap over the outside of the rim, their bottoms will be visible. I like to bevel or chamfer their bottom edges to make the posts more attractive.

IN DETAIL

Notching any 4×4 post by any amount will weaken it to the point where it may fail code requirements. While I've never seen one of my notched posts fail in 20 years of building, I've never subjected one to the measured stresses of code requirements either. So in the interest of safety…

- Don't notch your posts unless they are larger than 4×4 or are securely tied to each other with connecting rails.
- Don't notch more than an inch.
- Use defect-free material.
- Don't notch where a post failure would be a disaster and never on decks more than 4 ft. off the ground.
- Don't even consider using notched 2×4s, a common but frail railing post that I see too often.

A dado in the railing post to support the bottom rail will strengthen this joint, which often bears the weight.

After layout, make closely spaced cross-grain cuts with a circular saw set to the dado depth.

Clean up the bottom of the dado with a sharp chisel.

the posts have been installed, cutting in the horizontal position is awkward (and more risky). Don't forget that end posts near openings or walls probably won't need notches on both sides if there aren't railing segments.

If the posts are going to be bolted to the outside of the rim, this is a good time to lay out and predrill the post bolt holes. (Posts mounted inside the rim are not predrilled before installation.) This is also the best time to add a decorative finish to the top of the posts if they aren't going to be covered by a cap rail.

+ SAFETY FIRST

Although you can use a circular saw instead of a power miter saw to bevel-cut the bottoms of posts, this can be dangerous. For one thing, the base doesn't have a lot of support, making the saw unstable. You may also be tempted to manually hold the blade guard up, since many guards don't retract well when in this position. And the small wedge-shaped offcut can become a flying projectile or become wedged between the blade and the blade guard.

Bolting posts

Most posts are best attached with at least two ½-in.-diameter hot-dipped galvanized bolts. I locate these bolts as far apart as possible for stability, but not too close to joist edges, which can cause splitting and crowd washer and nut installation. The best location is usually about 1 in. away from the joist edges. I usually align the bolts directly on top of each other in the center of the post, but staggering them vertically will help minimize any chance of the post splitting under stress.

First, I hold the post in position (this is easier if I have a helper) and use a level to make sure the post is close to plumb in both directions. Then I continue the predrilled upper hole all the way through the post, rim joist, and blocking. I insert the upper bolt, using a hammer to drive the bolt in if the fit is snug, then add the nut and washer, and hand-tighten. After I check again that the post is plumb (especially left and right), I drill the lower hole and add the lower bolt, washer, and nut, then tighten both nuts securely from the back side with a socket wrench. I use this same sequence for the rest of the posts.

After the posts are installed and I've fastened the bolts wrench-tight, I check again for plumb. If the rim joist isn't exactly plumb or if the notches are uneven, chances are good that the post will lean slightly in or out. This may not matter much if the top rail is continuous, because the rail will help to hold all the posts in line. But if I need to correct for plumb, I remove the post and then plane or chisel the notch to correct the plumb. Another option is to add small cedar shims between the posts and framing to bring the posts to plumb.

Sometimes there isn't typical joist framing, so there's nothing to bolt posts to. This can be the case with a balcony, a roof deck, or a deck on sleepers over concrete. In these instances, the post has to be attached to a metal connector, which in turn has been anchored to something below. For these kinds of applications, a local steel supplier can fabricate a strong metal connector to your specifications. These connectors are typically thick metal base plates with a welded vertical component that attaches to the post.

The vertical component can be 1½-in.-diameter round pipe hidden and glued with epoxy inside a bored-out post or a single vertical steel plate that fits into a slot cut into the center of the post and is held in place with bolts. A third design features two vertical plates that form a "U" with the base and lap the outside of the post instead of fitting in a slot. This connector is easier

Before drilling, be sure the post is reasonably plumb. A second person is a big help.

After plumbing, continue the predrilled hole of the post into the joist.

Then insert the upper bolt and add the washer and nut, finger tight to the back side.

Double-check for plumb between holes.

Drill the lower hole and add nuts and washers.

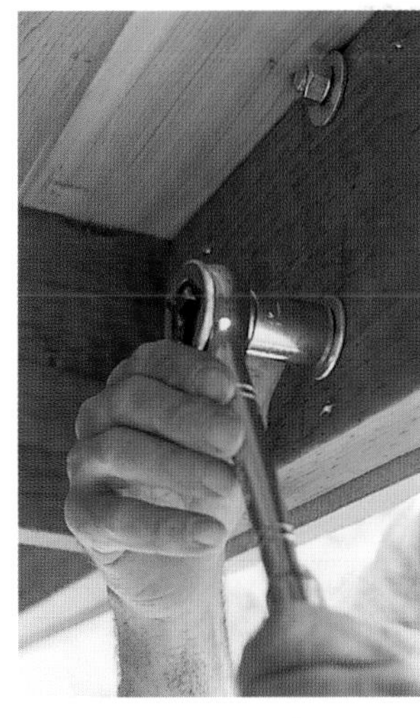
Finally, tighten the bolts and recheck for plumb in both directions. You might need to loosen nuts and trim the post or add shims to correct a lean.

PRO TIP

When fastening posts, I use carriage bolts, because they are simpler for one person to install and are less obtrusive. But hex bolts and washers also work.

TRADE SECRET

Accurately laying out the same two holes on 20 posts can be speeded up considerably by making a jig to mark the centers of the bolt locations. Made of scrap plywood and 1× stock, this jig aligns with one side and the bottom of the post. The hole locations are laid out on the jig and then drilled through so that when the jig is slipped over the post, a sharp pencil or awl can be poked through to mark the holes.

IN DETAIL

When I'm using bolts with softwoods, it's best if the posts and rim are drilled with the same diameter hole as the size of the bolt. Wood that is hard, very wet, or very dry may require a hole that is sized 1⁄16 in. larger than the diameter of the bolt.

Posts may need to be trimmed or shimmed (as shown) to keep them plumb.

to attach but more visible. The base plates need to be extremely well-anchored with long lags, through bolts, or concrete anchors, and special sealing precautions must be taken with gaskets, flashing, and caulk to prevent water from penetrating any untreated wood below.

Reinforcing the framing

The rim joist is usually attached to the ends of the regular joists with 16d nails. If posts are attached only to the rim joist, this connection may need to be reinforced. Using extra screws when attaching the decking boards to the perimeter of the framing is a good start. Another reinforcement is to add a heavy metal T-strap on top of the spot where the regular joists meet the rim, but this must be done before you install the decking. You may want to recess the strap a little into the framing with a chisel or router so that it won't interfere with the decking. Lag bolts through the rim into the joist ends will also help, though this is a bit of an ugly solution. The lags need to be driven at least 3 in. into the end of the joists.

Another way to reinforce the rim joist is with wood blocking, parallel to and either directly behind the rim or against the back of an inboard

Metal Brackets For Post Bases

If a post can't be bolted to the framing below, a fabricated metal bracket will hold it sturdy. Brackets need broad bases with long lags or through bolts and a sturdy connection at the top railing to tie posts together. On roof decks, flashing will be necessary if the bolts penetrate the waterproof layer.

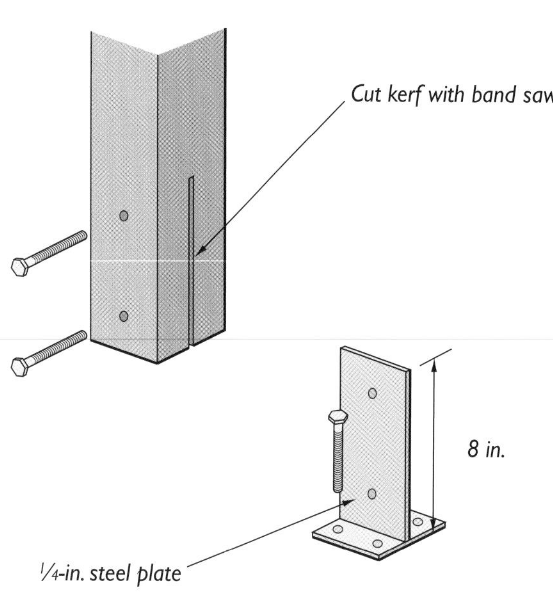

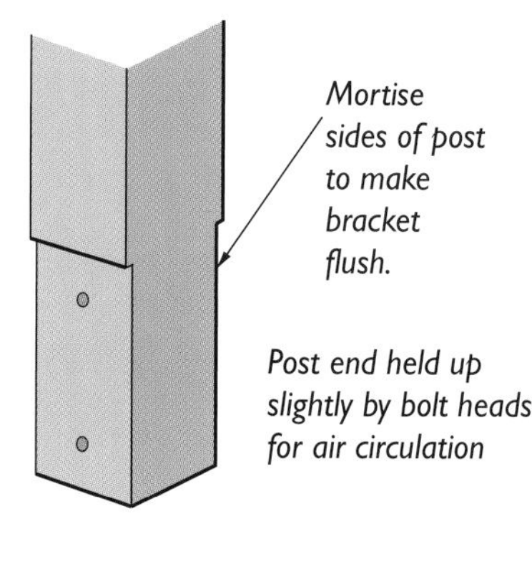

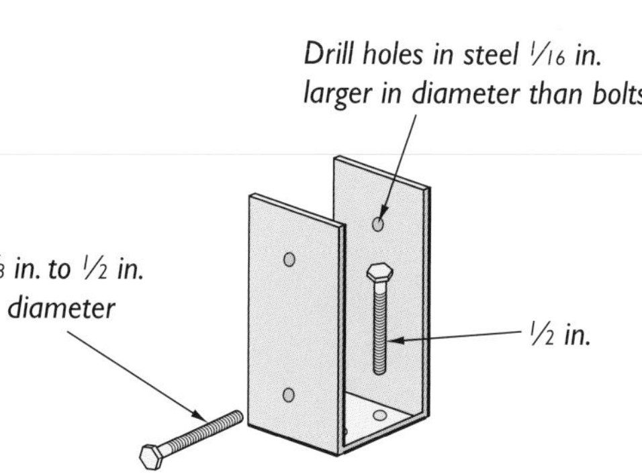

Metal bases need to be larger than posts unless the posts are stabilized by corner or top rails.

Blocking can be added between joists at railing-post locations to add stability.

mounted post. This blocking needs to be securely fastened to the framing with 16d nails or 3½-in.-long screws.

On the sides of the deck parallel to the joists, extra blocking is needed at least every 4 ft. to keep the end joist from bending in and out under pressure from the post. If the post is on the back side of the end joist, I position the blocking against the post so that the posts can be bolted to the blocking. Blocks can also be placed on either side of the post for an even stronger connection. If the posts are mounted on the outside of the joist, the blocks (like the rim) can benefit from reinforcement in the form of extra screws, straps, or lags.

Building a Balustrade

Just as there are many different styles of balustrades, there are many ways of building them. Depending on the design, the balustrade—the combination of top and bottom rails and balusters—can be built in place one piece at a time or installed as completed sections that start and stop at each post. The rails can either be laid flat and oriented horizontally, with balusters that butt into the face of the rails, or they can be oriented vertically on edge, with balusters attached to the side of the rails. Either type of balustrade can be topped with a cap rail.

"Ladder"-style balustrade between posts

This deck's railing system involves installing a 1½-in. thick top and bottom rail without balusters, covering the top rail and posts with a cap rail, and then filling in between posts with a sectional ladder balustrade using ¾-in. thick secondary rails. This yields a two-layer bottom rail and a triple-layer top rail. Simpler versions without secondary rails can be built in sections with balusters butting directly into 1½-in. thick top and bottom rails or with balusters attached to vertical rails (see pp. 138–139).

For systems with sectional balustrades, the rail lengths are measured between installed posts. Because the posts may not be exactly parallel at this stage, take your measurements for the top rail from post face to post face near deck level. After the top rail is installed, the posts will be brought into parallel. And remember to add extra length to

Balustrades can be built in ladder-like sections and added to already-installed upper and lower rails.

PRO TIP

On the sides of the deck parallel to the joists, blocking is needed at least every 4 ft. to keep the end joist from bending under pressure from the post.

IN DETAIL

Lag screws are a poor alternative to threaded bolts with nuts, but they are necessary when a carriage bolt won't work. In order to be strong enough, a lag screw needs to be long enough—about 8 or 9 in.—to go through the post, the rim, and on into the end grain of the joist by several inches. Predrill the post only for the shank of the lag screw, and use a smaller bit to predrill the rim and joist.

TRADE SECRET

When you push a bolt through a hole, chances are that the threads will pick up a lot of wood shavings. Be sure to clean them off with a wire brush before you try to add the nuts.

IN DETAIL

You may want to use lattice for your balustrade, but most manufactured wood lattice I've seen is too thin and splintery. Don't even consider the plastic variety; it has a hard time even holding itself up. If you want to use lattice, you're best off making your own out of properly sized and fastened stock.

Balusters

Balusters can be made from a variety of materials including steel, copper, or acrylic, but I usually use wood 2×2 balusters in the same material as my decking. I buy them premade in 10-ft. lengths with gently eased edges and in a clear grade for strength and longevity, and cut them to the final length on site.

The length for butted balusters on a 36-in.-tall railing is about 27½ in., which allows for a double top rail, a single bottom rail, and a 4-in. space above the decking. Balusters that lap almost the full width of top and bottom vertical rails measure about 30 in. long with a 1½-in. cap rail.

Balusters should be screwed (not nailed) to rails with high-quality screws for strength and corrosion resistance. Lapped balusters in brittle woods such as southern yellow pine may need to be predrilled to minimize splitting, but softer woods such as cedar may not need it. Butted balusters with screws entering their end grain usually will not require predrilling, but if yours do, keep the pilot hole as small as possible.

Because posts may not be perfectly plumb, measure rail lengths at deck level, being sure to add the depths of any notches to the length of the bottom rails.

the top rail measurement if your bottom rail fits into the post grooves that were cut into the posts.

I cut the 1½-in. rails to length on a chopsaw and attach them to the post with screws. Wherever possible on all designs, all railing screws should be placed so they are hidden from view and protected from the weather. On the top rail (which will be covered by a cap) railing screws can be toescrewed from above, with the holes predrilled if necessary to keep the rail ends from

First, predrill the top rail to keep the rail ends from splitting.

Then toescrew the top rail into the post, using at least two fasteners.

splitting. When you are fastening the top rails to the posts, a good way to ensure a tight connection is to pinch the rail between the posts with the aid of a nylon ratchet-type cargo strap.

The bottom rail can be toescrewed from underneath. I try to use at least two screws at the ends of each rail at each post; if the design doesn't give you room for enough fasteners, however, connections sometimes may need reinforcement with metal clips of some type. After the top and bottom rails are in place, you can install the cap rail, screwing up through the top rail to keep the screws hidden.

Now the horizontal distance between the posts can be double-checked, and the secondary rails cut to length to fit snugly. To get the baluster length, measure the vertical distance and subtract the thickness of the ¾-in. rails. (Here you need to measure carefully and accurately to avoid gaps or oversize problems later on.) Now all of the balusters (and there may be dozens of them) can be accurately cut to length.

Next, from a short section of 2×6, I make a spacer block that is the width of the space between balusters. Technically, the distance between balusters is 4 in. (maximum), but I make my spacer block about 3⅞ in. wide to allow some shrinkage of the balusters. This block will be used first to determine the location of the starting baluster and then to space balusters the correct distance apart as they are being screwed in place, one at a time.

A ratchet strap can be used to pinch the top rail tightly between the posts.

To locate the first baluster, find the center of the rails and mark it on the top and bottom rails. This mark represents either the center of a baluster or the center of the space between balusters. Using the spacer block in combination with a scrap of baluster. Step off a quick layout—first using a baluster centered on the rail center mark and then with the spacer block centered on the rail center mark—to determine the size of the last space at the end of the rail for both possibilities. The space between the last baluster and the post should be as large as possible, but not exceeding 4 in. It will be easier to gain momentum for this

Attaching the cap rail from underneath keeps the fasteners hidden.

Fastening the bottom rail from underneath helps keep the fasteners protected from the weather.

+ SAFETY FIRST

Horizontal balustrades must be stronger than vertical balustrades to accommodate the increased span of going from post to post. Instead of 2×2s, common horizontal baluster choices include metal tubing, 5/4×6 boards for privacy, and large-diameter wooden doweling. But before you build any style of ladder-type railing, check your local code. Some codes prohibit these types of balustrades, because they are so easy for children to climb.

PRO TIP

When attaching balusters, you may need to mark the baluster centers first and then predrill the rails before screwing to ensure a tight butt connection.

IN DETAIL

Cutting a few hundred balusters quickly and accurately requires a repetitive-cut stop block. You can mount your miter saw to an 8-ft.-long 2×12 using screws and washers so it can't move about. Add a couple of blocks on either side of the saw and at the same height, and fasten these blocks down with screws. Then screw down a 1× stop block located exactly the baluster length from the miter sawblade. A second block in line with the back fence of the miter box will help speed correct positioning of the baluster.

With the top and bottom rails in place, carefully measure the opening size for the rails of the ladder balustrade.

Balusters are cut most quickly and accurately using a power miter box with a stop block setup.

Use a spacer block to help lay out the balusters.

Spacer strips screwed to a scrap plywood help hold the balusters in the center of the rail.

Fasten the balusters to the bottom rail with 3-in.-long weather-resistant screws, using the spacer block to help position them accurately.

Once all the balusters have been attached to one rail, flip the unit over and attach the other rail, taking care to align the first baluster.

task if the posts are evenly spaced and the balustrade lengths are similar.

The balusters are attached to the ¾-in. thick secondary rail by screwing through from the outside of the rail into the end grain of the baluster. Place the rail on edge and set out a row of precut balusters. To help align the balusters across the width of the rail, I make a quick jig by screwing some spacer strips to a sheet of plywood. The strips should be of the correct thickness to hold the balusters so they are positioned automatically at the center of the rail. Once the first couple of balusters are in place, it's a simple process to continue fastening the rest of the balusters, leapfrogging with the spacer block to the end of the rail. When you have fastened the balusters to one rail, flip the assembly over and do the other rail, being careful to keep both rail center marks and first balusters aligned to produce a square balustrade. As a final touch to stop any chance that the balusters can rotate, I add a galvanized finish nail into the end of the baluster. Finally, each rail section can be lifted up (see the photo on p. 133), slid into place, and fastened to the already-installed main rails. I try to put fasteners every 8 in. or so, screwing up into the upper rail and lower rail to keep the fasteners concealed and protected from the weather.

Predrilling rails

When attaching balusters to a thicker or harder rail material, you may need to mark the baluster centers first and then predrill the rails before screwing to ensure a tight butt connection. First, find the location of the starting baluster as

A galvanized 6d nail set into the baluster helps keep it from rotating.

Fasten the lower rails, being sure to use appropriately sized screws that won't protrude through the rail.

Fasten the preassembled balustrade to the rail system by screwing up through the upper rails.

✓ According to Code

Most codes allow a maximum 4-in. spacing between balusters. This is simple enough to determine for straight vertical balusters, but if you introduce any curves, cutouts, or extra horizontal members, they too must meet the spacing requirement. But what about horizontal balusters that look like a ready-made ladder? A 4-in. spacing makes these hard to climb but not unclimbable, and while national codes don't prohibit horizontal balusters (multiple rails), some local codes might. Regardless of whether a railing is code-compliant or not, if you have small children you are better off building a railing system that is as safe as possible.

A finished balustrade.

PRO TIP

To save time, I predrill both rails at the same time by placing one on top of the other.

Laying Out Baluster Centers for Predrilling Rails

Layout of baluster centers can be done with dividers or a block. Lay out only one rail but drill both simultaneously.

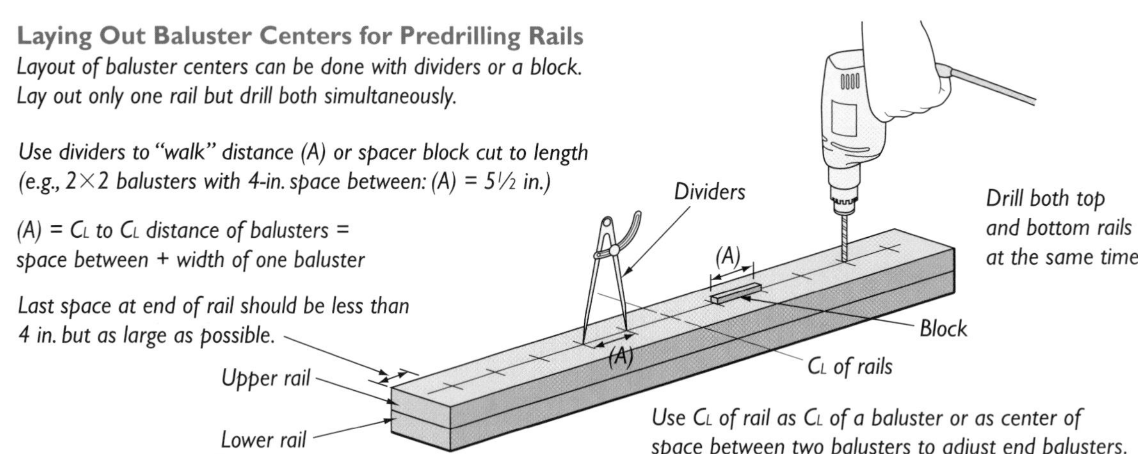

IN DETAIL

Depending on which code has jurisdiction, a railing might need to resist a concentrated load of 200 lb. applied outward at any point. It may need to resist a 50 lb./lf load applied horizontally at the same time as a load of 100 lb./lf is applied vertically or maybe just survive a simple 20 lb./lf horizontal load requirement. While the numbers are a minimum guideline and must be met for your location, practically speaking you don't want the railing to fail, ever. Your railing should survive one big bruiser hitting your rail at full speed at its weakest point, or 10 people at a party leaning over at the same time. Build it strong! If the posts wiggle and feel insubstantial before adding the rest of the rails, you've failed already and it probably will too.

Baluster Strength

Balusters have to be able to withstand a 200-lb. force applied horizontally to a 1-sq.-ft. section of the balustrade. This test not only determines the strength of individual balusters, but also whether they are adequately fastened to the rails. Unofficial tests have shown that 1½-in. square #2 yellow pine balusters can meet the first part of this requirement; (interestingly, so do ¾-in.-square yellow pine balusters, though I don't recommend using them).

My guess is that #2 cedar would pass the test too, but I don't risk it; I always use a stronger clear grade. Unofficial tests also show that a single 6d toe nail, driven into a predrilled hole and connecting the baluster to the rail, would meet the code's strength requirements. While I would never suggest using just one nail, these unofficial findings bolster my confidence in my attachment system. I always use at least two fasteners in each end—typically one screw and one small toenail. If you have any doubts about the strength of your system, decrease the spacing between members, increase their size, or add more fasteners.

described previously, but carefully step off and mark the other baluster centers using the spacer and baluster scrap combination. Alternatively, a pair of dividers can be set to the distance between baluster centers and "walked" down the rail. To make sure each baluster ends up centered across the rail width, use an adjustable square or marking gauge to draw a long line down the center of the rail on the hidden side.

An alternative rail system

A second railing system illustrates a slightly different approach to rail orientation and layout technique. The rails are aligned vertically and the balusters attached by screwing through the face of the rails. Although the balustrade is still built in sections, these sections are built long and then trimmed to the exact length, which minimizes layout at this stage.

First, measure and record the exact lengths of the rails between the post faces—(the top of a post can be a handy spot). Then cut the top and bottom rails so that they are at least 8 in. longer than the finished length of the section. Next, mark the center of the rails and use that as the center of the starting baluster, then continue adding balusters using a spacer block as before. It's important to make sure that each baluster is flush and square to each rail as it is fastened. Then flip the rail section over and fasten rails to the back side.

Screw through the face of each rail to attach it to the sides of the balusters.

When I cut the section to its final length, I want the distance from the post to the first baluster to be equal at both ends. So I pull my tape measure out to the required length of the finished unit and lay it on top of the rail, moving it back and forth until the zero end of the tape and the needed length measurement overhang the first and last balusters by the same amount. This measurement should be as close to 4 in. as possible without exceeding it; (you may find that you'll have to remove a baluster). This is where the rails should be cut to length, either with a circular saw or—with the rail section set up on supports—a power miter saw.

Continuous balustrade layout

If continuous rails are called for, you'll need to lay out and install the balusters after the rails have been installed. Although the layout for each section between posts is done individually, each section should be similar if the distance between posts is close to the same.

Once the position of the central baluster has been determined as before, the central baluster is screwed in place, plumb and square to both rails. Then, again using a spacer block, install the rest of the balusters, one at a time. I also use this method

Curved Rails

If your deck has curves, you'll need curved railings. Rails for curved deck sections can be laminated together from thin layers of wood or sawn from short mitered sections of stock joined end to end using waterproof glue and biscuits or splines.

1. Lay out the curves on a large piece of plywood. You can use a trammel, or use a string as shown in the drawing below.
2. Tack the string in one corner of the plywood, scribe the outside arc of the rail (taking into account the rail's position on the deck), then shorten the string by the design width of the rail and scribe the inside arc.
3. Then lay the rail stock (either laminated or glued together in sections) onto the plywood and retrace the scribes as shown.
4. Finally, cut out the curved sections with a jigsaw, sanding it smooth and profiling it to match the rails on the straight sections of deck.

Curved Railing

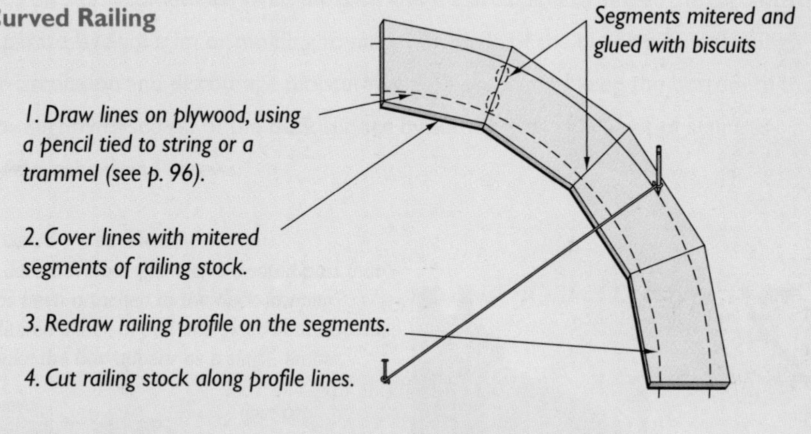

Screw each baluster through the rail on both sides.

PRO TIP

To help strengthen a railing system, run the railing or cap rail to the house wall and fasten it there with screws or metal connectors on the underside.

TRADE SECRET

As a final touch, ease the edges of the rails with a router before sliding them into place and fastening them to the posts with screws. Use the climb-cutting technique (cutting in the direction of rotation) to help reduce splintering, particularly with the splintery woods that are often used for decking.

Cap rail laps should fall over posts. When this beveled lap is slid home, it will stay tighter than a square butt joint.

Cap rails are mitered, predrilled, and screwed at the corners.

when there is no bottom rail and the balusters lap onto the rim joist framing.

Cap rail

Most railings are topped with a cap rail. I use a high-quality piece of 5⁄4 or 2× material in as long a length as I can find. The rail can be routed to ease hard corners or, if it's thick enough, beveled on top to aid drainage. The 5⁄4 cap rails are usually screwed through the exposed face into the upper rail and into the posts; 2× cap rails can be screwed from underneath through predrilled holes.

If there have to be any joints in the cap rail, I cut beveled lap joints and have them fall over something solid underneath so they can be well fastened. Like a simple butt joint, a beveled lap joint can open up over time, but the joint won't be as noticeable. I use screws to fasten all corner miters to

Railing deadends can be softened by clipping the corners.

Routing the long edges and ends of cap rails completes the installation.

each other and to the posts or rail underneath. If the cap rail ends at a corner post, I cantilever the end a little and cut it to a semicircle or nip the corners at an angle rather than just cutting it square. As a final touch, I run a run a router equipped with a ⅜-in. radius or ½-in. radius roundover bit over all the cap rail upper edges. This surface is what the eye sees and where the hands rest; this final detailing makes the rail more pleasing to the eye and smoother to the touch (and also helps to prevent splinters).

A cable railing made with marine-type hardware is weather-resistant and doesn't obscure the view.

Railing Options

Although wooden railings are probably easier and less expensive to build, there are a lot of alternatives to wood that will give your deck an entirely different look. Some systems use wooden posts and rails, but replace the balustrade with glass panels, pipes, or cables. Other systems replace all of the wooden components with metal or plastic materials (or combinations of the two). And while these alternative systems may cost more in materials, they may be quicker to install, less visually obtrusive, match a style hard to produce in wood, and radically decrease or eliminate maintenance.

Tempered glass panels instead of a wooden balustrade will keep a view unimpeded but requires some dedication to keep clean.

Glass panel railings

Large, tempered-glass panels can be used to make see-through railings that also act as windscreens. These panels are widely available and inexpensive, because they can come from failed IG (insulating glass) sliding door panels. The glass is tempered, which makes it strong but uncuttable, so spacing between posts must be done with the panel size in mind. The glass can be held in place with grooves cut with a dado blade in the sides of the posts and in the top and bottom rails before installation. Alternatively, the panels can be held in place with wooden stops applied to both sides around the perimeter of each glass panel, a system that allows the panels to be easily removed for repair or replacement.

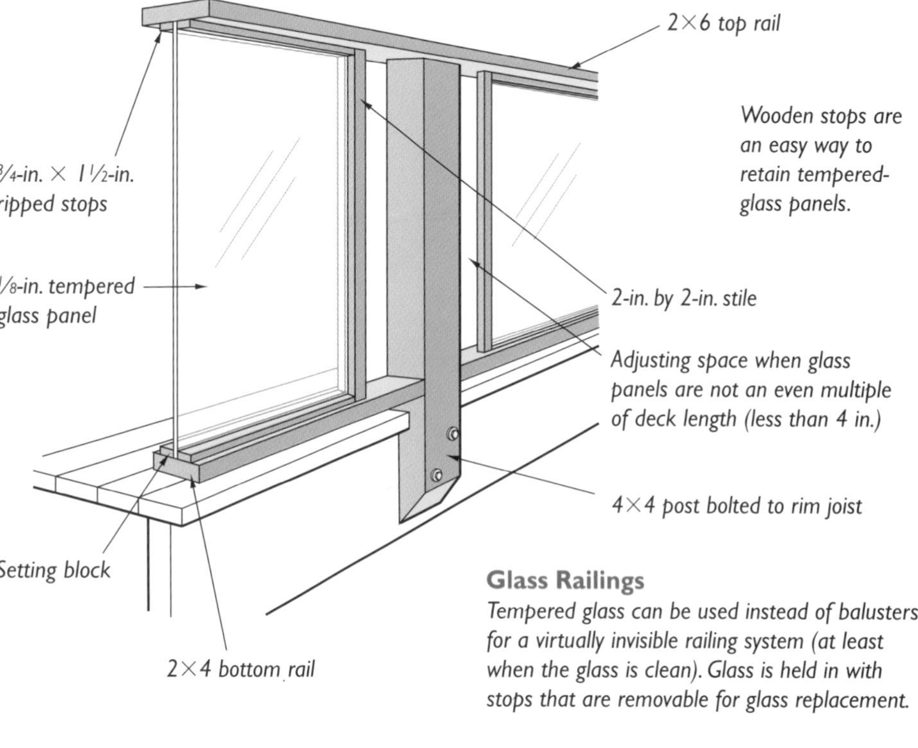

Glass Railings
Tempered glass can be used instead of balusters for a virtually invisible railing system (at least when the glass is clean). Glass is held in with stops that are removable for glass replacement.

PRO TIP

Polyvinyl chloride pipe is inherently too weak for long railings and often needs internal metal or wood reinforcement.

IN DETAIL

Glass panels should be set on thin rubber setting blocks, available from glass shops. Be sure to leave at least ¼ in. of extra space on the sides and top for expansion.

TRADE SECRET

Cables typically are run horizontally, but still need to comply with code-required spacing. I install them on 3-in. centers in order to maintain code compliance when they flex slightly.

IN DETAIL

The material costs for the cable and fittings that I generally use averages about $10 per lineal foot of railing. I order most of my supplies locally, but can also order by mail from the Feeney Wire Rope Co.

Cable rail

Over the last few years, cable rails have accounted for almost 25% of my railing installations. This system, which uses ⅛-in.-diameter stainless-steel cables with proprietary end fittings, is usually chosen for its unobtrusive presence rather than its beauty. (See the top photo on p. 141.) I first install wooden posts (although the posts could be metal too) with predrilled holes to accept the cable. Then I add a solid wood cap rail. I thread the cable through the holes and make the cable taut by tightening a nut on a threaded section on each strand.

When using cable, you have to take into account some special considerations, such as turning corners, using angle fittings for stairs, and carefully calculating the number of turns you can make with one cable, but these factors are clearly outlined in the manufacturer's literature. The woodwork involved in a cable rail system is standard fare and cable installation goes quickly, but like most manufactured systems (especially in stainless steel), material costs are more expensive than they would be for wood.

✓ According to Code

Most residential codes require the top of the highest rail in a system to be at least 36 in. from the deck surface. Typical commercial code height is 42 in., which makes a lot of sense on high decks but is also much more visually intrusive. Some codes require that the bottom rail be no more than 2 in. off of the deck, which doesn't offer a lot of clearance for shoveling snow or debris off the deck. I prefer to make this clearance 4 in., identical to the spacing between balusters. To meet code requirements in your area, you may be able to build some strategic sections with a higher bottom rail, then add a separate board or blocking that can be removed when necessary.

This cable end fitting has teeth that keep the cable locked in place. The other end is a nut-and-thread fitting for cinching the cable tight.

Manufactured railing systems

Just as there are lots of decking material alternatives to wood, there are also many different premanufactured railing systems built from composites, plastics, and metals.

These systems are far more expensive than wood railings, ranging in cost from $20 to $40 per foot uninstalled (with some urethane systems running over $150 per foot), but their big advantage is that they are largely maintenance-free. Some systems imitate wood, and others offer styles that would be difficult to duplicate in wood. Components are usually precut and ready to assemble because they have been ordered specifically for your deck's dimensions. Some railings may be broken down into individual pieces, and some may come in larger sections if components need to be welded or glued before shipping.

Polyvinyl chloride (PVC) railings. Like plastic decking, PVC railings are smooth and maintenance-free and can look like painted wood as long as you don't get too close. PVC is inherently too weak for long railings and often needs internal metal or wood reinforcement. Posts systems vary widely from posts with walls thick enough to stand alone to sleeves that cover a pressure-treated 4×4 to painted, galvanized, or aluminum pipe or square tubing with a mounting flange. PVC balusters and posts caps come in an amazing variety of shapes from simple squares to lathe-turned Victorian profiles.

Urethane. Another material that does a good job of imitating wood is high-density urethane foam. Although water-resistant, the foam will degrade in sunlight and so needs to be kept painted. Because urethane is easy to mold into forms, these pieces come in a larger variety of shapes than any other material except wood. One of the higher-priced systems available, urethane is often the material used on larger ornate pieces with classic, curvy shapes. Urethane takes skill and patience to install, and pieces are not usually preassembled into sections by the factory.

Fiberglass and other plastics. Some railings are made of fiber-reinforced plastic (FRP), or fiberglass, which is used on everything from boats to fishing rods. FRP is stronger than other plastics and can span larger distances without additional reinforcement. Less commonly available plastics made into railings include high-density polyethylene, acrylonitrile, and combinations of plastic with wood cores.

Metal. Metal railings are available that can be mounted to your own posts or factory-supplied posts. These are usually made from aluminum, and their higher strength can mean smaller sizes and less interference with a spectacular view. They usually come with a durable factory-baked finish.

Resin composites. One final material worth noting are the wood–resin composites. These contain recycled materials and do a pretty good job of imitating wood; they often are made by the same manufacturers that make decking composites. Composites won't shrink or warp and don't need a lot of maintenance. Some companies make components specifically for railings; others sell their material as a substitute for real wood, which you then fashion yourself using standard woodworking techniques. Some components are available with a smooth PVC colored coating or preprimed, but if not, most composites can be painted after a few months weathering.

Molded urethane can imitate ornate wooden railing parts and is durable and less expensive, but requires some specialized installation techniques.

Resin composite railing parts to match decking are available in various sizes analogous to wooden railings.

Plastic railing parts to match the decking are maintenance-free but require different installation techniques than wooden ones.

Factory-finished metal railings are durable and available in a variety of styles and colors that are hard to duplicate in wood.

Stairs and Ramps

CHAPTER SEVEN

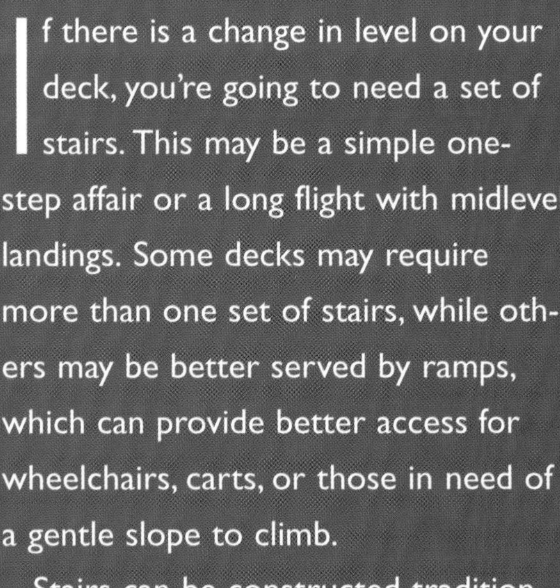

If there is a change in level on your deck, you're going to need a set of stairs. This may be a simple one-step affair or a long flight with midlevel landings. Some decks may require more than one set of stairs, while others may be better served by ramps, which can provide better access for wheelchairs, carts, or those in need of a gentle slope to climb.

Stairs can be constructed traditionally with a notched stringer for support or as a series of stacked boxes cascading down the slope. But regardless of how stairs and ramps are constructed, they need to be safely designed and constructed, with proper guardrails and handrails. In this chapter, I'll discuss several different approaches to stair construction, both how to build them and how to make them safe.

PRO TIP

Keep in mind that stairs with multiple turns or landings require extra foundation work.

IN DETAIL

Stairs should be shaped to fit their function. A set of stairs that traverses a large drop may need to be steeper, whereas a few steps between two levels can be long and wide, making them easier to navigate. Wider treads that are covered with ice are definitely safer than narrow, ice-covered stairs. For continuity and simplicity, I choose a tread width that is a multiple of my decking board width. For example, two 2×6s yield an 11-in.-plus tread. Three 2×6s yield a tread width of about 16½ in.

Single steps connect different deck levels.

Stair Location and Configuration

Stairs are built to get us from one level to another. On a deck, this typically means from the deck surface down to the surrounding lawn, driveway, or sidewalk. The stairs should be located with their frequency of use in mind. If the stairs represent the only access to a high-use area, then they should be placed squarely in the traffic pattern. But if the stairs serve an area needed only occasionally, they can be located out of the way so that they don't interfere with other deck uses. Siting stairs at the corners of the deck or alongside the house helps keep traffic patterns near the perimeter.

Stairs can also be used to connect two different levels of a deck. In this case, the stair location is less flexible. The only choice may be whether to make the stairs the whole width of the interface between the two levels, or just part of it. This will be determined by how adjacent areas are to be used, how many people will use the stairs, and whether the stairs will serve other functions, such as seating or support for planters.

+ SAFETY FIRST

When planning steps between level changes, give come consideration to the direction that the treads run. If possible, run the treads in a different direction from the main decking, which will help visually alert people to the approaching drop. It's amazing how much parallel decking board lines can disguise the top edge of a drop.

If possible, orient tread in a different direction than the decking to make a change in elevation easier to see.

Sizing the stairs

I like exterior stairs to be bigger than interior ones. Outside, you aren't faced with the same space constraints as inside, but there's also a difference of scale: Small steps surrounded by something literally as big as a house tend to look out of place. Another reason I built large stairs for my decks is that exterior stairs require separate railings, which tend to be bulky. In fact, the railings can use up to 6 in. to 8 in. of tread width on each side. My goal is for deck stairs to have an unimpeded tread width of at least 4 ft. and never less than 3 ft.

Exterior stairs should not be in a hurry to get somewhere. Even for long flights or utility stairs, I like to keep the rise of each step to about 7 in. maximum, with treads at least 11 in. wide. But for most shorter stairways, I aim for a rise of 6 in. and a tread width of 15 in. to 16 in. This will slow the pace (because you must pay attention to your feet) and help create a more visually grand and flowing appearance.

Construction options

Wide treads and shallow risers make stairways longer. Outdoors, this really isn't a problem, but it does influence the construction somewhat. Stringers that support these wide treads will be at more of a horizontal angle than they would be on a set of interior stairs; when there are more than a few treads, the stairs can start to feel bouncy. To solve this, I like to break up long stair runs into shorter flights connected to a landing. Sometimes I'll add supports midspan under full-length stringers. Another possibility on shorter flights with very wide treads is to build each step as a separate box that partially laps onto and is supported by the previous box (see p. 155).

A long stairway may need midspan support to keep it from seeming bouncy.

Stair Codes and Terminology

Deck stairs and handrails are generally governed by same codes as interior stairways. However, making exterior stairways wider and less steep makes them easier and more comfortable to use.

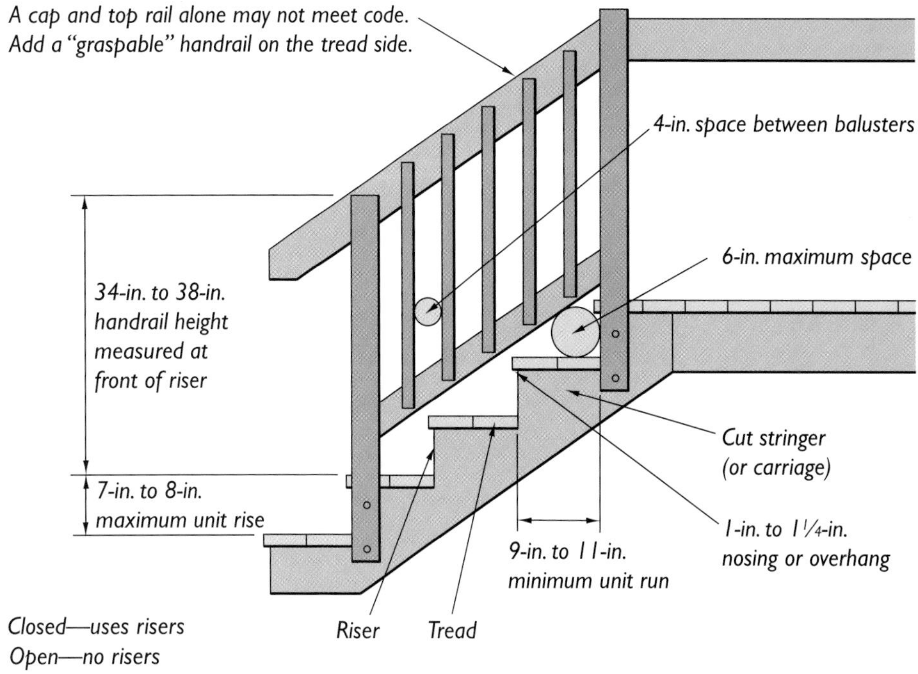

I usually build stairs with at least three stringers (or carriages) that are notched in a sawtooth manner to support the treads. The bottom of these stringers rests on a pad of concrete or gravel. If the top tread of the stringer is flush with the decking, a vertically cut face on the back of the stringer butts into the rim joist. But sometimes the rim joist will serve as the top riser, and then the top tread will be one step down from the decking surface. This second type of stringer usually will need extra blocking, strapping, or a longer carriage to be bolted up underneath the deck framing.

Whether notched or not, stringers should always be made from treated material. I usually use treated 2×12s, because they're readily available and have plenty of wood left after notches have been cut. Notched stringers should have their cuts treated with extra preservative if

PRO TIP

Exterior stairs should not be in a hurry to get somewhere. I like to keep the rise of each step to 7 in. maximum, with treads at least 11 in. wide.

IN DETAIL

Straight flights of stairs with more than six or eight treads might need some extra support under the stringers to help them feel solid. This is done just as you would decrease the span of deck joists—by adding a short beam with posts and small footings. The beam can be a 4×6 since it doesn't carry much weight, but it should have its top let into a *bird's mouth* cut in the underside of the stringer. Posts are attached to the beam with metal post caps; the posts themselves rest on simple premade pier blocks partially buried in well-drained soil or gravel.

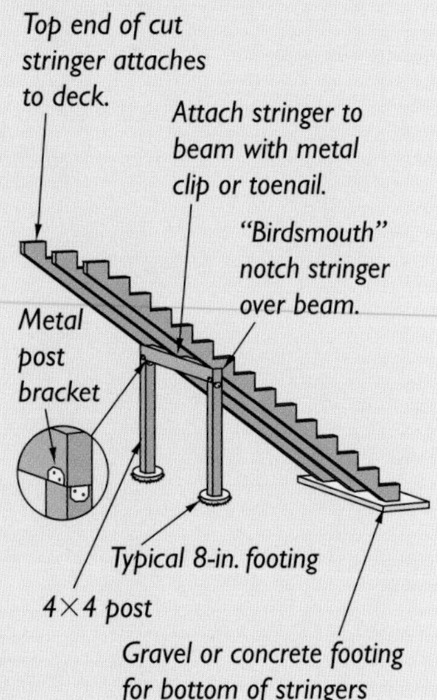

untreated wood is exposed, especially on the horizontal end grain under the tread. I usually make treads from the same material that I use for the decking.

Stairways and building codes

According to my residential building code, the maximum rise for a set of stairs (either interior or exterior) is 8 in., with a minimum run of 9 in. I think that this results in stairs that are too steep, so I prefer to follow commercial code guidelines. These specify shallower stairs, with a maximum rise of 7 in. and a minimum run of 11 in. Most stairs are required to be at least 36 in. wide (actual usable width after the guardrail is installed). However, code does allow the handrail to intrude several inches on the minimum width.

Like decks, all stairs that are 30 in. above adjacent areas are required to have guardrails with balusters spaced no farther than 4 in. apart. The bottom rail on a stairway guardrail creates a triangular area with the tread and riser and should be close enough to the front edge of the treads so that a 6-in.-diameter ball will not fit through. The guardrail requirement goes hand in hand with the need for a handrail on all stairs. Some codes only call for handrails on residential stairs with four or more risers, but again, I think the commercial code is a better choice as it requires handrails whenever there are more than two risers. Depending on the code, the top of handrails should be between 34 in. and 38 in., as measured vertically directly above the riser. I find that the lower end of the scale results in a handrail that is much easier to grab. The handrail must be between 1½ in. and 2 in. in cross-sectional dimension (measured in both directions).

+ SAFETY FIRST

A 5/4 or 2×6 cap rail is not a proper handrail for a deck stairway. Neither is a plain 2×4 bolted to the side of the stair guardrail. Handrails that meet code must be graspable, as shown. Handrails that will meet code can be easily shaped with a router or a dado blade on a table saw.

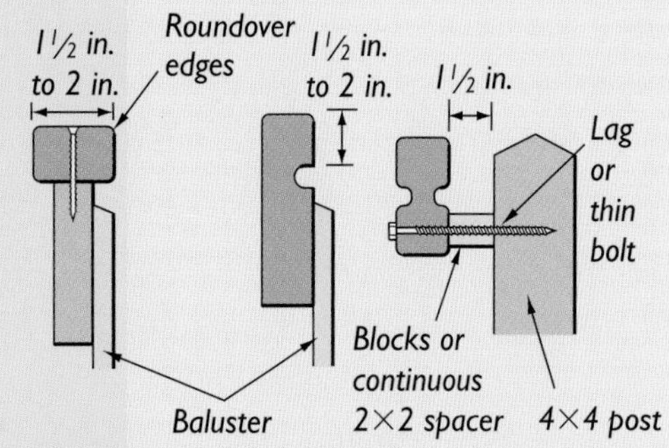

Handrail Profiles
Handrails (not guardrails) for stairs must be able to be gripped in the event of a slip. A plain 2×6 on edge will not meet code unless it has been profiled with a graspable top section (Figure 2).

Stair Layout

Once you've determined the stair location and configuration, you can calculate the rise and run of each step and then go ahead and lay out and cut the stringers. First, however, you need to determine the total rise and total run of the stairs.

Determining the rise

The vertical distance that a set of stairs must cover is called the total rise. This is always measured from finished surface to finished surface—that is, from the top of the decking to the ground level, which may be a gravel or concrete pad. This total rise is then divided equally among the individual steps, such that the distance from the top of each finish tread to the top of the next finish tread is the same for all of the steps in the stairway. The

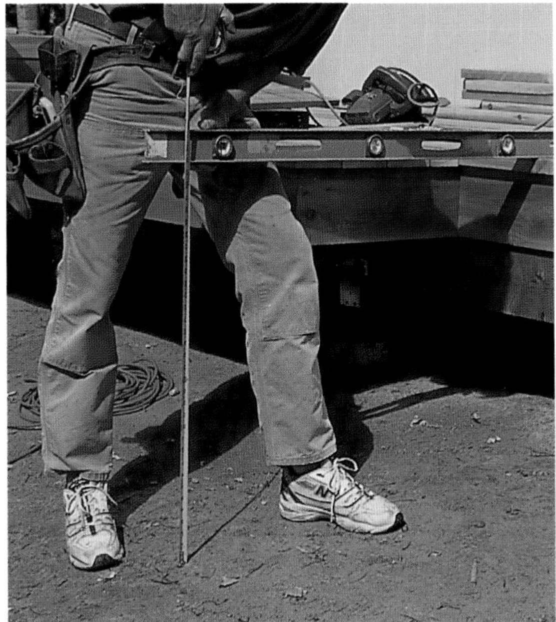

Use a level and a tape to measure the total vertical rise for the stairs.

number of vertical risers times the rise per step—the unit rise—should equal the total rise.

On longer flights of stairs, it won't be obvious how many individual risers are needed. To calculate the number of risers, first I take the total rise and divide it by what I consider to be an ideal rise per step. This will give me a number close to (but not equal to) the total number of risers, but will probably contain a fraction that needs to be rounded up or down. Now I divide this whole number of risers back into the total vertical rise to get the exact rise per step. Adjusting the total number of risers will change the rise per step. The final number of risers either will equal the number of treads or will be one more than the number of treads, depending on how the stringers are attached to the deck framing (see p. 151).

Determining the run

Once the number of treads is determined, that number can be multiplied by the chosen horizontal run of each tread to get the total run covered by the stairs. For example, if we determine that there are to be four treads with a 15-in. run per

Anchoring the Stairs

The most secure method of anchoring stairs is to add a concrete pad. This will mean a separate concrete mixing session, because most stairs are difficult to locate precisely at the time concrete is poured for the deck foundation posts. An extra concrete pad, which is not likely to be below frost levels in colder climates, should have a 6-in. layer of well-drained gravel underneath it to help prevent frost heave. A simpler method that I use on short flights (and that avoids the frost heave problem) also requires a 6-in.- to 8-in.-thick pad of gravel but no concrete. The stair stringers are attached to treated 2×6s that rest directly on the gravel pad.

Anchoring the Bottom of the Stair

The bottom of the stringers can land on concrete and be fastened with bolts to angle iron (no. 3) or a kicker (no. 2). Alternatively, you can have the stringers land on a pad of compacted gravel by adding 2× material across the bottom of the stringers (no. 1).

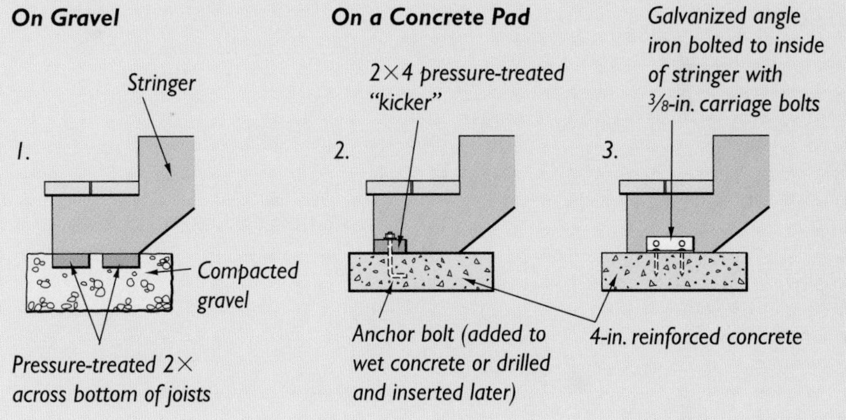

Calculating Rise and Run

The height of a riser—the unit rise—is determined by dividing the total rise by the number of risers. The total run of the stairs equals the unit run × the number of treads. Unit rise and unit run dimensions can be set with stair buttons on a framing square (as shown) to scribe the notches on a stair stringer.

PRO TIP

On longer flights of stairs, the number of risers needed won't be obvious. To get that number, I take the total rise and divide it by the ideal rise per step.

WHAT CAN GO WRONG

Use caution when reading codes or directions for building stairs; the *run* of a step is not the width of the tread. Rather, it's the horizontal distance covered at each step and is the length of the horizontal part of the notch. *Treads*, however, are wider than the run because they have an overhang—or *nosing*—on the front. A run of 10 in. plus a nosing of 1 in. equals a tread width of 11 in.

IN DETAIL

An *open* stairway leaves the vertical space between treads without any finished risers. But a finish riser of 1× material can create a *closed* stairway (with a more polished look).

IN DETAIL

The distance between stringers depends on the type of tread material being used and the span of the stringer. Stringers longer than 3 ft. to 4 ft. should be about 16 in. to 18 in. o.c.; stringers spanning shorter distances can be 24 in. o.c. In some cases, your local building code may dictate the required number of stringers.

After measuring the total rise and calculating the unit rise and run, you can determine the location of the landing. Here, the landing will be a gravel pad framed in with cedar.

tread, the total run of the stairway is 60 in. (4 × 15 = 60).

But there is a catch-22 in this process. To determine the exact location of the stair landing (and the pad that supports it), we need to go through the above calculations. But in order to have an accurate vertical measurement to do the calculations, the pad has to already be installed. In real life, what I do is predict the finished height of the pad after it's installed, do my rise and run calculations, then go back and put the pad in the right spot and at the right elevation.

Laying Out and Cutting Stringers

Once the rise and run dimensions have been determined, I can lay out the stringers and notch them for the treads. For my stringers, I use 2×12 treated lumber that is straight, uncupped, and free of large knots. I use a framing square to lay out the notches.

Stringer layout

The easiest and most accurate way to lay out notches is with a framing square set up with a pair of stair buttons or stair gauges (small screw clamps that attach to the square). I screw one button to the tongue of the square to mark the rise (7 in., in this example) and the other button on the wider blade of the square to mark the run (10 in., in this example). Then I slide the square along the edge of the uncut stringer and mark the notches to be cut, starting at the bottom and making sure that each tread/riser notch is marked the same.

After you have laid out the notches, you must make several important adjustments before you begin cutting. If you were to install the stringers with treads as they are now laid out, you would find that the top step and bottom step would be

Stair buttons attached to a framing square correspond to the rise of the run of the stairs, and make laying out the stringers more accurate.

After laying out the first tread, continue marking notches on the stringer for the rest of the stair.

Cut notches for stringers with a circular saw, being careful not to overcut the notch (which weakens the stringer).

too high by the thickness of a tread. You can easily solve this by removing the thickness of one tread from the bottom of the stringer. This is called "dropping the stringer." Mark the horizontal cut for the bottom of the stringer parallel to the tread cuts, with the lowest riser measuring one unit rise minus the thickness of one tread. If you plan on notching for a 2×4 kicker at the bottom, lay this out now too. (See the drawing on p. 149.)

The layout at the top of the stringer depends on how the stairs are attached to the deck. Some stairs simply butt into the deck rim joist, in which case the vertical cut on the back of the stringer is marked perpendicular to the treads. When I lay this out, I make sure that the top tread overhang matches the rest of the treads.

If the stringer continues back past the face of the deck rim joist, a slightly more complicated layout may be necessary and needs to include extra length for notching or bolting. This will depend on the size of the deck's framing and the rim joist thickness. In either case, adding finished risers for a closed-riser stairway will usually require shortening the horizontal cut for the top tread by the thickness of the riser material to keep the nosing overhang consistent. I draw these adjustments directly on the stringer, adding full-sized components with the proper dimensions.

Cutting the stringers

After the layout is complete and has been double-checked, I make the cuts on the waste side of the lines using a circular saw with a sharp blade. Once the first stringer has been cut, I use it as a template to scribe the others. In case the 2×12s have slightly different widths, I align the uncut straight edge of the notched stringer with the uncut one. And in case some of my cuts aren't perfectly square to the face of the stringer, I lay the face of the cut stringer with all my pencil lines against the face of the uncut one.

Attaching the top of the stair stringer

The method used for attaching a stringer to the main deck depends on the location of the upper tread. If the top tread is flush with the decking surface and there are the same number of treads and risers, stringer attachment is easy: A simple vertical cut at the top can butt into the main deck rim joist. Alternatively, the deck's rim joist can serve as the uppermost riser, with the first tread one step down from the deck. There will be one less tread than the number of risers, and the last railing post for the main deck also serves as the top post for the stair railing.

Depending on how I've laid out and cut the top of the stringer, I attach the stringer to the deck with corrosion-resistant lag bolts, 16d nails, or screws driven through the rim joist from the back side into the vertical cut of the stringer. If they can be hidden, I'll also add metal angle reinforcements (such as Simpson StrongTie® L50s or L70s) to the front of the connection.

Stringers with the first tread lower than deck level are harder to attach because they intersect with only a small area of the rim joist. These stringers require extra blocking and some creativity to ensure a solid, long-lasting connection. One way to attach this type of stringer is to con-

Use the cut first stringer as a template to scribe the remaining stringers.

PRO TIP

Whether notched or not, stringers should always be made from treated material.

IN DETAIL

The bottom tread of a set of stairs can land quite a few horizontal feet away from the top tread, and the ground between these points may slope considerably. When you are determining total rise, be sure to measure from deck's finished level to the anticipated finished level of the landing.

IN DETAIL

If the total measured distance (the *total rise*) between the deck and the ground is 29 in., and the desired rise per tread is about 7 in., divide 29 by 7 to get 4.14. Round 4.14 down to 4, and then divide 4 into 29 to get 7.25, or 7¼ in. per riser. If you wanted a more shallow riser, you could try dividing the total rise (29) by 5 treads, a riser height of 5.8 in.

WHAT CAN GO WRONG

A circular saw won't be able to complete the inside corner cuts for notches in stringers. Don't overcut the layout lines to finish the cuts. Instead, use a handsaw or jigsaw to finish the cuts.

Stringers can be attached to blocking added to the underside of deck framing.

Stringers can attached to a lowered rim joist extension by screwing through the back and adding metal reinforcement.

Where the top step is flush with the deck, the stringer can rest against and be attached to the rim joist.

To locate the top of the cut stringer, measure down one unit rise. In this case, the treads are the same thickness as the decking, so one unit rise down from the underside of the decking equals the top of the stringer.

tinue it up past the deck rim joist and bolt it to some added blocking within the deck's joist framing. I don't use this solution very often because it usually requires deep notching and leaves only a narrow, continuous section of stringer for bolting. The solution I use more frequently is to add a short section of joist material parallel to but directly underneath the rim joist. The stringers are then butted and attached to this short section in the same way stringers are attached when they butt into the rim joist. This horizontal section runs the width of the stairs and is attached to the rim on the back side with either a large, well-nailed rectangle of treated plywood or with bolted, vertical 2×4 blocks. In all these methods, the top tread is usually against the rim joist and helps lock the stringer system in place.

Once I've determined the position of the stringers on the rim joist, I tack them in place temporarily and use a 4-ft. level to check that the horizontal cuts are all in line. I also double-check that the stringer notches are level. If the layout was accurate, all the tread cuts should line up on all of the steps and be reasonably level in both directions. If one stringer is consistently out of line with the rest, it may need to be shimmed or trimmed at the bottom. Once the stringers are properly positioned, the connections at the top can be completed.

After the stringers have been toenailed to the deck framing (here, the beam supporting the joists) and checked to ensure that they are level and properly positioned, the stringers can be securely fastened with joist hangers.

Joist hangers fastened to the stringers and the framing with screws offer a more secure connection than simple toenailing.

Anchoring the bottom of the stair stringer

Depending on the length of the stairway and the amount of use it's likely to see, the bottom of the stringer can be anchored in a few different ways. In most cases, I've already planned and poured a concrete pad, from which I've determined the rise and run of the stair. If I've already cut the stringers when I pour the pad, I can use them to help me locate J-bolts into the wet concrete. I use these J-bolts to anchor a 2×4 "kicker" that fits into a notch cut into the front edge of the carriage. Alternatively, I can use these bolts to anchor a short section of metal angle, which I then bolt to the side of the carriages. The bolts can also be added later by drilling into the cured concrete and using concrete anchors.

A simpler method that I use on short flights (and that avoids the frost heave problem) requires a 6-in.- to 8-in.-thick pad of gravel, but no concrete. Before I install the stringers, I turn them over and nail two treated 2×6s across the bottom horizontal cut. These 2×6s will rest on the top of the gravel pad, connect all the stringers into a unit, and distribute the load across the gravel. Adding a final layer of gravel surrounding these extra boards locks the bottom of the stairs in place.

Installing treads

Once the stringers are solid, I field-treat any raw wood with preservative. Then I install the treads, which I always make from decking material. I typically use two 2×6 boards to make an 11-in.-wide tread, since a single, wider board would quickly split in an outside environment. And as with decking, I use the best-looking side facing up. I hang treads over the side of the stringer by the amount that I hang my decking over the rim joist, about 1¼ in. To determine the tread length, measure from outside to outside of the stringers, adding the overhang amount on each side.

Stringers are fastened to a pressure-treated board supported by a level gravel pad. The special end stringer is designed to allow the treads to end at a 45-degree angle. While the unit run for the stringer could be calculated trigonometrically, a safer method is to make a full-scale plan view drawing.

PRO TIP

You can strengthen notched stringers by bolting or nailing a treated 2×4 to one or both sides of the unnotched part of each stringer.

Treads can be fastened to unnotched stringers with manufactured steel brackets.

IN DETAIL

In some situations, I'll use heavy-gauge, galvanized steel L-brackets (either Simpson StrongTie TA9 and TA10) to fasten my treads to unnotched stringers. The brackets are bolted to both the stringers and the treads with short 1¼-in.-diameter lag screws. These are useful when notching the stringer would weaken it too much.

Once the stringers are in place, you are ready to add treads (and risers if the stairway is a closed one).

Treads are installed with the same fasteners as the decking—two screws per tread into each stringer. Start at the bottom and work toward the top so there is always a finished tread to kneel on. Slide the back half in place up against the riser cut and fasten it, then fasten down the front board using the same board spacing that you used on the decking.

Stair Railings

Stair guardrails are similar to the guardrails on the main deck, except that the ends of the rails and balusters need to be cut at an angle. Posts at the top and bottom of the stair support the rails.

Installing stair posts

Stair posts can be located either inside or outside the cut stringers, but I usually keep the same relationship that the posts on the main deck have to the rim joist. Typically, I notch the posts when they're outside the stringer and install unnotched posts on the inside. When mounting the posts inside, I make sure the stringers are set far enough apart to compensate for the space used by the railing.

If the top tread of the stairs is flush with the surface of the decking, I use two posts on that tread that are the same height as the deck posts. One will be a corner post in line with both deck posts and stair posts; I bolt this post at the inside corner created by the deck rim joist and the cut stringer. The other is the top stair post; its front face is even with the top riser cut on the stringer. If the top tread is one step down from the deck, there will be only one post, located in the corner between the rim and the cut stringer and at the same height as the other deck posts.

Whenever possible, I mount the bottom post flush with the front of the second riser, because this offers more stringer to bolt to than the front of the bottom step. However, to meet code, handrails will need to be cantilevered past this post at least until even with the bottom riser.

The height of posts is determined by several factors. I plan the height of the guardrail on the stairs so that the cap rail won't interfere with the positioning of a handrail. The height and style of the stair guardrail also affect how it intersects with

✓ According to Code

Accuracy is critical when you are calculating, laying out, and cutting stair stringers. To minimize the possibility of tripping, codes allow only up to a ⅜-in. height difference between the tallest and shortest riser. So measure and cut your stringers carefully.

Railing posts are more stable if attached to the stringer at the second riser instead of at the short section at the lowest riser. The handrail will have to be cantilevered past the post until it's even with the first riser.

STRINGERLESS STAIRS

Once stair treads get much wider than 16 in., notching a stringer starts to get impractical. Instead, I build stairs with extra-wide treads just as I would a series of small overlapping decks. For example, the step can start with a large box that supports a series of successively smaller boxes. The lowest box is big enough to support the boxes above and provide framing to support the lowest-level tread, while the highest box is sized only to support the tread itself. Rise and run calculations must be done not only to determine the size of the boxes but also so that the joist framing boards can be ripped to the unit rise for each step. It's important that the bottom box be installed so that it's level and solid. This may not entail deeply buried concrete footings, but you should excavate down to stable soil, adding plenty of gravel to assist drainage. If the stairway has more than just a few treads, it makes more sense to install each box separately, with only the front face of each box resting on the rear face of the box below. This means that the rear of each box needs separate foundation work.

Instead of stringers to support wide treads, a series of boxes or minidecks, stacked on each other will do the job. Getting the bottom box level and well supported is crucial to success.

A completed stack of boxes ready for decking "treads"

Wide tread stairs use deck boards installed in the usual manner.

Completed wide tread stairs ready for railing.

PRO TIP

It's simpler if you wait to install treads at post locations. After the posts are in place, the tread notches are easier to measure and cut.

This stairway is built with decking for treads but uses stacked timbers instead of cut stringers for support.

IN DETAIL

Treads can be formed by stacking timbers next to or on top of each other. This usually requires at least two 6×6s side by side to form an 11-in. tread with a 5½-in. rise, but 6×8 or 8×8 timbers can be substituted to make wider treads or taller rises. Typically, each step is supported by sections of timber running perpendicular to the tread on the step below.

IN DETAIL

Stair posts are usually spaced a bit more closely together than deck posts are. Stairs less than 6 ft. long usually need only a top and bottom post, but longer flights will need intermediate posts. Try to space middle posts equally.

A top cap intersects the post below the main rail.

A continuous flat top cap makes a smooth transition over the post.

A continuous top cap continues over one post and abuts the next.

Blocking should be added between stringers near the base to reinforce railing posts.

the main deck guardrail. My typical solution is to have the stair cap rail butt into the post just underneath the main-level cap rail. However, with a little planning, the stair cap rail can intersect the upper cap rail to form a continuous railing.

Once I've determined post heights and locations, I add in the amount of lap onto the stringer to get the total post length. For maximum stability, I lap the posts onto the stringers as much as possible. The bottom of the post is usually cut square, but it also can be cut at the stair angle or to match the other deck posts.

Stair posts are attached just as deck posts are—by bolting through the post and stringer, typically with two ½-in.-diameter bolts per post (see the bottom photo on p. 154). You can increase post stability by blocking between stringers and adding additional bolting (similar to blocking between end joists on the main deck).

Installing stair rails

Because stair rails are set at an angle, I find it easiest to first attach vertically oriented rails to the installed posts and then add balusters one at a time. If the balusters are butted to horizontally oriented top and bottom rails, I prebuild the balustrades and install them as a unit between the posts. Flat bottom rails won't have anybody standing on them so I don't notch them into the posts for support as I would on the main deck railing.

The top rail location is determined by the style of the system. The bottom rail is usually set with only a ¼-in. space between it and the front edge of the treads. This keeps the open triangle formed

The angle-cut stair balusters are secured to rails using a spacer block and screws, just as the main balustrade was attached.

Completed stairs with railing

After post installation, obtain angles for rail cuts by laying the rail on the stringers and scribing it with a pencil.

After the rails have been scribed and cut, toescrew the rails to the posts and the space measured for a railing unit built with angled cuts on the end of the balusters.

by the treads and risers under it to a minimum. I usually determine the length and angle of cut for rail system components by laying them in place and scribing them. When I can, I attach the rails to the posts by toescrewing from underneath where the screws can't be seen. Toescrews through the face may be needed on thin rails that would split otherwise.

Cutting and installing balusters

After the rails are in place, lapped balusters are installed one at a time. Balusters that lap onto sloping vertical rails are usually square-cut with a decorative bevel on the bottom. The tops of balusters can be cut either square or to the angle of the stairs. Their length will depend on the railing style and can be measured in place after the rails are installed.

Lapped balusters are screwed to the face of the rail with corrosion-resistant screws. Start either in the middle or at one end (depending on your layout), and use a spacer block to set each adjacent baluster. It's a good idea to double-check the balusters occasionally with a 4-ft. level to be sure that they are plumb.

Butted balusters are attached to precut horizontal rails by screwing up or down through predrilled holes. Because these holes need to be drilled at an angle, I find it easiest to drill both rails at once by setting them in place on the treads between the posts and using the posts to help me visually plumb the drill bit. Like railings, the balustrade can be built as a complete section, and then attached to the upper and lower rails that are already in place.

✓ According to Code

Handrails are added after the guardrail system has been constructed. Code-approved handrails can be bolted to the posts with rustproof metal brackets, but usually I screw a 1½-in.-thick block to the post first, and then secure the rail with a long lag or carriage bolt that goes through the rail and the block and into the post.

The completed stair balustrade is added as a unit to the already-installed top and bottom rails.

PRO TIP

Make landings large enough so that the bottom of the stringer of the upper flight rests on the decking surface, which makes a secure connection.

IN DETAIL

Traditionally, stair treads overhang the stringers. To change the look, cover the tread ends by adding unnotched finish skirts that run parallel to the stringers. These skirts are usually made from 5/4 or 2× material and should be separated from the cut stringer with a thin spacer to encourage drying. Skirts are added after stringers have been set in place but before treads are installed. Then the treads are cut to the correct length between the skirts. These skirts also can be added to help strengthen notched stringers, in which case the skirts should be securely bolted every couple of feet.

Adding boards to the sides of notched stringers creates a more finished-looking "housed" stringer.

An L-shaped stairway with a landing breaks up a long flight of steps.

Landings and Ramps

Landings and ramps are built just as small deck sections are. I make them with the same type of joists and decking used for the rest of the deck, using the same joist sizing tables. Landings offer more flexibility when you are designing and building stairs; ramps offer an alternative way of accessing a deck.

Landings

If stairs are too long or need to turn a corner, a landing is necessary. A landing is built in the same manner as a freestanding minideck, and needs foundation supports similar to the main deck (although a landing can be sized smaller because loading conditions are minimal). A landing can take the place of the uppermost tread, allowing stairs to make a quick turn after leaving the main deck, or it may be located somewhere in the middle of a stairway if needed to break up a long span.

The elevation of the landing's decking isn't arbitrary; it should be thought of as a tread in a long stairway. To find the landing elevation, the rise and run calculations for the entire stairway from the main deck surface all the way to the ground must be calculated first as if there weren't a landing involved. Then the landing elevation can be chosen as a multiple of the unit rise for the stairs and measured from either the upper or lower finished surface.

The lateral position of the landing in relation to the main deck is also derived from rise and run calculations. The landing should be placed so that the upper flight of stairs ends with the bottom of the stringers resting fully on the landing. If space is a problem, the lowest riser should just reach the face of the landing's rim joist, with the bottom of the stringer cut with a long vertical face that butts into the rim joist of the landing.

Once the landing location is established, the stringers for the flights above and below the landing can be thought of as independent stairways and are laid out, cut, and anchored the same way.

Ramps

For ramps to meet code and replace a set of steps, they should have a slope no steeper than 1 in 12; a shallower 1-in-15 pitch is even better. However, I

Ramps to decks make access easier not only for wheelchairs but also for other means of transportation. This ramp has joists attached to the main deck rim joist.

Sloped walkway ramps can be built as a series of little decks with separate posts and beams.

often make utility ramps with a 1-in-6 slope. And I plan them so they have a usable width of at least 4 ft., which may require an overall width of 5 ft., depending on the type of guardrails and handrails.

Most of the ramps that I build are permanent and have sloping joists. I anchor them to the rim of the main deck with joist hangers, cutting a bevel at the end and a bird's mouth on the bottom of the joist to accept the horizontal seat of the hanger. Long ramps that exceed the maximum span of the joists will need some midspan support from short cross beams and a couple of footings.

All ramps should end with a level landing pad at the bottom. However, backyard ramps for private use can be made simpler than public-use ramps accessing a front deck from the street. Occasional-use ramps that end near unpaved areas can simply be buried in the ground so the decking can be brought to ground level for a smooth transition.

Ramps that land on a hard surface (a deck landing, for example) will need the bottom end of the joists cut to a long, pointed taper. If the ramp has a rise of 1 in 12 and is built with 2×8 joists, this taper could extend almost the entire joist length for an 8-ft. ramp, in which case the entire taper should be supported. The bottom can be held in place with treated-lumber blocking nailed on the flat between joists and then bolted down.

Ramp Construction

Ramp joists typically are hung off of the main deck's rim joist with joist hangers, and slope to the ground where they are attached to a concrete pad with metal anchors or set on compacted gravel (as shown), which is later backfilled to bring grade up to ramp level. A removable ramp has a separate rim joist and is bolted to the main deck with ½-in.-diameter bolts.

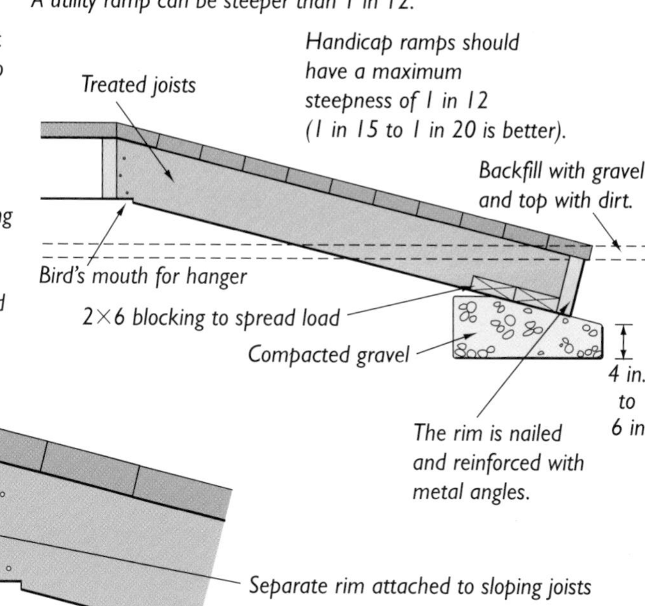

This ramp allows the owner, an avid bicyclist, to ride right onto his deck.

✓ According to Code

Although ramp handrails are always a good idea, most building and handicap accessibility codes require them on both sides of the ramp whenever the ramp rises more than 6 in. or is longer than 6 ft.

Special Cases and

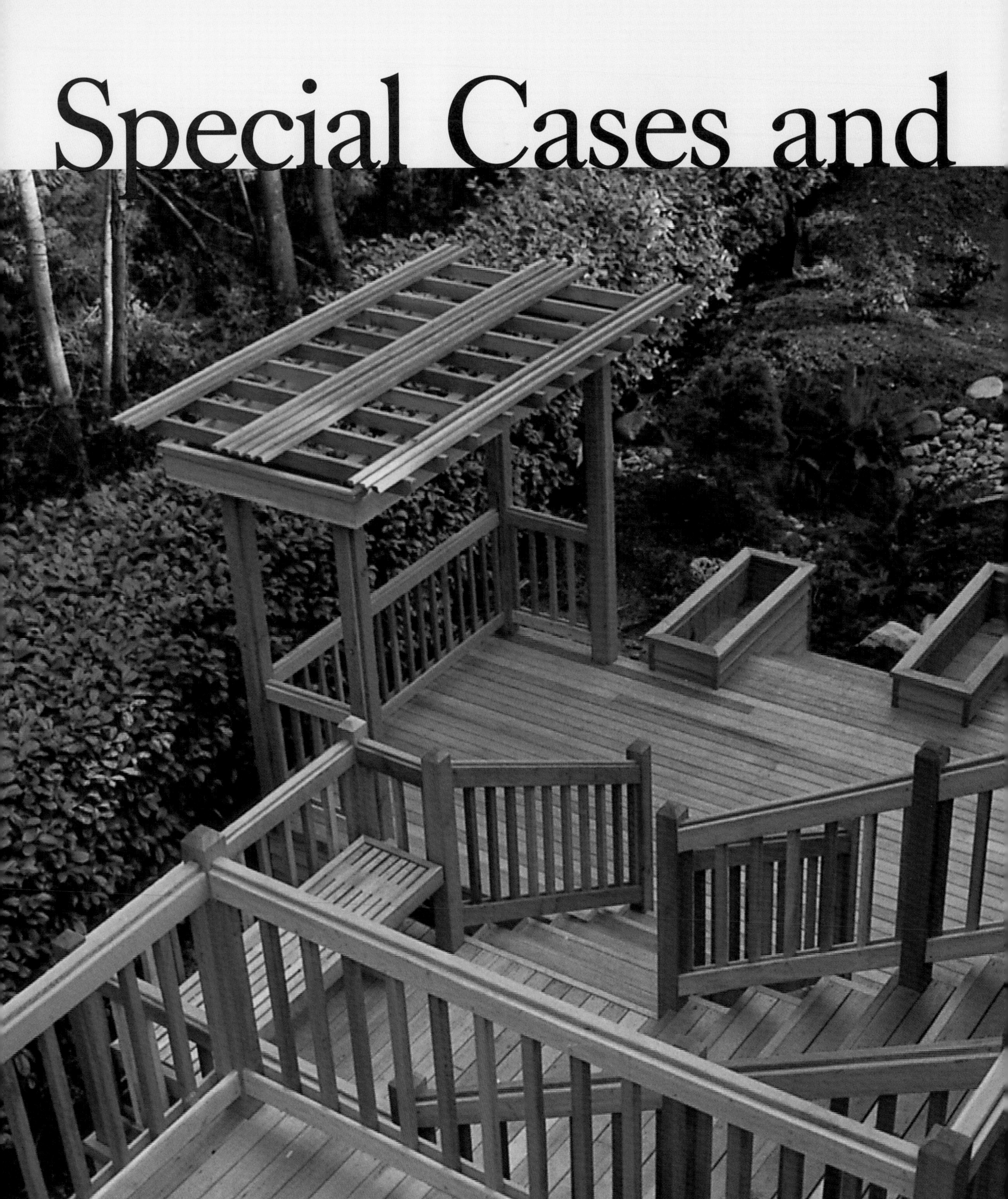

CHAPTER EIGHT

Custom Details

Once the essentials of framing, decking, and railings have been constructed, it's time to add benches, planters, or other features that can help make your deck even more attractive, interesting, and fun. These features—and others such as trellises and lighting—will make daytime use of the deck more comfortable and extend the amount of time the deck is used after the sun sets. In addition, there are some less pleasant jobs that still need attending to (such as dealing with the area underneath the deck). Although these tasks may not feel urgent, they need to be finished before you can call your project complete. And finally, some decks (including those built over roofs or crumbling patios) need special techniques to help turn or return them into pleasant and useful outdoor spaces. This chapter will help you finish up these important but often neglected final items.

PRO TIP

The best option is to build a bench with a back that is independent of the railing system.

IN DETAIL

While built-in deck seating has its advantages, outdoor furniture can be inexpensive, comfortable, and easily rearranged to suit the situation. Moveable furniture can be temporarily dragged out into the yard, over to a table for family functions, or around the corner to get some respite from the midday sun.

IN DETAIL

The surest way to get a comfortable seat is to use your favorite chair as a model. But here are some general guidelines to get you started:

- Seat height: 14 in. to 18 in.
- Seat depth: 16 in.
- Too deep a seat cuts into the back of the knees.
- For a sloped backrest, make the seat about 1 in. higher in front than in back.
- Benches intended for reclining need to be flat and at least 30 in. to 32 in. wide.

Benches can be used for seating or as a barrier on the edge of a deck.

Benches and Planters

Built-in benches are a good way to provide seating for a lot of people at social gatherings. Permanent benches near doors are a convenient place for changing muddy shoes or resting bags of groceries while you fumble to unlock the door, while seats built into deck corners can foster private conversation. If your deck has long sections of railing, attractive built-in seating can add character and break up the monotony. And on a low deck that doesn't require a railing, a perimeter bench is a useful and appealing addition.

Fixed planters can be incorporated into bench design.

Having said this, though, I must admit that I'm not a big fan of built-in deck furniture. For one thing, hard benches offer seating that is less than comfortable. And built-in seating usually faces the wrong direction if you want to see a view. My advice is to limit built-ins to small benches that are located near doors and serve dedicated functions. But if you need a lot of seating regularly, benches can be the way to go.

Planters, on the other hand, are a natural for a deck—they can be as important as pictures on a blank wall. Planters can be built in a variety of shapes and sizes to fit their location. They can be built in pairs. They can frame the opening of a stairway or door, define an access, or delineate a level change. Planters can serve as dividers or barriers, adding privacy by replacing sections of railings.

Built-in benches

There are several ways to construct built-in benches. You can simply modify a section of rail-

A frame attached to the railing supports seat and backrest planks. A simple jig (see the drawing at right) makes the construction of multiples of this frame quick and accurate.

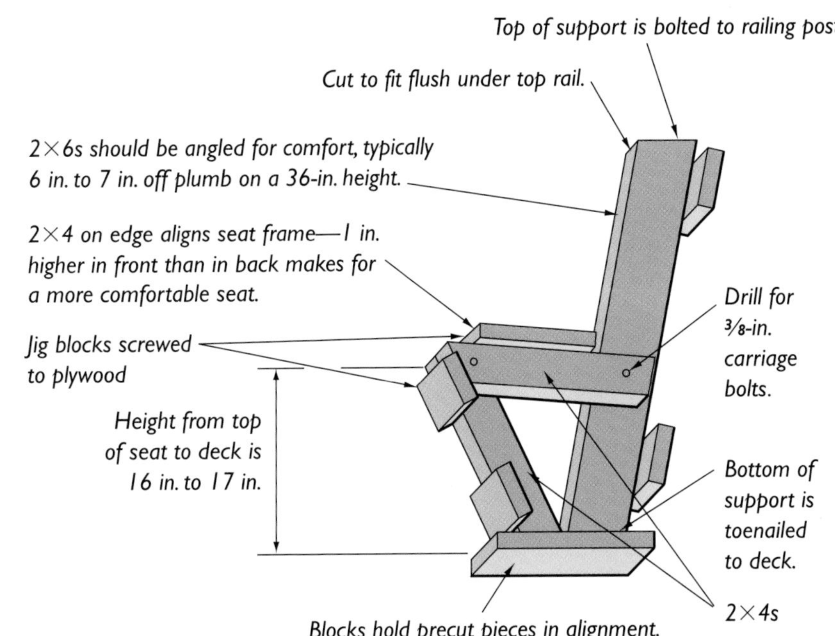

ing to form an angled back for the bench (though this creates a mismatch with the rest of the railing that is very visible from the outside). Another option is to build a bench without a separate back, but this isn't very comfortable for long sits. I think the best option is to build a bench (with a back) that is built independently of the railing system. Although this bench style requires only a little more work and material than the other two options, it does need advance planning to make sure that posts are located in the right position. The benches can be added after the deck and railing are built, and they can be removed in the future without affecting the railing's integrity.

I use an angled support system for the bench and back support, which I build with the help of a simple jig. The bench support involves only three pieces: a long back leg, a horizontal base for the seat, and a short front leg. I precut the pieces, place them in the jig, then drill and bolt them together. Then I attach the supports to existing deck posts with bolts (built-in benches need legs about every 4 ft. for adequate support). Finally, I use decking material to connect the supports and form the seat and back.

For the sake of convenience, I make the seat width a multiple of my decking. For example, if I'm using 2×6 decking, three full boards will give me a total seat width of 16½ in. (though the boards could be spaced slightly from each other and from the back support to provide extra width). I make sure to design and build the supports so that the horizontal section supporting the seat is slightly shorter than the planking to allow the seat to overhang. Two or three 2×6s also work well for the backrest.

Making Bench Supports

Bench supports can be built assembly-line style by precutting the parts and using a jig to assemble the frame components. Scrap blocks screwed to a piece of plywood (as shown) help ensure that the bench supports are consistently sized.

This bench starts with a 5/4 × 4 cedar frame with nailed and mitered corners that is sized to allow a small overhang of the finished seating surface of cedar deck boards.

PRO TIP

Planters should be made of rot-resistant material—a great way to use leftovers from deck construction.

TRADE SECRET

A bench with a vertical, flat backrest should have a 4-in. to 6-in. gap between the back and the seat to make the bench more comfortable. Continue the backrest up to 32 in. to 36 in. above the floor. For the most comfort, a backrest should be angled between 15 and 20 degrees from vertical (or a 10-in. to 12-in. tilt over 36 in.).

Benches with backs are definitely more comfortable, but require a sturdy connection so that the backrest remains firmly attached.

Adding some 2×4 cross blocking will give more support for attaching the legs and seat boards.

I also add 2×4 rungs between the legs and nail them in place.

Then use screws or bolts to attach 2×4 legs to the cross blocking and 5/4 frame.

Adding a simple bench

Benches without backs can be added just about anywhere. Although flat benches aren't as comfortable as sloped seats with back supports, they're great for casual sitting and can be a good place to take a nap.

A quick and easy freestanding bench without a back may be a good option for your deck. This bench starts with a 5/4 × 4 cedar frame with nailed and mitered corners that is sized to allow a small overhang of the finished seating surface of cedar deck boards. Adding some 2×4 cross blocking will give more support for attaching the legs and seat boards. Then use screws or bolts to attach 2×4 legs to the cross blocking and 5/4 frame. To keep the legs more stable and to improve the styling, I also add 2×4 rungs between the legs and nail them in place.

Although any thickness of seat material would work, here we used extra 2×6 deck boards, which are screwed in place as you would the deck surface. After completing the bench, clean up the sawn edges with a block plane or router to

Here we used extra 2×6 deck boards, which are screwed in place as you would the deck surface.

improve the look of the bench and minimize splinters. The completed bench is flanked with matching planters on either side.

A more elegant alternative is a freestanding bench that includes a backrest (though this bench takes a little more work to notch the legs). For added stability, these kind of benches can be screwed temporarily to the deck.

Planters

Simple wooden boxes are at the heart of both plain and fancy planters. Planters can be built with a false bottom to hold only the minimum amount of soil needed for some flowers, or they can be sized to hold a removable plastic liner. They should be designed to allow a maximum amount of air circulation, especially between the planter and the deck surface. The bottom needs to be sturdy enough to handle the load, but it also needs to allow excess water to drain through.

Planters should be made of rot-resistant material (usually there are plenty of leftovers from deck construction). Boxes can be made from treated

Clean up the sawn edges with a block plane or router.

The completed bench is flanked with matching planters on either side.

plywood and then sheathed with cedar siding or trim. The boxes can also be made from heavier 2× material that is fastened together with rustproof screws. It's seldom necessary to use waterproof glue unless you are making a planter that needs to have all of its fasteners hidden.

To assemble the planters that flank the bench on this deck, I first precut enough 1×8 material for the vertical parts of all the sides. Boards can be

Corners

Grooves cut in the 4×4 corners with a router or table saw equipped with a dado blade accept leftover decking material. Adjust the grooves to match the siding material thickness.

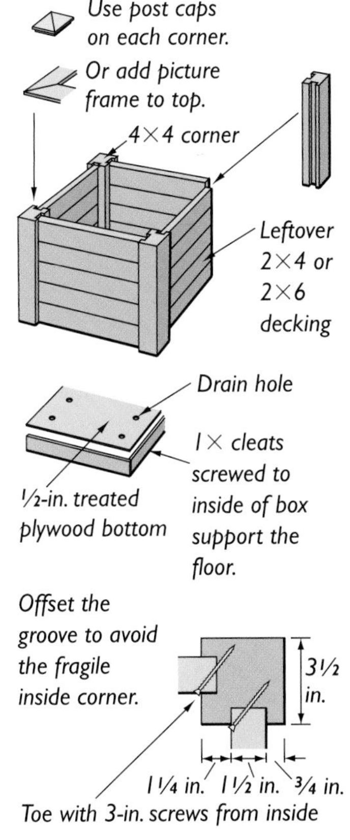

PRO TIP

Remember to account for the weight of soil-filled planters in your deck design.

IN DETAIL

Some vegetables grow quite well in containers, especially new "patio" varieties developed for container growing. If you plan to grow edibles in your planters, you probably want to avoid pressure-treated lumber. There is a small possibility of anti-decay chemicals leaching into the soil.

Building a Simple Planter

This planter can be made from decking and trim scraps. Most of the screws are hidden inside. Add a plastic liner and drainage holes to protect the interior of the planter from moisture. Small feet underneath the planter promote air circulation and keep the deck and planter dry.

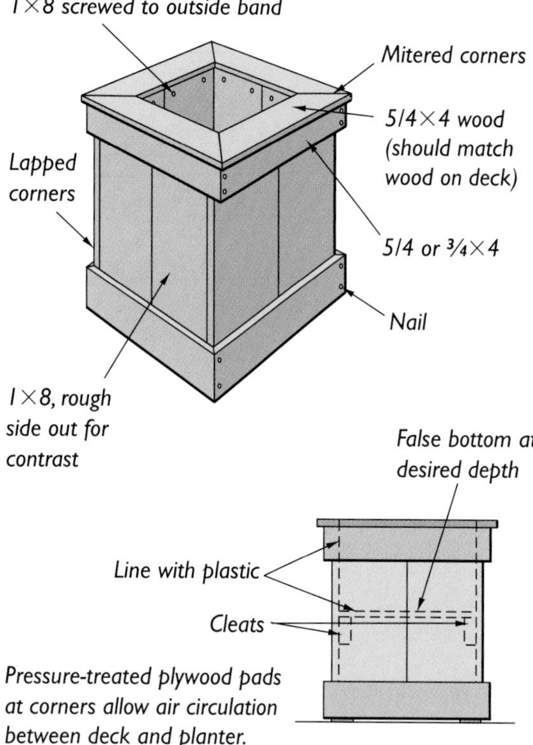

Boards can be ripped to fit a predetermined planter width, or the planter size can simply be a multiple of whole boards.

These side boards are then screwed from the back side to horizontal 5/4 bands that are mitered on the ends.

ripped to fit a predetermined planter width, or the planter size can simply be a multiple of whole boards. These side boards are then screwed from the back side to horizontal 5/4 bands that are mitered on the ends. I make the length of the bands longer on two opposite sides to accommodate lapping of the vertical pieces at the corners.

+ SAFETY FIRST

Use caution when choosing a planter liner, particularly if your planters are used for growing food. Petroleum-treated products and treated plywoods may leach unwanted chemicals into the soil, as will extra preservatives used to treat cut lumber.

1. The sides are then nailed together through the miters in the bands and along the vertical laps of the side boards.

2. After assembling all the sides, I nail on a 5/4×3 mitered top cap that slightly overhangs the sides and band.

3. At the bottom, I attach cleats that I rip from leftover stock, screwing them to the inside of the box at a height to accommodate pots or a liner.

4. Finally, I attach boards to the cleats, leaving spaces between the boards for circulation and drainage. The completed planter can be placed on the deck, or attached with screws for a more permanent installation.

Planter Liners

I prefer to build planters that have removable plastic pots and trays. However, permanent liners can be installed in a couple of ways. Sheet liners can be made from heavy polyethylene sheeting or tar paper, but will need to be replaced each season. Better are sheet liners made from scraps of sheet vinyl from swimming pool suppliers or rubber membranes from roofing suppliers; both of these materials are made to last a long time outdoors. Sheet liners should be held in place near the top of the planter with rustproof staples, or sandwiched behind a thin wooden cleat attached with stainless-steel screws. The weight of the soil will hold the liner at the bottom. Another option is to have a galvanized sheet-metal liner bent to your specifications at a local shop. Keep in mind, though, that none of these will last forever in the moist and dirty environment of a planter.

No matter what you use for a planter liner, it must have drain holes at the bottom so that your planter doesn't become a swamp. Adding a layer of coarse rock under the soil will help keep the drain holes from clogging.

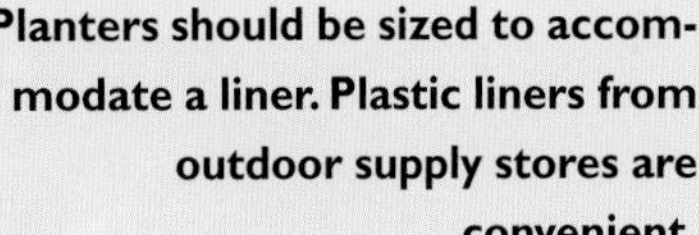

Planters should be sized to accommodate a liner. Plastic liners from outdoor supply stores are convenient.

PRO TIP

To avoid the need for diagonal bracing, trellis posts must be designed and built so that they provide structural rigidity to the overhead structure.

IN DETAIL

You can estimate the load a trellis will have to carry by figuring out the percentage of area overhead that is covered by boards or slats compared with the total area of the trellis. Multiply this percentage by the anticipated snow load in your area to get the live load you will need to design for. Don't forget the loading must also consider the weight of the framing materials themselves, typically about 5 psf.

IN DETAIL

Many trellises require diagonal post-and-beam bracing. Braces are added as needed (as for decks) but with more care given to the finished appearance. Braces can be utilitarian—simply 2× material lag-bolted to the outsides of the posts)—or decorative—bandsawn 4×4 knee braces butted into the face of the post.

and a transformer—and simply plugged into an outlet. In a low-voltage system, a transformer converts standard 120-volt house current to 12 volts (the same found in your car). Fixtures are available that mount in posts, on posts, or as strings of lights that can be attached under railings, benches, or nosing on stairs. Most codes will permit you to install your own 12-volt wiring.

Outdoor circuits

Whenever I'm adding lighting, either by tapping into an existing circuit or by installing a completely new one, I like to add a receptacle in the first box. An extra deck outlet is always handy, and if I use an oversized box, it can also serve as a junction box for wires that extend to switches and lights. However, some codes have specific requirements for outside receptacles, so check the codes when you're planning your wiring.

All codes will require outside receptacles to be waterproof. At minimum, this means a box with a gasketed cover, though some codes will require larger rain-tight hoods that cover the extension cord end as well. All outside receptacles will also need to be protected by a ground-fault circuit interrupter (GFCI), an important safety device that shuts off the flow of electricity at the slightest hint of a current leak to a grounded source. This protection can be provided by a GFCI outlet that offers protection for itself, as well as devices wired downstream from it. Or the entire circuit can be protected by a GFCI circuit breaker in the main panel. If you have a hot tub to power, it will have its own appropriately sized and GFCI-protected circuit.

Trellises

A trellis may be added to a deck for architectural embellishment or to provide shade from the sun through a system of wooden slats or with supported greenery. Trellises are built in the same manner as a deck or a roof but usually won't have the stabilizing action of a continuous layer of plywood or decking to add rigidity. Instead, to keep the open feeling on top and still be sturdy, trellises need to be anchored to the house or built with rigidly installed posts or knee braces.

Most of the structural considerations for decks hold true for trellises, except that trellises are not called on to carry the same loads if the covering boards are far apart. A support system for trellis rafters usually requires at least two posts and a

This elegant trellis structure matches the style of house.

Adding wide rafters in two directions will provide more shade at different times of the day than a single set running in one direction.

In addition to providing shade, a trellis can exhibit quality craftsmanship as demonstrated by the joinery shown here.

beam at each end. Sometimes trellis rafters can be hung (like deck joists) from a ledger attached to the house. Although this may simplify trellis framing, I prefer to build freestanding trellises in order to avoid complications from debris shedding off the roof and piling up behind the trellis framing, interference with the guttering system, or the guesswork of whether the house can support the extra weight of the trellis.

If you're building in snow country, you will have to take loading considerations into account. Overhead boards standing vertically are stronger and catch less snow, but they provide less sun protection. Flat boards offer more sun protection, but are structurally weaker and will catch more snow. Fortunately, snow loading isn't a big concern in those areas of the country that need maximum sun protection.

Trellis construction

Most trellises are built like decks, with posts, beams, rafters (equivalent to the joists), and a covering (equivalent to the decking). If you want to avoid diagonal bracing, the posts will have to be designed and built so that they provide structural rigidity to the overhead structure. Simply bolting the posts to the side of the deck joist framing will not be sufficient by itself. The best solution in this case is to extend posts up from the foundation level. Alternatively, trellis posts can be bolted to the deck framing and then extend down to their own separate foundation pads. In either case, you may want to integrate them into the railing design.

Overhead beams and rafters usually can be of a lighter weight than those used in the deck framing, but are installed similarly. Beams are attached to posts, and rafters rest on the beams. But because

2×s bolted to each side of the post make an attractive beam to support rafters.

PRO TIP

A roof to be decked should have enough slope to drain water, but not so much that it is unsafe to walk on.

IN DETAIL

The minimum amount of slope for a roof deck will depend on the roofing material, but I try for a slope of ¼ in. per ft. You can achieve this slope by simply raising the rafters at one end during installation. Alternatively, if you need to keep a flat ceiling below, the tops of the rafters can be ripped to this slope.

WHAT CAN GO WRONG

Any roof-mounted deck greatly increases the chance of a roof leak. When building the deck, take care to remove any gravel or debris, because the weight of the deck will eventually force down any irregular objects through the roofing and cause leaks. And the roof will need periodic cleaning so that debris doesn't accumulate underneath joists or sleepers.

the trellis (unlike the framing of a deck) is designed to be seen, joinery details need to be considered and executed more carefully. For example, instead of using 4× beams on top of posts, I suggest using 2×s bolted to each side of the post. This eliminates the utilitarian metal post caps and adds a lighter feel to the overhead work. Rafters—typically 2×4s or 2×6s on edge—can be attached to the beams with discreet metal clips or by careful toescrewing.

If your trellis rafters are supporting slats, they need to be spaced properly so that the slats don't sag. Rafter spacing should be no more than 24 in. for 1×2 (or thinner) slats, no more than 32 in. for 1×4s or 2×2s, and no more than 48 in. for bigger 2× material.

After the rafters are installed, a final layer of material may be added to provide more shading. These may be 1× or 2× boards lying flat or 2× material on edge, which are simply screwed or nailed to the tops of the rafters. The covering material should be chosen and sized to match the style of the deck and to provide strength (if the covering is to support planters or greenery or if rafters are widely spaced); of course, the material should also be rot-resistant or easily replaced. With widely spaced lumber coverings, it may be necessary to add galvanized metal mesh to support greenery.

In addition to common lumber, some choices for overhead covering materials are thin lath, grape or tree stakes, fencing material, woven reed, bamboo, or premade cedar or redwood lattice panels. You can check lumberyards as well as gardening and landscaping supply yards for other alternative materials.

Building a Roof Deck

Adding a deck over a roof isn't difficult, and it will be even easier if you plan on the dual function right from the beginning while the roof is under construction. First, make sure that the roof is strong enough to support the added load of a deck. Second, the deck and roof will need to be detailed so that water can't penetrate into the living area below. And finally, because this type of deck is high off the ground, special care needs to be taken to ensure that the deck is safe.

Basic Trellis Construction

Post-and-beam trellises are built just as beautiful deck framing is constructed. Unlike decking, however, the final layer can be varied to match your needs. The beam can be either a solid timber (below) or a built-up beam bolted to the unnotched post (right), a simpler alternative that is structurally adequate in most cases.

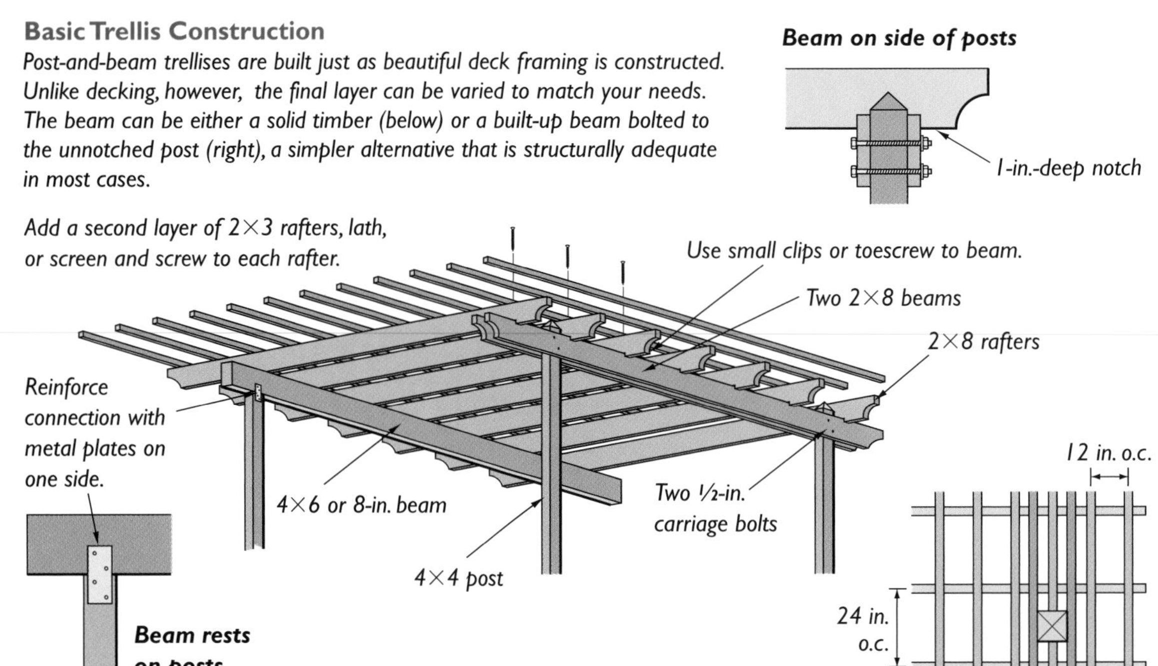

Low-Cost Flat Roof Deck

For some low-pitched roofs, 36-in.-wide, double-coverage roll roofing can be used as a low-cost roofing material under a roof deck. The roof should be pitched at least ¼ in. per ft., and the roofing requires careful application to remain leak-free. Duckboards are sections built of thin decking screwed to 2× sleepers and use gravity to remain in place. Choose a size and pattern of removable units that are easy to handle and fit the area.

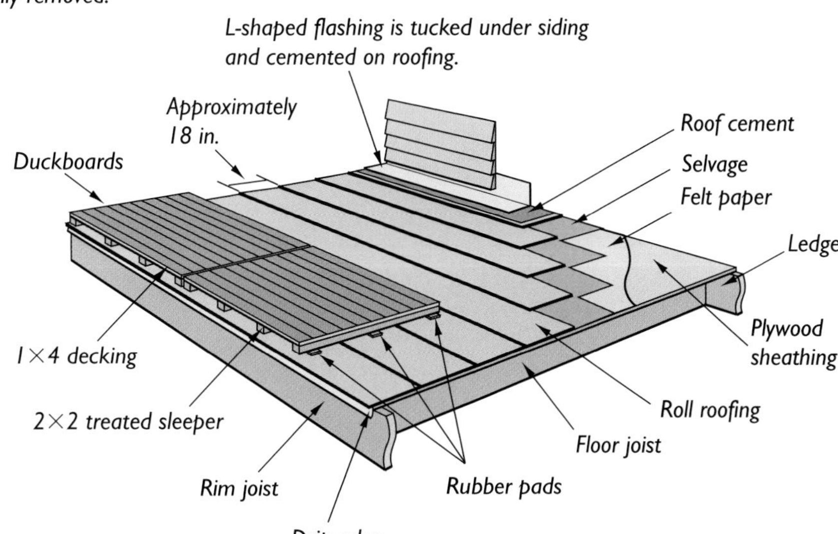

Structural considerations

At minimum, a roof that will also be used as a deck needs to be built to meet the code live-load requirement for a floor, which is typically 40 pounds per square foot (psf) (see Chapter 3). A roof in snow country may have even higher requirements, as will roof decks with special considerations such as a hot tub. Rafter sizes and spans will need to take these loads into account. Rafters should normally be spaced at least 16 in. o.c. and sheathed with ¾-in.-thick tongue-and-groove plywood for a sturdy substrate without any give. It's best to check with the local building department to find out the requirements in your area.

Also, remember that a roof to be decked should have enough slope to drain water, but not so much that it is unsafe to walk on.

Roofing

Shingles, metal, and other standard roofing materials won't work on a roof with a shallow pitch. Instead, you'll need a roof covering that is seamless or that has sealed seams.

Roll roofing. The least expensive roofing choice is double-coverage roll roofing, preferably installed over a layer of tar paper. This roofing comes in 3-ft.-wide rolls, and each row overlaps the previous one by one-half its width, resulting in a double layer everywhere. This type of roofing shouldn't be installed on roofs with a slope less than one inch per foot (steeper than I would recommend for a deck). I would consider this a risky roofing material for anything other than an easily inspected porch ceiling.

Hot tar. This kind of roofing is most commonly seen on flat-roofed commercial buildings. A layer of roofing felt is "glued" down to the sheathing with melted tar, and then covered with

+ SAFETY FIRST

If you want to add a deck to an existing roof, it is essential to check into the roof's framing and carrying capacity. Even if you can accurately determine the size of rafters, you will also need to take into account such considerations as attachment method, support below the rafters, and extra loading. And if your house has trusses, it may be impossible for you to figure out the carrying capacity of the roof. I recommend an engineering evaluation before adding any deck to an existing roof.

PRO TIP

One treatment for the underdeck area is to screen it off building a lightly framed wall that runs from the beam down to the ground.

IN DETAIL

Paneling or lattice under the deck can be attached to treated framing added between foundation posts and beams. Holding the paneling or lattice up off the dirt will keep it looking better; any wide cracks at the bottom can be sealed up with gravel or a 1×4 attached to the back side.

SAFETY FIRST

If you choose to screen off the area under the deck with solid siding, be sure to provide ventilation. One way to do this is by providing screened openings in unobtrusive sections of the deck. Another solution is to stop the solid siding a foot or two below the underside of the deck and change to a pattern using lattice with large ventilation spaces.

A torch-down modified bitumen membrane applied over a base of tar-saturated asphalt felt guarantees a no-leak roof, but needs professional installation (with a fire extinguisher nearby). Post flashings are sealed to the membrane in several layers with plenty of cement.

more melted tar and a protective layer of washed gravel. Because special equipment is used to melt the tar, a hot-tar roof needs to be applied professionally.

Single-ply or membrane roofs. Hot tar is giving way to a newer generation of single-ply or membrane roofing materials made from modified asphalt or rubber. Some require adhesives, some need heat for adhesion to the substrate (called torch-down), some can be left free-floating, and some are applied as a liquid and then cured to form a skin. Most of these roofing materials should be professionally applied.

Decking over the roofing

A separate deck can be built right on top of the roof, provided there is enough vertical room without encountering a door threshold. Using a conventional ledger and pressure-treated joists ripped to a taper negates the roof pitch and yields a level deck surface. And since the joists are supported by the roof, they can be smaller than if they were free-spanning. A rim joist will cap the ends of the joists, and it can be covered with a wider fascia that will cover any exposed roofing membrane or flashings. Decking can be any thickness or material desired but should be installed with screws so that boards can be removed occasionally to facilitate cleaning underneath.

Instead of building a conventional deck, you can install removable panels, called duckboards. These rely on gravity to stay in place, but can be easily lifted to inspect underneath and remove built-up debris. Duckboards are built in sections that aren't too heavy, usually no larger than 6 ft. by 6 ft. Each section has several runners, or sleepers, of flat 2× material; the sleepers act like joists, and the decking is screwed into them. The sleepers should align with the roof rafters for support, and

Deck boards are attached to sleepers with screws to make future inspections easier. Small pads of membrane under the sleepers help protect the roof.

should be oriented so that they run downhill and don't trap water. (See the drawing on p. 173.) It's best to use lightweight cedar or redwood for decking, but use treated wood for the sleepers so that screws hold better. For low-use areas, using 1× deck boards with an extra sleeper or two will result in the lightest unit.

Railings

Railings are the hardest part of a roof deck, because often they need to penetrate the waterproof layer. However, you can avoid this problem if you've chosen to build a separate deck over the roof and the joists are at least 2×8s. In this case, the posts can be installed conventionally, simply bolted to the rim joist. Even a 2×6 rim joist covered with a wider fascia usually can be reinforced adequately with extra joist hangers or bolts to

Another Roof Deck
Construction of this deck is similar to that of a regular deck. Deck joists can have spans that are longer than normal. The construction is similar to a regular deck, but the joists must bear on and align with the roof rafters rather than on a beam and posts.

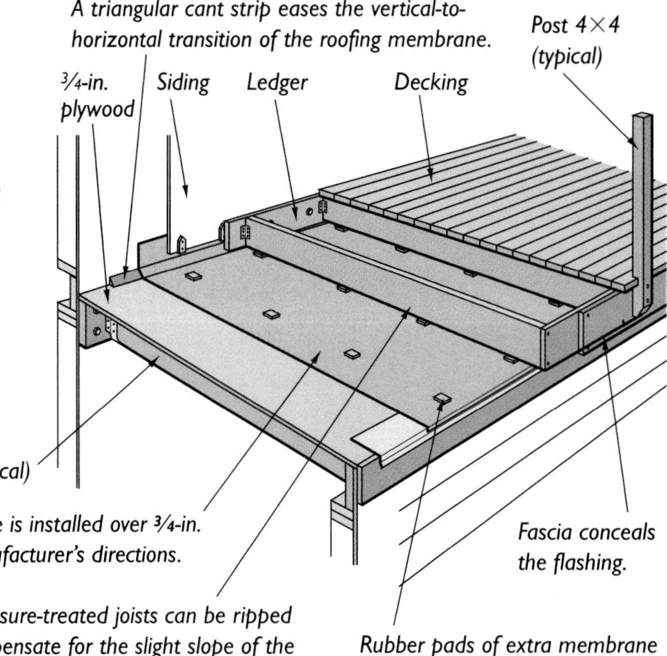

Roof Deck Post Flashing
Deck posts attached to roof rafters need a seamless flashing that can be sealed to the waterproofing layer. Adding a counterflashing or sleeve will keep water from getting behind the base flashing.

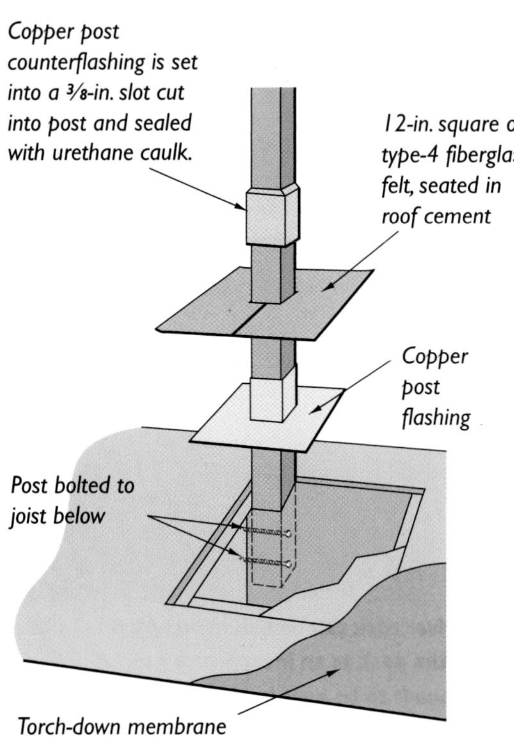

Rubber Roofing

Ethylene propylene diene monomer (EPDM) membrane roofing is a good solution for flat roofs under a deck. It can be left loose for small spaces (called a *ballasted* installation) or glued down on larger roofs. If your roof is relatively small and simple, a ballasted membrane roof is a good alternative to other roofing options. For a roof that needs to support a deck, I recommend thicker 0.060-in. material. The sheet usually laps over the edges around the outside perimeter of the roof and is held down with screws through a special metal strip, called a *termination bar*. Metal flashing under this edge is common to ease the corner, protect the roofing, and aid drainage. Corners and penetrations are sealed with a special uncured form of EPDM; patches and seams need special adhesive.

EPDM (ethylene propylene diene monomer) rubber membranes come in large sheets and are easy to handle. Lapping them onto the wall provides a good corner seal.

PRO TIP

If you have a concrete patio in good shape, you may be able to build a deck right on top of it, using the patio itself as the foundation.

IN DETAIL

A small storage area enclosed with lattice and a door provides a place to keep deck and patio accessories. The walls are built using typical frame construction, with extra footings added as needed. Screening behind the lattice helps keep out bugs. Adding a 2-ft.-tall band of plywood around the inside will help make the structure rigid and keep the lower screening and lattice from getting damaged.

TRADE SECRET

While powder-actuated nailers offer a fast and easy way to attach sleepers to sound concrete, they can be less than successful on old or weakened concrete. In this case, you may need to use concrete anchors instead.

support a railing post. (See the top drawing on p. 175).

If you use duckboards, narrow joists, or no joists at all, the posts will need to be mounted differently. They can be bolted to roof rafters that have been reinforced with extra blocking, then flashed with soldered or seamless flashings that are thoroughly sealed to the roof membrane. To keep water from getting behind the top of the base flashing, you will have to seal the top edge of an added counterflashing with polyurethane caulking or add a separate finish sleeve over the post.

Alternatively, posts can be installed using metal brackets (see the drawing on p. 132). On duckboards, these brackets can be through-bolted to sections that have been reinforced with extra sleepers and possibly a reinforcing metal plate on the underside of the duckboards.

Ground-Level Details

Because decks are elevated above the ground, the area underneath them usually doesn't get a lot of attention. But this area gets dusty and weed-infested and provides a great (though unintentional) home for animals and insects. I like to screen this area off from view or finish it with ground cover.

Ground cover

If the area below the deck is too low or doesn't serve as access to the house, an inexpensive and easy cover is clean, graded stones of any size. A border of small staked boards or timbers will help keep the stones from spreading into lawn areas. To prevent weeds, I cover the ground with black plastic before putting down the stones, but I slit the plastic frequently to encourage drainage and eliminate insect-breeding pools. Other possible ground covers include tree bark (though bugs may find this attractive), concrete pavers, and bricks.

Screens

Instead of sprucing up the underdeck area, you can screen it off by building a lightly framed wall that runs from the beam down to the ground. The framing can be prebuilt in sections to fit between the foundation posts, or added in place, piece by piece. Extra posts may need to be added and set on separate concrete piers if the deck posts are spaced too far apart to support the framing, and the vertical support spacing should be close enough to properly support the screening material.

After framing is completed, siding or a screening material can be added to either match the house or extend the deck styling. A typical solution is to cover the framing with prebuilt wood lattice, a simple approach that provides plenty of ventilation. In some cases, you may want to add a layer of screen on the back side of the lattice to keep out insects.

Gravel or river rock can be extended around and under the deck as an inexpensive ground cover, but needs to be kept in place by wood or plastic lawn edging.

A door needing access under the deck benefits from a small patio built with pavers to help keep dirt from being tracked inside.

Underdeck areas walled off completely with solid wood paneling applied over a treated wood frame look great ,but adequate ventilation must be provided.

Decking a patio

For many people today, decks serve the same function that patios did a few decades ago. If you have an existing patio made of brick, stone, or concrete that is not extensively broken, misaligned, or settled, you may be able to build a deck right on top, using the patio itself as the foundation.

If there is a doorway over the patio, the deck will probably need to have a very low profile. This is best done by attaching 2×4 treated sleepers, flat side down, directly to the concrete to act as joists. These should be spaced like regular joists, typically 16 in. or 24 in. o.c., depending on your decking material, and fastened to the concrete using a powder-actuated nailer. Low spots underneath the sleepers should be shimmed with treated wood or layers of asphalt shingles.

The sleepers should be oriented so that they don't impede drainage (typically, perpendicular to the house foundation and sloping downhill). The sleepers on the outside should be flush with the patio edges or overhanging slightly so they can serve as a base for attaching a fascia to cover the edges of the sleepers and concrete. Decking is installed in the usual manner.

Building a Deck Over an Old Patio

An old concrete patio in good condition (no major cracks or settling) can be covered with a wood deck. Treated sleepers installed as shown provide nailing for the new decking. Be sure that the extra thickness of sleepers and decking doesn't interfere with door thresholds.

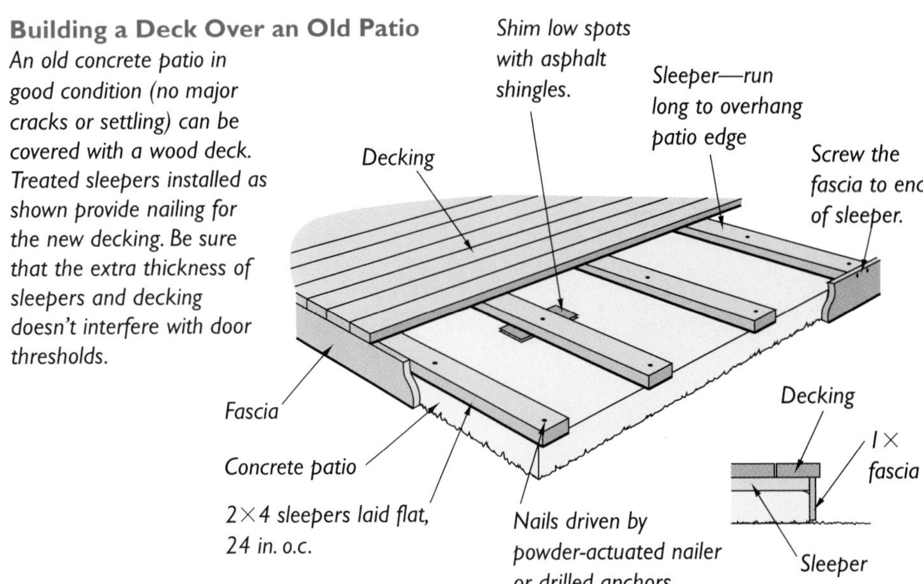

Appendix

Sample Lumber and Materials List

This list is based on a typical 14×20 ft. deck.

FOUNDATION

- 10 1x4x8 ft. S4S common pine bracing
- 2 8-in.-diameter x 12-ft.-long fiberboard concrete tube forms
- 1 yellow masons' line
- 5 40-in. pieces of steel rebar; no. 4, grade 60
- 18 0.45-cu ft sacks of premixed sack concrete
- 5 4x4 metal post bases
- 50 (1 bundle) 1x2x24 wood stakes
- 2 8x100-ft., 6-mil polyethylene sheeting
- 1 lb. 3-in. drywall screws
- 1 roll orange flagging

FRAMING

- 4 2x10x20, KD, pressure-treated, select, hem-fir – ledger, rim and beams
- 11 2x10x14, KD, pressure-treated, select, hem-fir – joists
- 2 4x4x8, pressure-treated, no. 2 and better, hem-fir- foundation posts
- 3 1/2-inch pressure treated plywood-beam and ledger spacer
- 5 pair post caps
- 12 2x10 joist hangers
- 10 lb. 8d hot galvanized nails
- 15 lb. 16d hot galvanized nails
- 5 lb. 10d hot galvanized nails
- 3 lb. 1 1/2-in. galvanized joist hanger nails
- 20 1/2-in. x 4 in. hot galvanized lag bolts
- 20 1/2 galv. washers
- 1 box 1/4-in. staples
- 2 tubes polyurethane caulk
- 3 tubes silicone caulk
- 4 10 ft. 2 1/2-in.x4 in. galvanized L metal flashing

DECKING, RAILING, AND STAIRS

- 38 2x6x20, #1, S4S, KD, tight-knot, western red cedar—decking
- 5 2x6x14, #1, S4S, KD, tight-knot, western red cedar—decking
- 3 2x4x20, #1, S4S, KD, tight-knot, western red cedar—rail
- 5 2x4x14, #1, S4S, KD, tight-knot, western red cedar—rail
- 6 2x4x8, no. 2, untreated fir—stair pad forms
- 180 2x2x3-in., clear, all-heart, KD, western, red cedar—balusters
- 9 4x4x8, #1, green, western red cedar—posts
- 1 2x12x16, select, KD, pressure treated hem-fir-stair stringer
- 30 1/2 x 5-in. hot galvanized carriage bolts, nuts, and washer
- 1 1/2 x 7-in. hot galvanized carriage bolts, nuts, and washer
- 15 lb. 3 1/2-in. weatherproof deck screws
- 5 lb. 3-in. weatherproof railing screws
- 2 1/2 in. x 4 concrete expansion anchors

FINISHES

- 1 5 gal. natural wood weatherproofing, clear
- 1 gallon paint thinner
- 1 9-inch roller cover
- 2 disposable tray liners
- 1 4-in. brush
- 2 pairs disposable gloves

Resources

Products

Ercon, Inc.
275 N. Franklin Turnpike
P.O. Box 369
Ramsey NJ 07466
(201) 327-1919
A-Square

F&S Manufacturing, Inc.
RR #1 Mahone Bay
Chester Basin, Nova Scotia, Canada BOJ 1KO
(800) 934-0393
Bigfoot

Feeney Wire Rope Co.
(800) 888-2418
www.cablerail.com
Cable and Fitting

Johnson Level and Tool
6333 West Donges Bay Rd.
Mequon, WI 53092
(262) 242-1161
Deckmate®

Mayhew Products
P.O. Box 68
Shelburne, MA 01370
(800) 872-0037
The Tweaker

QPI Tools
Freeport Road
Cheswick, PA 15024
(800) 469-5522
Stud Tuner

Manufactured and Composite Decking

Carefree U.S. Plastic Lumber™/ Earth Care Products
2300 Glades Rd.
Suite 440 W.
Boca Raton, FL 33431
(888) 733-2546
www.smartdeck.com
Smart Deck

Louisiana-Pacific
(800) 521-4316
www.weatherbest.lpcorp.com
See Web site for local distributors.
WeatherBest

McFarland Cascade®
P.O. Box 1496
Tacoma, WA 98401
(800) 426-8430
www.ldm.com

Nexwood Industries Limited
1327 Clark Blvd.
Brampton, Ontario, Canada L6T 5R5
(888) 763-9966
www.nexwood.com
Ewood®

Royal Crown Ltd.
P.O. Box 360
Milford, IN 46542
(800) 488-5245
www.royalcrownltd.com
Brock Deck

Thermal Industries Inc.
301 Brushton Ave.
Pittsburgh, PA 15221
(800) 245-1540
www.thermalindustries.com
Dream Deck

TimberTech Limited
P.O. Box 182880
Columbus, OH 43218
(800) 307-7780
www.timbertech.com

Trex
Winchester, VA 22601
(540) 678-4070
www.trex.com
See Web site for local distributors.

Weyerhauser
Bloomington, MN 55425
(612) 893-1717
www.choicedek.com
See Web site for local distributors.
Choice Dek

Factory-finished Decking

Arch Wood Protection, Inc.
1955 Lake Park Drive
Suite 250
Smyrna, GA 30080
(770) 801-6600
www.wolmanized.com
Wolmanized® Extra

Chemical Specialties, Inc.
One Woodlawn Green
Suite 250
Charlotte, NC 28217
(800) 421-8661
www.treatedwood.com
Ultrawood®

Thompson Co.
Cleveland, OH 44135
(214) 373-1601
www.thompsonsonline.com
Thompsonized® Lumber

Stainless Steel Fasteners

Manasquan Fasteners
P.O. Box 669
Allenwood, NJ 08720
(800) 542-1979

McFeelys Square Drive™ Screws
1629 Wythe Rd.
Lynchburg, VA 24506
(800) 443-7937
www.mcfeelys.com

Swan Secure
7525 Perryman Court
Baltimore, MD 21226
(410) 360-9100

Coated Fasteners

Grabber Construction Products
205 Mason Circle
Concord, CA 94520
(925) 680-0777
www.grabberman.com
Deckmaster®

ITW® Buildex®
1349 West Bryn Mawr Ave.
Itasca, IL 60143
(800) 323-0720
Dek-King screws

Concealed Fasteners

Cepco Tool Co.
P.O. Box 153
Spencer, NY 14883
(800) 466-9626
www.cepcotool.com
Bo Wrench

EB-TY
P.O. Box 414
Califon, NJ 07830
(888) 438-3289
www.ebty.com

Maze Nail Co.
P.O. Box 449
Peru, IL 61354
(800) 435-5949
www.mazenails.com

Simpson Strong-Tie Co.
Pleasanton, CA 94566
(800) 999-5099
www.simpsonanchor.com
Special decking nails

Plastic Rail Components

CertainTeed® Corporation
750 East Swedesford Road
Valley Forge, PA 19482
(800) 333-0569
www.certainteed.com
PVC

Dayton Technologies
351 N. Garver Rd.
Monroe, OH 45050
(800) 432-9250
www.daytech.com

Fypon®
P.O. Box 365
Stewartstown, PA 17363
(800) 537-5349
www.fypon.com
Urethane

Gossen Corporation
2030 W. Bender Rd.
Milwaukee, WI 53209
(800) 558-8984
www.gossencorp.com

Kroy Products
P.O. Box 636
York, NE 68467
(800) 933-5769
www.kroybp.com

L.B. Plastics
(800) 725-7739
www.lbplastics.com
See Web site for contact information.

Polyvinyl Co.
Drawer 300
Sheboygan Falls, WI 53082
(800) 832-8914
www.polyvinyl.com
Color Guard®

Royal Crown Limited
P.O. Box 360
Milford, IN 46542
(800) 365-3625
www.royalcrownltd.com

Style-Mark™
960 West Barre Rd.
Archbold, OH 43502
(800) 446-3040
www.style-mark.com

Thermal Industries
301 Brushton Ave.
Pittsburgh, PA 15221
(800) 245-1540
www.thermalindustries.com

FRP and Other Plastics

Avcon®
1451 Rt. 37 West
Tom's River, NJ 08755
(800) 242-8266
www.avconrail.com

HB&G
P.O. Box 589
Troy, AL 36081
(800) 264-4442
www.hbgcolumns.com

Pultronex™
(800) 990-3099
www.ezdeck.com
See Web site for local distributors.

Shakespeare Composites
P.O. Box 733
Newbury, SC 29108
(800) 800-9008
www.shakespeare-ce.com

Metal Railing Components

DEC-K-ING
1160 Yew Ave.
Suite 84
Blaine, WA 98230
(800) 804-6288
www.globaldecking.com

DecKorators®
2222 Schuetz Rd.
Ste. 102
St. Louis, MO 63146
(800) 662-3325
www.deckrail.com

Duradek
(800) 338-3568
www.duradek.com
See Web site for local distributors.

Resin Composites

Fiber Composites LLC
(Fiberon®)
34570 Random Dr.
New London, NC 28127
(704) 463-7120
www.fibercomposites.com

Trex
(800) 289-8739
www.trex.com
See Web site for local distributors.

U.S. Plastic Lumber/Earth Care Products
2300 Glades Rd.
Suite 440 W.
Boca Raton, FL 33431
(888) 733-2546
www.smartdeck.com

Post Caps

Boston Turning Works
120 Elm St.
Watertown, MA 02472
(617) 924-4949
www.bostonturningworks.com

Maine Ornamental Woodworkers
Kittery Point, ME 03905
(800) 556-8449
www.postcaps.com

Lumber information

Bear Creek Lumber® Co.
P.O. Box 669
Winthrop, WA 98862
(800) 597-7191
www.bearcreeklumber.com

California Redwood Association
405 Enfrente Dr.
Suite 200
Novato, CA 94949
(888) 225-7339
www.calredwood.org

Southern Forest Products Association
P.O. Box 641700
Kenner, LA 70064
(504) 443-4464
www.sfpa.org

Southern Pine Council
2900 Indiana Ave.
Kenner, LA 70065
(504) 443-4464
www.southernpine.com

Western Red Cedar Lumber Association
(604) 684-0266
www.wrcla.org
See Web site for list of certified cedar distributors.

Western Wood Products Association
522 SW Fifth Ave.
Suite 500
Portland, OR 97204
(503) 224-3930
www.wwpa.org

Deck Lighting

American Lighting Association
P.O. Box 420288
Dallas, TX 75342
(800) 274-4484
www.americanlightingassoc.com

Kichler Landscape Lighting
7711 East Pleasant Valley Road
Cleveland, OH 44131
(800) 875-4216
www.kichler.com

Kim Lighting®
16555 East Gale Ave.
City of Industry, CA 91745
(818) 968-5666
www.kimlighting.com

Lighting Research Center
21 Union St.
Troy, NY 12180
(518) 276-8716
www.lrc.rpi.edu

The Lighting Resource
P.O. Box 48345
Minneapolis, MN 55448
(952) 939-1717
www.lightresource.com

Nightscaping
1705 East Colton Ave
Redlands, CA 92374
(800) 544-4840
www.nightscaping.com

World's Greatest Lighting Manufacturing List
www.lighting-inc.com
See Web site for list of lighting manufacturers.

Membrane Roofing Manufacturers

Firestone Building Products Company
525 Congressional Blvd.
Carmel, IN 43032
(317) 575-7000
www.bridgestone-firestone.com

Goodyear
1144 East Market St.
Akron, OH 44316
(800) 321-2136
www.goodyear.com

Grace Products
P.O. Box 161196
Austin, TX 78716
(501) 296-6861
www.trulytexan.com/grace/index.htm

Johns Manville Roofing Systems
P.O. Box 5108
Denver, CO 80217
(800) 654-3103
www.jm.com

National Roofing Contractors Association
10255 W. Higgins Rd.
Rosemont, IL 60018
(708) 299-9070
www.nrca.net

Owens-Corning
Toledo, OH 43601
(419) 248-8000
www.owenscorning.com
See Web site for regional information.

Resource Conservation Technology
2633 N. Calvert St.
Baltimore, MD 21218
(410) 366-1146

Single Ply Roofing Institute
200 Reservoir St.
Suite 309A
Needham, MA 02494
(781) 444-0242
www.spri.org

Photo Credits

Photos © Jim Hall except as noted below:

Photos © Jeff Beneke—pp. 20 (top), 90 (top left), 120, 144, 159 (right).

Photos © Laurie Black—p. 14.

Photos © Cliff Chatel—p. 160.

Photos © Leon Frechette—pp. 121, 152, 158 (bottom left).

Photos © Susan Gilmore—p. 24 (top).

Photos © Anton Grassi—p. 15 (right).

Photos © Michael Howley—p. 18 (left).

Photos © Michael Mathers—p. 125.

Photos © Keith Mazzarello—pp. 161 (second from bottom), 174 (center and right).

Photos © Keith Moskow—p. 25 (bottom).

Photos © Randy O'Rourke—pp. 45, 59 (bottom), 61 (bottom), 89 (bottom center), 109 (bottom), 111 (left), 112 (right), 126 (top), 136 (bottom left), 139, 140 (top and bottom left, top center), 142 (bottom), 155, 157 (top right), 169 (bottom right and left).

Photos © Steven B. O'Sullivan—pp. 145 (top), 146 (top).

Photos © Byron Papa—p. 32.

Photos © Ted Putnam—pp. 96, 97.

Photos © Scott Schuttner—p. 145 (second from bottom).

Photos © Edward Sprouts—p. 124 (center).

Photos courtesy *Fine Homebuilding* magazine, © The Taunton Press, Inc.—pp. 16, 18 (right), 19, 20 (left bottom), 21 (top right and bottom), 22 (top), 100 (right), 101-104, 105 (bottom), 106 (bottom), 107 (top), 114 (right), 115 (right), 123, 141 (second from top), 158 (bottom right), 161 (third from top), 162 (bottom), 169 (top left), 170, 171 (top right), 175.

Photos © Robert Viviano—pp. 22 (bottom), 113 (top and bottom left), 158 (top), 161 (second from top), 161 (bottom), 162 (top), 165 (bottom left), 166 (top), 167 (top right), 168, 169 (top right), 171 (top left and bottom), 174 (left), 177.

Index